Mogadishu on the Mississippi: Language, Racialized Identity, and Education in a New Land

Language Learning Monograph Series

Lourdes Ortega, Series Editor
Nick C. Ellis, General Editor

Schumann:
The Neurobiology of Affect in Language

Bardovi-Harlig:
Tense and Aspect in Second Language Acquisition: Form, Meaning, and Use

Kasper and Rose:
Pragmatic Development in a Second Language

Seedhouse:
The International Architecture of the Language Classroom: A Conversation
Analysis Perspective

McNamara and Roever:
Language Testing: The Social Dimension

Young:
Discursive Practice in Language Learning and Teaching

Bigelow:
Mogadishu on the Mississippi: Language, Racialized Identity, and Education
in a New Land

Mogadishu on the Mississippi: Language, Racialized Identity, and Education in a New Land

Martha H. Bigelow
University of Minnesota

Blackwell Publishing was acquired by John Wiley & Sons in February 2007. Blackwell's publishing program has been merged with Wiley's global Scientific, Technical, and Medical business to form Wiley-Blackwell.

Registered Office
John Wiley & Sons Ltd, The Atrium, Southern Gate, Chichester, West Sussex, PO19 8SQ, United Kingdom

Editorial Offices
350 Main Street, Malden, MA 02148-5020, USA
9600 Garsington Road, Oxford, OX4 2DQ, UK
The Atrium, Southern Gate, Chichester, West Sussex, PO19 8SQ, UK

For details of our global editorial offices, for customer services, and for information about how to apply for permission to reuse the copyright material in this book please see our website at www.wiley.com/wiley-blackwell.

The right of Martha H. Bigelow to be identified as the author of the editorial material in this work has been asserted in accordance with the Copyright, Designs and Patents Act 1988.

Library of Congress Cataloging-in-Publication Data

Bigelow, Martha.
  Mogadishu on the Mississippi : language, racialized identity, and education in a new land / Martha H. Bigelow.
     p. cm. – (Language learning monograph series)
  Includes bibliographical references and index.
  ISBN 978-1-4443-3874-4
  1. Second language acquisition. 2. Immigrants–Language. 3. Somalis–Minnesota.
4. Immigrants–Cultural assimilation–Minnesota. 5. Language attrition. I. Title.
  P118.2.B543 2010
  418.007109776–dc22
                              2010026301

A catalogue record for this book is available from the British Library.

Set in 10/13 pt TimesNRPS by Aptara

01—2010

**Mogadishu on the Mississippi:
Language, Racialized Identity,
and Education in a New Land**

Contents

Language Learning   ISSN 0023-8333

Series Editor's Foreword

This book by Martha H. Bigelow is seventh in the *Language Learning* Monograph Series. The volumes in the series are intended to serve as benchmarks for interdisciplinary research in the language sciences in the years to come, and *Mogadishu on the Mississippi* sets itself as a benchmark for future research on the relationships among racialization, identity, literacy, and education, exploring in novel ways how multiple-language learning and use are at the heart of these relationships, mediating them and being mediated by them.

Since the beginning of the Somali Civil War in the Horn of Africa in 1991, and all the way to the continuing conflict of the present day, the Somali diaspora has grown large and diverse across many parts of the world: in Eastern Africa (Ethiopia and Kenya), the Middle East (Yemen, Saudi Arabia, and the United Arab Emirates), and the Western world, particularly the United Kingdom, Canada, the United States, and northern Europe. Close to half of all Somalis live outside Somalia today. In her book, Bigelow recounts her 5-year-long research engagement with the Somali community of the Twin Cities of Minneapolis and Saint Paul in Minnesota, the largest population of Somalis living in any given area of the U.S. geography. In a truly interdisciplinary and transdisciplinary spirit, Bigelow mobilizes knowledge across a dauntingly diverse number of areas inside and outside applied linguistics in order to do justice to her complex object of inquiry: poststructuralist theories of identity (chapter 1), psycholinguistic research on adults without alphabetic print literacy (chapter 2), critical theories of multiliteracy (chapter 3), sociology of minoritized identities (chapter 4), and educational research on English language learners with limited prior formal schooling capital (chapter 5). Remarkably, each of the six chapters could be read on its own, and in any order. Yet, each chapter carefully builds on one another and offers a needed piece of the rich, complete landscape that is host to the main argument of the book, which is indeed powerful and simple at the same time. Namely, highly contested racialized, religious, and gendered identities are intermeshed with in-flux oral and literate identities, and these processes of hybrid and multiple identity construction among vulnerable youth offer educators and researchers a central site for both understanding and supporting the struggle for access to equitable education by Somali and other refugee and immigrant youth in our societies.

I anticipate at least three ways in which the research that Bigelow reports in this book can influence the direction of future research undertaken by applied linguists, second language acquisition scholars, and educational researchers. First, her research on psycholinguistic processing by Somali youth with low print literacy points at the staggering gap in our disciplinary knowledge regarding how literacy and orality contribute to the psycholinguistic mechanisms of language learning. This question has attracted little empirical effort to date. Yet, the application of this new lens of literacy versus orality to old second language research problems would shed novel knowledge on constructs that have always been central in second language acquisition research, most particularly in ongoing debates regarding the theoretical status of implicit, explicit, and metalinguistic knowledge, which are relevant to most approaches to second language research. Second, in the notion of (in)educability, Bigelow's research offers an astute account for the social construction of blame when education fails. Through minoritization, racialization, and other oppressive ideological processes, powerful players in key institutions of our society, such as officers of the court (judges, attorneys, experts) and school leaders (teachers, administrators), place the responsibility on allegedly inherent characteristics of the youth whom we all fail. The construction of ineducability makes it possible for our institutions and their actors to continue their business as usual and to make themselves impervious to change. Much can be achieved if educational researchers and applied linguists are willing to engage in future studies designed to illuminate the inner workings of these ideological processes and help us see productive ways in which they can be subverted. Third, Bigelow's research will provide a model for other researchers who wonder how to balance the demands of academia and advocacy, because at a meta-level, the book is destined to be a guide to advocacy-integral research. The scholarly journey across multiple fronts that this book chronicles—the school and after-school life of Somali youth, their neighborhoods and community organizations, and the law enforcement and courts that interact with them—is fueled by Bigelow's determination to generate usable and useful research that helps "dismantle structural barriers in schooling, document the struggles and strengths of youth and their families, and help educators be more effective both within and beyond the walls of academia" (chapter 1, p. 2). She does not purport to hold definitive answers in this regard. Much to the contrary, she lets her book transpire vulnerability and honesty in her willingness to engage with the painful contradictions that characterize advocacy-integral research; nevertheless, the value and success of the integration will be undeniable to readers. Bigelow's research articulates and analyzes the abysses of experience that arise between literate educators and oral students (chapters 2 and 3) and the power-laden misconstructions of other and self that undermine our social structures, our scholarly disciplines, and our futures (chapters 4 and 5). Additionally, it documents agentive and affirming sources of strength among Somali youth and identifies transformational opportunities for action-oriented scholarship.

The *Language Learning* Monograph Series aims to advance knowledge in the language sciences with authoritative volumes that review recent findings and current theoretical positions, present new data and interpretations, and sketch interdisciplinary research programs. It began in 1998 under the editorship of Richard Young of the University of Wisconsin–Madison, who spearheaded it to the highest levels of scholarship by commissioning titles that have attracted repeated international recognition, including the Sage/International Language Testing Association award for best work in language testing and assessment, which went to McNamara and Roever's monograph in 2006, and the Kenneth W. Mildenberger Prize from the Modern Language Association to the outstanding scholarly book of the year, which went to Seedhouse's monograph in 2004. It has been a great pleasure for me to serve as editor for the past 4 years and two volumes. Mary Schleppegrell of The University of Michigan succeeds me as new Series Editor, and I know she will enjoy as much as I have the charge to identify innovative lines of interdisciplinary research in the diverse language sciences and invite leading scholars to craft volumes that are authoritative statements of the given domain.

It has been humbling and exhilarating for me to have played a small part in making Bigelow's *Mogadishu on the Mississippi* happen. I leave my role as editor of the *Language Learning* Monograph Series by offering readers her book, with pride and admiration. Few scholarly works can be read not only for their sheer research value but also for their intense moral and aesthetic enjoyment, and I commend this book to readers as one of such rare cases.

Lourdes Ortega
University of Hawai'i at Mānoa

References

McNamara, T., & Roever, C. (2006). *Language testing: The social dimension*. Malden, MA: Wiley-Blackwell.

Seedhouse, P. (2004). *The interactional architecture of the language classroom: A conversation analysis perspective*. Malden, MA: Wiley-Blackwell.

Acknowledgments

A book of this nature could never be produced in a vacuum. I am grateful to the Somali youth and elders whose words and wisdom give this book meaning. I am continually amazed and educated by their experiences and insights. Their resilience in the face of injustice, discrimination, and bias is humbling. I have tried to represent their experiences and views, but I know that this account will remain incomplete. I do hope that this book captures some stories of the Somali Diaspora in Minnesota in a particular point in time. I would like to especially acknowledge Ladan Bashir Yusuf, who mentored me as I learned to respond to the advocacy and activism demands that were springing from the research. I am forever appreciative of her patience and the opportunity to learn from her. In 2009, when I was working most intensely on this book, I was afforded the privilege to work in Hanna Malone's English-as-a-second-language classroom at Ubah Medical Academy High School. I benefited greatly from the opportunity to observe, tutor, and teach East African teens who were confronting the academic and literacy demands of a U.S. high school for the first time. My interactions with them were constant reminders of why it is important to understand their experiences and invest in their schooling.

I am grateful to the following friends and colleagues who gave me helpful and encouraging feedback on drafts of the chapters as they developed and as I learned: Connie Walker, Cynthia Lewis, Kendall King, Letitia Basford, Elaine Tarone, Kit Hansen, Sandy McKay, Bic Ngo, Jill Watson, Bonnie Swierzbin, Vichet Chhuon, Timothy Lensmire, Michael Anderson, and Marta Ljungkull. Their conversations and critique as I was writing were invaluable. I also must give special credit to Tara Fortune, who gave me many forms of intellectual and tangible support as I was in the final stages of writing and revision. Finally, I am particularly indebted to Lourdes Ortega, the editor of this series. She believed in this project from the beginning and masterfully guided me through multiple writing decisions that have helped me to communicate the breadth and depth of this book better. Her commitment to the roles of advocacy, activism, and social justice in SLA inspired and challenged me as this book was taking shape. Of course, none of these wonderful colleagues is responsible for the many limitations of the book, but I am so indebted to all of them for the help I received. They have added in countless ways to the potential of this work.

Heartfelt and humble gratitude to all of you.

Language Learning   ISSN 0023-8333

CHAPTER 1

Engaged Scholarship in the Somali Communities of Minnesota

We must probe to find the sites of intellectual
leverage, responsibility, and obligation
through which our work can begin
to fissure public and political discourse . . .

From Fine, Weis, Weseen, and Wong (2000, p. 124)

Introduction

This book brings together 5 years of interdisciplinary research with the Somali community in Minnesota and seeks to understand central and contemporary problems that tie the language learning of Somali youth in the diaspora to their broader experiences at school and home and how they experience the institutions of the dominant society. I chose the title *Mogadishu on the Mississippi* to locate the work solidly in the Midwest United States and evoke the sense of the large Somali community there. The subtitle *Language, Racialized Identity, and Education in a New Land* hopes to convey the interdisciplinarity of the endeavor, which taps into the fields of Applied Linguistics, Second Language Acquisition (SLA), Sociology, Anthropology, and Education. It also merely outlines the content of the book, which aims to connect dimensions of literacy and language learning to gendered, religious, and racialized identity. These descriptors are just some of the ways Somali youth are minoritized in the mainstream and dominant culture in Minnesota. The issues are old, and the experiences of Somali youth in U.S. schools and communities are highly theorizable and do compare with and contrast to experiences of other immigrant and refugee groups. On the other hand, the players and the context are new and require a reexamination of generally accepted theories and the way gendered, religious, and racial identities are shaped in a city in the upper Midwest elucidates various blind spots in the field, which will be explored throughout the book. Therefore, this book also aims to offer a model for how Applied Linguists can contribute to social justice and advocacy agendas that align with the communities in which they work, forwarding another argument for the centrality of sociopolitical issues in language learning and the schooling of immigrant youth. A strand throughout this book is the exploration of the question "What are some of the limits and possibilities of activist research?" This includes and goes beyond Applied Linguistics and SLA to include research that can be used to dismantle structural barriers in schooling, document the struggles and strengths of youth and their families, and help educators be more effective both within and beyond the walls of academia. Critical issues to be explored include how choice of methodology, choice of research question, and methodological rigor contribute to the usefulness of research for the communities studied and served.

The book is organized as follows. In this chapter, I introduce readers to the research and key constructs discussed in this book. To help me do so, I have chosen to narrate two pivotal events that drew me across institutional, professional, and personal barriers, real or imagined, and into adversarial conversations on behalf of Somali youth. In chapter 2, I depict the geographic and political landscape in which this research took place, providing information about the Somali Diaspora community in Minnesota and discussing some of the ways Somali traditional cultural perspectives and practices matter in today's Diaspora societies. In addition, chapter 2 offers an overview of research in the areas of orality and literacy among adolescents and adults as well as some of the documented consequences of limited formal schooling. In chapters 3–5, I report on the research I have carried out with Somali adolescent refugees since 2004. These chapters follow the chronology in which the research was conducted, which allows for an understanding of the progression and deepening of my understanding of the issues I saw in the community as well as my growth as an advocate. Specifically, chapter 3 reports on a case study focused on becoming print literate for the first time. In this chapter, I concentrate on the experiences of four Somali girls. Chapter 4 focuses on racialized identity formation among Somali youth in multiple contexts (home, school, community) and with a range of people (elders, peers, police). Chapter 5 offers an analysis of a lawsuit in which I served as an expert witness. This chapter explores issues of education and equity for adolescent refugees with limited formal schooling. The book closes with chapter 6, which distills what has been learned from all this research for theory building in Applied Linguistics and discusses and problematizes advocacy research in light of being an outsider.

Diaspora as a Construct and a Research Context

The Somali Diaspora is the result of the massive involuntary migratory displacement since 1991 of hundreds of thousands of Somalis due to the chaos and violence of a civil war that is still unresolved after almost 20 years. Diaspora is a powerful and useful construct in this research because, as Paul Gilroy (1993) said, "it breaks the dogmatic focus on discrete national dynamics" (p. 6) and "is cherished for its ability to pose the relationship between ethnic sameness and differentiation: a changing same" (p. 90). In other words, Diaspora communities retain unifying cultural or historical threads among them but change and adapt in innumerable ways across the places where those communities evolve around the world.

I choose the construct of Diaspora in discussing some of the research presented in this book because of the fact that being "Somali" still matters to many who have left Somalia; and that the notion of "Somaliness" still has great power in the ethos of Somali communities and identities around the globe. The concept of Diaspora has come to have local meaning for Somalis living in different countries and continents and the circumstances of the sudden creation of so many large Diaspora communities unifies many (not all) Somali communities in disparate places of the world. However, "[Diaspora] is not a matter of classification, but of being. It is an ontological question" (Echeruo, 1999, p. 9), and it includes a tangible feeling of connectedness to the nation state of Somalia and the imagined community (Anderson, 1983) of Somalis. It is imagined in the sense that it is not a concrete, actual community in everyday terms but rather a sense of belonging, an abstract affinity, and even a sense of loyalty associated with the community or, in this case, nation. Yet, the concept of Diaspora that I embrace allows for variations in and connections between communities around the world—from Canada (Ajrouch & Kusow, 2007; Berns McGown, 1999; Collet, 2007; Kusow, 2006), to Britain (Arthur, 2003; Berns McGown, 1999; Griffiths, 2002), to the United States (Bigelow, 2007; De Voe, 2002). This notion of Diaspora also embraces the pervasiveness and importance of mass media (see Appadurai, 1996). Media and technology connect Somalis through multilingual and interactive Web sites such as www.hiiraan.com as well as inexpensive telecommunications between individuals.

Evidence of the vibrancy and transnational nature of the Somali Diaspora includes many Somali organizations around the world that advocate for the stability of Somalia. For example, the Somali Canadian Diaspora Alliance states that their "vision is to strive for a sovereign and peaceful Somalia that is politically, socially and economically independent and just, a Somalia that is united and free from institutionalized tribalism" (http://www.somaliDiasporaalliance.com/). Attempts to influence politics in the country of origin from the Diaspora is what Laura Pires-Hester terms a *bilateral Diaspora ethnicity*. In her research with Cape Verdean-Americans, she defines this as "a strategic use of ethnic identification with an original overseas homeland to benefit that homeland, through relations with systems and institutions of the current actual homeland" (Pires-Hester, 1999, p. 486). Bilateral Diaspora ethnicity is seen among Somalis, including adolescents. It takes shape through sending money to relatives in the Horn of Africa and travel back to Somalia and neighboring countries. Although individuals and families take short-term trips back, there have been reported instances of sending young people back to Somalia and Kenya for long or indefinite stretches of time (Integrated Regional Information Networks, 2003). Some of these young people have been returned for religious education, to recuperate Somali language skills, and to be culturally "reschooled." Sadly, there have been recent reports of Somali youth being recruited to join the ongoing fighting in Somalia (Ephron & Hosenball, 2009). These acts speak to a powerful diaspora identity in the Somali communities in Minnesota and elsewhere.

As immigrants before them, many Somali youth and their families live actual and figurative transnational lives, thus broadening the sociohistorical context beyond the borders of Minnesota or the United States. The examination of immigrant identity today should acknowledge that immigrant youth construct and contest identity in transnational worlds influenced by world and local political and historical events. The identities and allegiances of Somali youth often cross national borders, particularly when they still have family members in Somalia, Kenya, or Ethiopia, and when inexpensive telephone calls and Internet connections link them to friends, family, and news from friends and relatives around the world, including the Horn of Africa. Somali youth, like so many other immigrants, inhabit figurative borderlands (Anzaldua, 1987; Lam, 2006, 2009) where they move between religions, cultures, nationalities, and languages. Transnationalism adds another layer to the importance of understanding the identity of immigrant youth and families as multiple and shifting. In this sense, transnational identity is an important aspect of Diaspora that goes well beyond the scope of this book but is in need of further exploration in future work.

The way Somali adolescents imagine themselves within their local and global worlds influences the meaning they find in learning English, persisting through school and envisioning options for themselves beyond school. These identities (subjectivities) play a role in their investment in all manner of family and community activities. By understanding the experiences and views of Somali teens, educators will gain a broader view of immigrant students who experience the intensely racialized environments of our public schools and urban communities. Hoping to improve our schools for immigrant students, this research begins by letting us see our schools and communities through these students' eyes and allows them to correct, complicate, or contest people's misperceptions of them.

Public Engagement Story #1: Meeting with the Police

As part of my ongoing research, I had gathered interview and focus group data on racialized identity among Somali youth and adult community members (see chapter 4). Ladan Bashir Yusuf, the president of a nonprofit agency called CrossingBarriers, helped organize and facilitate the focus groups with me. Ladan's organization advocates for and with immigrant youth, particularly in relation to issues involving secondary public education and equity. For example, she has worked with schools to afford immigrant students access to honors classes, communicating graduation requirements clearly to parents and students, and, in general, helping schools become more welcoming places for immigrant youth and their families. CrossingBarriers focuses on academic success through institutional transformation. Ladan knows how to organize and mentor young people and immigrant families. She is originally from Somalia and is bilingual.

Part of the interview protocol with the focus groups of Somali teens and young adults included the simple question "Have you ever been mistaken for someone you aren't?" Many, many of the participants reported having had this experience. They spoke of being mistaken for other East Africans (e.g., Oromos) or for African Americans by teachers or peers. Girls talked about how Somali girls who did not wear a *hijab* (veil) had more instances of mistaken identity. Sometimes they said they could not recognize co-ethnic Somali peers because they talked like (African) Americans. They spoke indignantly about how their elders mistakenly thought they were turning into criminals because of the way they dressed or wore their hair. However, the majority of the stories about mistaken identity had to do with our local law enforcement. The youth felt that they were treated unfairly and even criminalized. Many of the experiences they reported happened after the terrorist attacks of September 11, 2001, and seemed deeply anti-Islamic in nature. At the same time, participants said they were often mistaken for being "Black."[1] Many Somali youth were having experiences with authorities that were distinctly racist *and* Islamophobic.

As the focus groups unfolded, Ladan and I were disturbed by what the participants said and we discussed how important these data were. Admittedly, my outrage and sadness about what was happening would likely have remained within the walls of academia without Ladan. Particularly angered by the accounts of educators discriminating against Somali youth and by hearing so many stories of police harassment, she took immediate action. She contacted the Somali Student Association at the University of Minnesota and arranged a meeting with a city council member. She invited me to come and present data from the focus groups. I had not analyzed my data but agreed to present the stories, but not without much discomfort in sharing data that I did not thoroughly understand, in a venue I had never traversed.

In attendance were two police chiefs and other police officers, many Somali community members and leaders, and numerous members and interns from the Department of Civil Rights. Ladan facilitated the meeting. Many of the young people who attended were angry at the police. They wanted to tell about their experiences and complain about how they were treated. Nevertheless, Ladan and the members of the Somali Student Association facilitated the meeting in a way that gave all of the young people present the opportunity to communicate their stories and ask questions about law enforcement procedures. This gave them the opportunity to say that they felt racially profiled, to say that they felt discriminated against because they are Muslim, and to complain that they felt their community did not get high-quality policing. To their credit, the police officers listened and there seemed to be an exchange of information, albeit through palpable tension.

As a result of this first meeting, leadership from the Somali Student Association and Ladan organized numerous follow-up meetings with the police chiefs, who cooperated in sponsoring a community event that would begin to repair the relationship between the community and the police forces. The police officers were asked to attend without their uniforms or guns. They spoke with a largely Somali audience about how to file a complaint, what to do if a police officer stopped them, and many other things everyone had agreed would be helpful and improve relations between the police forces and the Somali youth on campus and in the neighborhood. This work continues to this date and although some of the faces of those involved have changed, these early efforts undoubtedly mattered to some and empowered others.

The events portrayed in the Meeting with the Police story illustrate some of the ways research can link to engagement with communities beyond the university and serve concrete purposes of members of the community. The story also serves to exemplify how the academic exploration of the construction of identity among Somali youth intersects with a local problem: the racial and ethnic profiling among Somali youth. The phenomenon of profiling is an outcome of the racism in the United States—past and present. Discrimination is also part and parcel of life for Muslims in the United States and many other parts of the world after the terrorist attacks of 9/11. Racism and Islamophobia are intertwined in this case, and among Somali youth, it is practically impossible to treat either system of oppression or Othering as a separate phenomenon distinct from the other. These systems of oppression also inform the multiple ways that Somali youth see themselves and each other and how they choose to display or contest representations of identity.

The Fluidity of Identity

Bonny Norton has framed identity as "how a person understands his or her relationship to the world, how that relationship is constructed across time and space, and how the person understands possibilities for the future" (2000, p. 5). She acknowledged identity as a site of struggle and sometimes contradiction; as constantly transforming across time and space and related to the desire for affiliation, recognition, and security (Norton Peirce, 1997). Norton demonstrated in her work that identity must be "understood with reference to larger, and frequently inequitable, social structures which are reproduced in day-to-day social interaction" (2000, p. 5). I add Stuart Hall's (1996) caution that identity is not so much about "being" but rather a "process of becoming" (p. 4), as well as his point that symbolism and representation are at constant play in identity processes. Following Norton, I see language and discourse as mediated in macro and micro ways by racialized, gendered, academic, religious, and other identities, all of which may be characterized by ambivalence.

Ambivalence, according to Block (2006), "is the natural state of human beings who are forced by their individual life trajectories to make choices where choices are not easy to make" (p. 26), because, clearly, an individual is not simply "half of what he/she was and half of what he/she has been exposed to" (p. 26). Ambivalence involves uncertainty that is heightened or lessened according to the situation. However, uncertainty in immigrant identity construction does not necessarily imply conflict. As Bic Ngo (2008) pointed out, "culture clash" is often an unhelpful metaphor in understanding cultural adaptation because it reinforces false dichotomies between cultural groups. She argued:

> The cultural difference model for understanding immigrant experiences
> sets up binary oppositions between tradition and modernity, East and
> West, and First World and Third World, among others. This oppositional
> framework is problematic for at least two reasons. First, the emphasis on
> traditional cultural values reifies the notion of culture, positioning it as
> something that is fixed or a given, rather than as a social process that finds
> meaning within social relationships and practices. Second, binary
> oppositions inscribe judgment and a pecking order (i.e., good/bad,
> ours/theirs) into cultural practices and values. (p. 5)

"Culture clash," if not an accurate metaphor for the experience of immigrant youth, is certainly pervasive and even adopted by youth themselves, resulting in an obstruction to ways of being in the world that are more fluid across time and space.

One of the persistent answers to the problem of binary oppositions comes from cultural studies theorists Homi Bhabha and Stuart Hall. Bhabha (1994) used the terms *hybridity* and *third space* to describe the cultural space that is created by an individual. Rejecting the definition of cultural identity based on an understanding of a singular "one true self" or a self -belonging simply to a people of a common history and ancestry, Hall particularly argued for a concept of identity based on the constant process of differentiation and the recognition of difference (Hall, 1989, 1990, 1996). Hall contended that identity is constructed through discourse and representation and involves the play of power. He conceived identity as constituted through alterity: "the relation to the Other, the relation to what is not, to precisely what it lacks" (Hall, 1996, p. 4). Any notion of identity, therefore, depends on its difference from or negation of some other term. Because identity is constructed through social and discursive practices (e.g., De Fina, 2003; Gee, 1990; Lin, Wang, Akamatsu, & Riazi, 2002; McKay & Wong, 1996), identity is a *positioning*—unstable, incomplete, and always changing (Hall 1989, 1990, 1996). Bhabha (1990) explained:

> For me the importance of hybridity is not to be able to trace two original
> moments from which the third emerges; rather hybridity to me is the
> "third space" which enables other positions to emerge. This third space
> displaces the histories that constitute it, and sets up new structures of
> authority, new political initiatives, which are inadequately understood
> through received wisdom. (p. 211)

This understanding of multiple identities within the self that emerge through discourse and representation allows for sites to continuously open for reidentification and resignification—for the construction and reconstruction of identities (Bell, 2007; Bhabha, 1994; Hall, 1990). However, identity construction and the creation of a third space need not only be the result of immigration and need not always involve blending of minoritized ethnicities with the most obvious culture(s) of power. Bhabha's (1994) theory is more about performative contestation of identity, understood in the broadest terms, rather than simply or only about ethnicity or colonialism. In this book, I am concerned with the performance, representation, and struggles related to racialized identity and the racialization of religion in the particular U.S. setting where this research takes place.

Racialized and Ethnic Identity

The construct of racialized identity emerged as central to the Meeting with the Police story, which revealed the problem of racial profiling and the need to work with the police to eliminate it. Racialized identity is a key facet of this research that will be explored and critiqued through the experiences of Somali adolescents living in the United States. Racialization is an historically specific ideological process whereby racial meaning is given to a social practice or group, according to Omi and Winant (1994). The limits of understanding the racialization and minoritization of Somali youth through notions of the third space (Bhabha, 1994) will be tested in this book. The stance that I will take is that "race" is deeply situational as well as structural (Kusow, 2006) and that linguistic, religious, gendered, and other social identities are created and negotiated through interactions with others as well as the institutions of the local and global society (e.g., schools, courts, refugee services). Unfortunately, race often eclipses other potentially preferred identities among Somali youth, such as religious or national identities. Often, in the public lives of visible ethnics, they are defined by an identity tied to their ethnic heritage—or rather, by people's perceptions, stereotypes, or partial understandings of their heritage.

As visible ethnics, Somali refugees and immigrants have different experiences with identity than White Americans. This is due, in large part, to the ways race and racism undergird U.S. social institutions (Bell, 1992; Crenshaw, Gotanda, Peller, & Thomas, 1995; Omi & Winant, 1994) and inform our national discourse on identity (Feagin, 2000). Somali immigrant youth navigate unique religious, ethnic, and gendered identities (Collet, 2007; Zine, 2001) that mediate constructed and co-constructed processes of racialization. Like other minoritized racial ethnics, Somali immigrants' "racial and ethnic identities crosscut and compete with each other for dominance, with race almost always overriding ethnicity" (Tuan, 1998, p. 22). Thus, although a first-generation Somali American immigrants may wish to be identified as "Somali" or "Somali American," they are more likely to be identified by others as "Black" or "African American," as has been the case of other Black immigrants to the United States (e.g., Bryce-Laporte, 1972; Traoré & Lukens, 2006; Vickerman, 1999; Woldemikael, 1989a). Unlike White North Americans, who have the option to evoke a symbolic ethnic heritage (e.g., choosing a German ethnicity during a soccer match), racially minoritized immigrants have a socially imposed racial-ethnic identity. Although ethnic identity may be an option in their private lives, in their public lives, ethnic identity is not voluntary.

It is, however, too simplistic to take for granted that an other-imposed racial identity is rejected by all Somalis. In his seminal study, Ibrahim (1999) found that many African adolescents in Canada embraced a new Canadian African identity including ways of talking and types of music associated with a sort of "prepackaged" or stereotypical racialized identity. Likewise, Khadar Bashir-Ali (2006) found that some immigrant adolescents who were not phenotypically Black might embrace Blackness as an identity. She wrote about a Mexican girl who rejected the identity of "ESL student" and embraced a Black racialized identity. She chose as her target a variety of American English that approximated African American vernacular, not mainstream American English. It is also too simplistic to assume that just because in the United States race is one of the most visible and common other-imposed identity markers, this is the aspect of identity that most challenges Somali youth. That would assume that identity construction always occurs with and in opposition to groups outside the Somali community. The reality may be that visible identity markers *within* the community are those that matter most. This will be explored further in chapter 4.

The continuum of cultural practices among phenotypically Black immigrants varies greatly among ethnicity, families, and generations. The "Diaspora experience" is a constant process of recombination and hybridization (Hall, 1996). Many first-generation immigrants express great concern that the younger generation is "losing" its culture and tradition (e.g., Woldemikael, 1989a). Although this may be what appears to be happening, another option may be that youth are engaged in the creation of new identities in third spaces. Youth are hybridizing and negotiating new identities that have very much to do with who they were, who their families are, and who they are hoping to become.

It is uncommon to hear Somalis draw a clear separation between what they understand as Somali culture and the tenets of Islam, or Islamic religious practices. How does culture intersect with religion and how does this relate to an ethnic identity? The post-9/11 anti-immigrant and anti-Muslim sentiments as well as the dramatic differences between religious norms and the norms of the dominant U.S. society can challenge the maintenance of a religious identity among Muslim immigrants. On the other hand, there are strong cultural and economic forces from within the society that have the potential to radicalize Somali Muslims (Abdi, 2007). In this case, fronting a strong Muslim identity may be for the sake of other Somalis, rather than an assertion of a minoritized religious identity within the majority population. Being Muslim creates a dynamic of hybridity where youth may negotiate a Muslim identity between home and public life. As Sarroub (2005) said, Muslim youth are often "triangulators of identity, and, as a result, culture is enacted in the in-between places they occupy in their home and school worlds" (p. 7).

Ethnic identity can often become important when members of one ethnic group are mistaken for members of another group according to race. In the urban contexts of this research, this can occur in the following ways: All Asian students are assumed to be Hmong, all Latino students are assumed to be Mexican, and all African students are assumed to be Somali. This lumping of ethnic groups along racial lines occurs at school, in communities, and in the media. It is often the group whose ethnicity is ignored (e.g., Oromo, Burmese, Ecuadorian) that feels compelled to display an alternate identity. This display may be lost on members of majority ethnicities but likely noted by those with whom they are typically lumped. The lumping of students' identities across and within ethnic groups can be detrimental because it ignores the fluid nature of identity and the ways in which students are actively creating and contesting what it means to be "Somali," "urban," "female," "student," or "Muslim" in U.S. schools and society. This research explores how identity is embraced, contested, and newly minted.

In some social contexts, people of a particular race are often linked to a particular religion in popular discourse. This "racialization" of religion can compound the ways in which groups are minoritized. Khyati Joshi (2006) has written about this in terms of how people from India, who are largely Hindus, Muslims, and Sikhs, experience Othering as non-Christians in U.S. contexts. Joshi drew on Higginbotham's (1992) idea that race is a metalanguage and builds force only when given social meaning (Joshi, 2006, p. 211). She argued that it is important to distinguish social contexts in which race and other identity markers are conflated or mutually marked categories. It is in the contexts in which the two are blurred that the racialization of religion occurs— where an individual's religion stands in for his/her race, and vice versa (Joshi, 2006). Specifically, "the racialization of religion is a process whereby a specific religion becomes identified by a direct or indirect reference to a real or imagined ethnic/racial characteristic" (Joshi, 2006, p. 216). This phenomenon is how a religious group becomes recast as a racial group.

In the context of this study, the upper Midwest United States, there is great potential for Islam to become racialized. A very small percentage of the population of the state of Minnesota is Muslim, and many of the visible Muslims in the state are from East Africa, specifically Somalia (Hallman, 2006). This would be unlike other areas in North America (e.g., Dearborn, New York City, Toronto), where there are more and more diverse Muslim communities that span many generations and countries of origin. In fact, during the 1920s and 1930s when Islam began to have a critical mass in the United States, it was characterized by the diversity of backgrounds and orientations of Muslims, including the emergence of African American Islam (Hudson & Corrigan, 1999). However, in the context of this research, Islam is often associated with East African immigrant groups and the differences between their religious philosophies or ideologies are often masked by lumping according to racial phenotype.

Although Muslims are grouped across racial lines, what should be more salient is how Muslims differ across ideological lines. Differences among Muslims are historic and contemporary and not exempt from influences of globalization. For example, partially in reaction to Westernization in Middle Eastern countries, Muslim immigrants may have religious ideologies that are more conservative or nationalistic than those of their American Muslim counterparts. This phenomenon of Islamic nationalism has reinforced ethnic differences among Muslims, resulting in Muslim identities being closely linked to political discourses (Hudson & Corrigan, 1999). Minnesota continues to resettle Somali refugees and therefore has a constant flow of home-country religious ideologies that may not necessarily align with the views of Muslims born in the United States or who have been in the United States longer. A powerful public discourse regarding Islam in Minnesota has taken place in the media and has focused on high-publicity events, such as taxi drivers refusing to transport passengers who are carrying unopened bottles of alcohol from the airport, Target employees refusing to scan pork products, and labor disputes involving factory workers who wish to pray during the work day. In large-scale public disputes such as these, as well as in the local day-to-day conflicts Somali youth may face at school, it is often unclear if their minoritization is rooted in racism, anti-immigrant views, xenophobia, or Islamophobia. For all of this murkiness, it is worth exploring how and when race and religion are conflated and whether the racialization of religion is a reality in this particular Midwestern setting, given the powerful role of religion in the lives of Somalis in Minnesota.

The relevance of racialized identity to Somali adolescents in Minnesota can be found in their daily negotiation of essentializing practices in the cultural spaces where Somalis live and work: at school, in the mainstream community, and at home. Examples of racial and religious bias can be found and explicated in the media that is produced locally, nationally, and internationally (e.g., Anderson, 2009). On the other hand, the challenge of achieving affirmation of multilingual, multicultural, third-space identities can conflict with trying to maintain a "pure" Somali identity that may bring approval among some members of the co-ethnic community (Shah, 2000). Essentializing language, value judgments, or stereotyping, in any guise, can hinder the development of positive identities for immigrant adolescents. These damaging processes also thwart any opportunity for two-way enrichment during which all involved have the opportunity to choose to learn from others' values, resources, and competencies in a mutually hybridizing manner (Lin, 2008). Optimistically, these circumstances may result in acts of great agency that create opportunities for youth to find ways of being Muslim and Somali at the same time they are wearing other identities they embrace, such as student, artist, or provider.

Public Engagement Story #2: Suing the School

The second story of public engagement, and another personally critical experience, again brought me into public contact with authorities on behalf of East African immigrant youth. I was called to serve as an expert witness in a lawsuit filed against an alternative school and the school district in which it was located. Again, I collaborated with Ladan Bashir Yusuf and CrossingBarriers, who helped organize the plaintiffs in the lawsuit. The school was housed within a large school district, but its status as an alternative school meant that it had a great deal of fiscal, administrative, and curricular independence. I am generally supportive of finding flexible ways of educating adolescent immigrant and refugee newcomers, particularly those with limited formal schooling.[2] Furthermore, I have done work in alternative and charter schools and have seen excellent examples of administrative leadership and instruction in these settings. Such schools are often able to accommodate students who work full time or have children in ways large public schools cannot. They can also be excellent places of transition for students who need initial support before moving to a traditional high school setting.

Given these antecedents, it was painful to see the many ways that this school seemed to have failed some of their neediest students. I was asked to offer an expert witness report and deposition based on my analysis of a set of documents gathered from the school. In my assessment, the school personnel did not do enough to overcome language barriers to give students full access to the district's curriculum. I found failings mainly in the areas of their choice of educational programs and curricula. Essentially, the school had adopted traditional approaches to language instruction when the students needed innovative approaches. Despite being in operation for many years, it was my conclusion that they had not established effective placement, assessment, and monitoring systems for their students with limited prior schooling. There did not seem to be articulation between the levels of the classes meant to develop language skills. School personnel seemed generally unable to communicate graduation requirements to students and their guardians, resulting in much confusion over how to obtain a high school diploma. Because so many of the student body had low print literacy and limited formal schooling, there was an unmet need for staff development to address the learning needs of the school population in a meaningful way. The school administration also had erroneous interpretations of state policy regarding assessing students with special education needs— physical, emotional, and cognitive. Students and their families had attempted to initiate changes in the school. They had complained to school leadership and then filed an official complaint with the Minnesota Department of Education. This complaint resulted in an investigation that uncovered many of the problems that led to the lawsuit. The details of the lawsuit will be further elaborated upon in chapter 5 in relation to how limited formal schooling is a reality that schools have generally not accepted or addressed programmatically or instructionally. The lawsuit gave my research on youth with limited formal schooling direct application in the form of community involvement and advocacy. The experience was challenging and interesting and fueled by the desire for all schools to address the language learning and academic needs of this unique population of English language learners. I learned more about the laws and policies that impact English language learners as well as powerful lessons about how scholarship can be used in legal disputes.

The young people involved in suing the school gained from the experience as well. By contesting the school, a powerful institution, the students (plaintiffs) developed confidence and leadership skills. I noticed that all of the people involved with the case learned to name and talk about structural and racial obstacles to education with community members, policy makers, and within the court system. They could explain, with the confidence of educators, why a program model technically cannot be called "immersion" if it is linguistically subtractive (Fortune & Tedick, 2008) and why content classes in the native language and content-based English-as-a-second-language (ESL) classes for newcomers with limited formal schooling would have gotten them closer and faster to graduation (Adamson, 1993; Bigelow, Ranney, & Hebble, 2005; Crandall & Kaufman, 2005; DeCapua, Smathers, & Tang, 2009; Zwiers, 2006). Together, we came to identify some of the policies schools follow as pure fiction. This knowledge, which was co-constructed with the community, the attorneys, and the young people involved, became valuable, homemade local knowledge that spread through Somali communities as newfound cultural capital about how schools and schooling work. Since the events took place to this date, the lawsuit has not only generated dialogue and activity among those involved, but it has also reached into the public realm through newspaper articles and word of mouth.

The Suing the School story of my involvement as an expert witness raises a number of interesting issues. It exemplifies how a relatively new refugee community can organize and contest institutionalized educational practices that directly impact their youth. It also raises many controversial issues in education and public policy about how to educate newcomers with limited formal schooling and, possibly, late-onset print literacy in any language (Tarone, Bigelow & Hansen, 2009). Chapters 3 and 5 explore these issues and problematize the fact that there is still relatively little SLA research available to date about the strengths and challenges these learners have while acquiring a new language. Even more disconcerting is the finding in chapter 5 that some may believe these students to be uneducatable.

Educating Newcomers

English language learners with limited formal schooling are unique because although they have a host of language and life skills, they do not have experience with print literacy (Medina, 2009), particularly academic language (Adamson, 1993; Colombi, 2002; Kidd, 1996). Yet, most instruction at the secondary level assumes and relies heavily on print. Secondary teachers are not typically prepared to teach students with large gaps in the sort of content knowledge valued in formal schooling and without the ability to access this knowledge through grade-level texts. Instructional modifications to scaffold basic print concepts or engage the oral modalities more significantly in all phases of instruction and assessment may suggest differentiation techniques that are beyond the usual repertoire of many teachers.

Students with limited formal schooling challenge the services that public schools offer in other ways as well. They may have experienced extreme levels of violence and trauma that may make it difficult to conform to the ways students are expected to learn in U.S. schools (e.g., in groups, through interaction, and independent projects) (Frater-Mathieson, 2004). In addition, they may be living with family members or guardians who are also experiencing the aftereffects of trauma (Tummala-Narra, 2004). To make matters worse, it is common for psychological and emotional needs to go unaddressed in this population (Scuglik, Alarcón, Lapeyre, Williams, & Logan, 2007).

Identifying students who have had little or no schooling is often not systematized but handled in an ad hoc fashion within the ESL program in the given school, if one exists. Typically, in U.S. public schools students with limited formal schooling are not identified or served in any formal way (Medina, 2009). Although they may be multilingual, their native language literacy or knowledge in any of the content areas is rarely assessed. Not assessing students in these areas may be due to the lack of assessments of native language literacy or to the inability to assess content knowledge independent of print literacy and oral language proficiency. Ironically, although students with limited formal schooling may not be assessed in these crucial ways, they are often required to sit for standardized tests before they are prepared to succeed on these measures. This experience often results in repeated and demoralizing failing, as described in chapter 3 and elsewhere (e.g., Shepard, 2008; Stone, 2008). If students are not identified and determined to have very low levels of print literacy or academic content knowledge, they usually do not have a particular curriculum that would be tailored to their learning levels and needs. They are more likely to encounter sheltered curricula that are designed for English language learners with print literacy and background knowledge in the content areas. All of these issues are typically framed as challenges embodied in the individual rather than challenges to educational institutions.

The exploration of what it is like to become literate for the first time in a language one is beginning to learn must be located in broader conversations about language and literacy use among bilingual and multilingual adolescents who must relate to text and high school experiences in processes of literacy learning that are situated and intensely personal (e.g., Block, 2003; Gee, 1996; Hornberger, 2003; Street, 1993, 1995). Youth are socialized into new social and academic settings through language and use language to express new ways of being in the multiple contexts through which they move (Schieffelin & Ochs, 1986). For example, hip-hop literacies (Alim, Ibrahim, & Pennycook, 2009; Richardson, 2006) may be very important to second language learners and users and this may influence their choice of language variety (Bashir-Ali, 2006; Ibrahim, 1999; Rampton, 1995). Other primarily oral language traditions such as storytelling and reciting poetry transform in the many arenas of language use in Diaspora communities. As Somalis from different regions are brought together, the memorization of poems as a common practice slips away with other forms of orality, and improvised poems include topics of life in the Diaspora. For youth who are just becoming literate due to limited formal schooling, the task of appropriating academic literacies in a new language is formidable.

Language and literacy processes among adolescents such as those who inhabit the chapters of this book intersect necessarily with processes of agency and identity. As such, the research I will present will also examine their investment (Norton Peirce, 1995) in engaging with academic print materials well beyond their literacy levels. This investment to engage with academic text involves the difficult process of appropriating linguistic skills or habits of interacting with text as well as the belief that in so doing, newcomer refugee youth with little prior schooling will benefit socially and economically. Some of the overarching assumptions implicit in this book with regard to language and literacy acquisition include the assertion that youth identities and investment influence how they use language and for what purposes. In addition, I recognize that many public high schools are ill-equipped to teach adolescent emergent readers the most basic literacy skills, and by not doing so, students are faced with a structural obstacle to their academic progress. Falling outside the norm in terms of prior schooling, native language literacy development and traditional preferences for orality versus literacy are all problematized in terms of how U.S. public schooling chooses to educate immigrant or refugee youth.

Research to Advocacy to Research

Research can lead to advocacy (ideally, in partnership with community members) and advocacy can lead to new paths of scholarship. It should be clear to readers by now that I firmly believe in this symbiotic relationship between research and advocacy. The personal experiences of community involvement outside the walls of academia that I have recounted, and many more I choose to leave out of this book, have propelled and guided my research agenda for the past 5 years. The Meeting with the Police and Suing the School stories, in particular, are noteworthy because they came to symbolize the broadening of my role as a researcher in ways that included advocacy. Thus, this book is grounded in multiple social concerns that work as a backdrop for sustaining the interdisciplinarity and larger social issues that have come to characterize the research.

I believe that it is important for researchers to engage in the issues that are relevant to the populations they study. With the leadership of Ladan, a strong community partner, my work was used to try to disrupt institutionalized racism at school, challenge deficit discourses, and educate the broader community about cultural and linguistic difference. All of these activities are suitable activities to engage in as an applied linguist and educator. The challenge is finding a meaningful way to do these things where we work in conjunction with others who have complementary skills and assets.

For example, take the Meeting with the Policy story. The dynamic of the encounter—a White professor talking about/for Somali youth—was layered with symbolic power of race and privilege, and this was not lost on the Somali young people present. Yet, Ladan felt that this was the way the meeting should be conducted, because until the police had heard that "a professor" was involved, they were not interested in meeting with her or the Somali youth. Because I had a perceived position of power as a professor, and was White, I was able to have the floor first. The Somali youth present said later that it was strange to hear me telling stories that represented experiences like the ones they had had, but they accepted it because I gave their stories more credibility and my being there sanctioned the telling of their stories in this public forum. There is a serious tension with *both* the research and the advocacy resulting from this work. I am not only an "outsider" but an outsider who has gotten involved in a way that inadvertently reifies a racist system, demonstrating the power of the capital I have to the activist youth involved.

Engagement through the lawsuit is instructive as well. I was energized by seeing firsthand how the status quo in education policies and practices did not work for students who were marginalized and minoritized in multiple ways. This experience broadened and deepened my understanding of the structural obstacles that adolescents with limited or interrupted formal schooling face in U.S. public schools. The experience also afforded me a new understanding about how SLA research is urgently needed to inform educational decisions about how to teach language and literacy to newcomers without prior schooling or literacy. At the same time, and as I will discuss in chapter 5, I also became aware of the fact that educational scholarship intended to help can be subverted in ways that contribute to a destructive rationale for why these learners may not be able to be successful in school.

There were also other much less public aspects of my work with Somali youth that had levels of community engagement that were new to me as a researcher and even as an English as a second/foreign language teacher. A good case in point is the research I carried out with four Somali teenage girls and that I will report in chapter 3. The focus of this work was to learn what it was like, socially and academically, to be a recently resettled Somali refugee with limited formal schooling and be enrolled in a large public high school in the United States. I met with the girls for over 2 years, and during that long period, our contact was even more intense for 16 months, when I would meet with the girls two to four times a month in order to gather data. I had the opportunity to be a mentor, resource, tutor, confidante, and friend. In some research paradigms, these sorts of interactions with participants would compromise the study, but in this case, it was both part of the research design and necessary for the experience to be sustainable, reciprocal, and fair. Practically speaking, without academic and social reasons to meet, it would have been difficult to follow the girls and my view of their worlds would have been much more limited. Sometimes my role in the group meant coaching the girls on their state-mandated basic skills tests. Other times my role was to listen to their complaints and worries about school. We came together to work on job and scholarship applications as well as homework. My inquiry into their schooling and literacy development began for me what Buroway et al. (2004) called the restoration of a balance between basic research and a commitment to social justice. In this sense, it was an intervention on my own learning and development as a researcher.

"Getting involved" can begin to reduce the asymmetry sometimes experienced between researchers and participants by balancing the sacrifices, benefits, and rewards of all involved. Partnerships with community members and organizations have the potential to reduce the gap between the questions researchers ask, often derived entirely from scholarly literature, and the questions community members or teachers ask, often drawn from their observations and experiences (Crookes, 1997). This practitioner-scholar divide, however, is a somewhat false dichotomy because academics in higher education can develop programs of research and advocacy within the academy—for example, in their own teacher education programs (Bigelow & Ranney, 2005), with other educators outside of higher education (Dyer, 2008; Gibbons, 2008)—or they can find research questions closely tied to their work as, for example, graduate student mentors (Waring, 2007).

Engagement with those outside the academy is different. It requires different skills and processes to gain access to a community and, furthermore, grounding research in issues that the community cares about (e.g., education, language learning, racial profiling). It takes more time to develop a well-rounded sense of the research context within which data are gathered and analyzed. Additionally, there are structural barriers to equity in research endeavors in terms of how participation is rewarded. For example, in funded projects, participants and community partners often collaborate with little or no monetary support, whereas researchers and research assistants receive reduced teaching loads, tuition, health benefits, and so forth. Products from the research (e.g., publications, presentations) may result in merit pay increases, whereas the rewards community collaborators obtain may be far less tangible.

Despite the challenges involved in doing publically engaged research, the process of committing research to the community it ultimately benefits can be of great value. This process, however, is infrequently reported or problematized in the Applied Linguistics scholarship. In addition, advocacy activities can be uncomfortable, call upon skills that researchers do not necessarily have, and therefore can feel risky. For this reason, I hope to problematize the issue of advocacy or activism in research and contribute to a response to Foley and Valenzuela's (2006) invitation to publish my collaborative practices and efforts to affect change.

When research and advocacy can mutually inspire each other, this creates a healthy purpose for scholarship and grounds the research in broader social dimensions. For some, however, it may create tension: Is the researcher's objectivity compromised because she has become an advocate? This is a serious and legitimate concern, but advocacy and research are not necessarily mutually exclusive or sequential processes. In my experience, engagement with an immigrant community results in learning what their perspectives and concerns are regarding their lives in this new land.

Researcher Identity and Disclosure

The research process must include a certain level of disclosure. The work of a researcher should include an attempt to examine and reveal biases to build credibility. My co-authors and I have attempted to do this in Tarone et al. (2009). We described ourselves this way in an effort to reveal our own ethnicity, race, and political views with regard to immigration and immigrant education:

> All three primary researchers identify as female, White, and middle-class. Religiously, we are within the dominant Judeo-Christian traditions in the United States. When we are treated as minorities, it is typically due to our gender. Tarone draws on her Scottish and Italian immigrant grandparents to define herself ethnically. Bigelow draws on her German and Irish heritage, or the myth of that heritage, to situate herself as a great-granddaughter of immigrants. Hansen too, is of European— German, Danish and Irish—heritage. We share an identity as advocates for immigrants—particularly in the realm of education. Our views are progressive, both with respect to immigrant policy (e.g., we support amnesty for undocumented immigrants and would like to see the numbers of refugees resettled in the United States increase) and with respect to

language policy (for example, we support multilingualism and multiculturalism). Our stance as educators and teacher educators is squarely within perspectives that promote culturally relevant pedagogy and additive bi/multilingualism. (p. 37)

Obviously, no research is without bias, and bias is revealed in all dimensions of scholarly work: in the questions asked, the scholarly literature chosen to review, the participants chosen to study, and so on. However, for the research to have the potential to be useful to specific communities, groups of people, or higher social justice aims, it has to be of high quality and be accessible to stakeholders, perhaps in unconventional forms such as Web sites, pamphlets, videos, or nonacademic presentations in community spaces (Fine et al., 2000). Even if researchers begin with social justice aims and conduct their research in thoughtful, ethical, and participant-focused ways, there is no guarantee that the process will unfold as planned and be of direct benefit to participants or the populations from which they came. Perhaps there are other ways that the researchers can reciprocate (e.g., giving workshops for teachers, serving on the boards of community organizations). However, this way of "giving back" takes the research out of the engagement. There is also no guarantee that the researcher will not make mistakes in interacting with community members. It is my hope that the risk of failure or conflict not be cause for preventing researchers from attempting collaborative work in unfamiliar settings with underrepresented communities.

Working in an unfamiliar setting can add an insider-outsider dichotomous dimension to the research. The advantages and limitations of each cannot be assumed (Banks, 1998). As a cultural outsider working with Somalis, I am limited by and also benefit from participants' assumption that I do not understand their lives. For example, participants may explain ideas more thoroughly to me because they assume that I do not share their experiences (Twine & Warren, 2000). On the other hand, it is impossible to understand fully stories of survival and loss, racial discrimination, and Islamophobia. This is why it is important for me as a White researcher to examine my White privilege and think about my own racialized identity. Although I am far from done with this process, it is essential for navigating issues of power that arise in any type of research and particularly research that deals with topics on race (Fine, Weis, Powell, & Wong, 1997). In the new and unfamiliar Somali cultural context in which I hoped to work, it was important for me to engage all of my personal and scholarly knowledge of racial and cultural awareness and positionality (Milner, 2007). The work by Peggy McIntosh (1988, 1990) is helpful to White researchers like me to begin to understand White privilege. Thandeka's (1999) work is also helpful. For example, Thandeka can guide White researchers through childhood memories of racism by explaining how "the first racial victim of the White community is its own child" (p. vii). Although this is undoubtedly tragic, a Somali student in one of my graduate classes reminded me that it is even more tragic to be a racial victim of the White community as a Black child with no power (Abdullahi Bashir, personal communication, September 23, 2009). Bashir also pointed out that White people have the option to engage (or not) in explorations of White privilege and identity, whereas people of color often experience race and the development of a racial identity personally, through societal injustices. White researchers must be reflective as they carry out their work and build relationships in minoritized communities, such that the work has the potential to be both meaningful and appropriately grounded.

Writing and Reporting Research as an Opportunity for Advocacy
Before moving to chapter 2 and the report of the research in this book, I wish to offer a final thought on how researchers report their research findings and discuss the implications of their work. It is common or sometimes required for Applied Linguists to advocate for the relevance of their findings in the implications sections of their articles, despite the distance of the linkages between the findings and the implications (Han, 2007). For instance, the *TESOL Quarterly* instructs authors in their submission guidelines that "theoretical articles and reports of research must contain a discussion of implications or applications for practice" (TESOL Quarterly Submission Guidelines, 2009). This is a slightly different stance from earlier work in Applied Linguistics that problematizes research that draws conclusions too vast for the research that was conducted (Swain & Fathman, 1976), perhaps causing researchers to be too hesitant to speculate about the meaning of their work. I believe that it is possible to do both: craft a discussion of the data that does not go beyond what the data have to offer as well as speculate about the implications and future directions of the research.

Conclusion: Engaged Research

I hope that readers do not see advocacy as the result of research—something that begins when the research is complete. Rather, advocacy can occur when the inquiry is in its earliest stages. By crafting research questions that are relevant to the intended beneficiaries of the work, researchers are better able to undertake research that will matter both along the way and in the end (Allen,

2007; Ortega, 2005). If the research is of interest to those who are meant to use it, there will be more opportunities to use the research for advocacy purposes at multiple places during and beyond the activities of a study.

One of the most fruitful outcomes of research is when the research(er) can serve as a catalyst for dialogue and activity among individuals. Engaged research, or research including stakeholders from the public, has the potential to inform policy and raise public awareness of issues. It is my hope that the work in the community and dissemination of the research and its subtexts in this book serve to share some of the perspectives of Somali immigrant youth as well as the issues that affect their lives. The opportunity to gather these perspectives and understand how various institutions interact with their lives only occurred through close collaboration with community partners. I find it difficult to imagine how engaged research could occur without the insight and good sense of strong partners, particularly when the researcher is not a member of the community. Through collaboration, researchers can act publically and politically in ways that have the potential to inform policies and practices in U.S. institutions. As Applied Linguists, we should consider these activities as part of our role as scholars as well as a way to maintain the integrity of our research among stakeholders and foster social justice.

Notes

1 The construct of race embraced in this book is that race is not a biological fact (thus the quotation marks) but rather a socially constructed set of assumptions based largely on visual and assumed identification of physical or phenotypic physical characteristics of an individual.

2 I am aware I use the term "limited" in reference to learners who have had interrupted or no formal schooling. For now, I will persist with this descriptor, knowing that it contributes to the discourse of deficiency and does reduce individuals to a single label. The fact that I struggle with another word to speak of the plaintiffs and students like them speaks to the power of the construct within the social structures that gave rise to the term. However, I do wish to note that students are categorized as "limited" only within the institutions of schooling. I have found that their identifications and descriptions are more complete and positive in community, work, and family settings.

Language Learning   ISSN 0023-8333

CHAPTER 2

Orality and Literacy Within the Somali Diaspora

Do you see why it's amazing,
When someone comes out of such a dire situation
And learns the English language,
Just to share his observation!
Probably get a Grammy without a grammar education.

From the song "Somalia" off of Troubadour album by K'naan,
a Somali-Canadian musician and poet

Introduction

It is within the larger context of migration that the research in this book was conducted. Although the research that will be discussed in this and the following chapters is highly contextualized in local social structures and ideologies, it is also part of a profoundly global phenomenon of transnational movement due mainly to civil strife in the Horn of Africa.

Somali refugees face a continuum of challenges as they resettle and become part of communities around the world. At the same time, the possibility still exists that Somalis from the Diaspora will return and help rebuild Somalia once there is finally an "outbreak of peace" (Roble & Rutledge, 2008, p. 182). Roble and Rutledge (2008) offered this statement of hope, which is the view I share about how Somalis are living in the West:

> Somali members of the Diaspora are far from home, but they have learned to participate in the economic and cultural environments in whatever country they find themselves. They are caring for themselves and their families . . . but the journey continues. These traditionally nomadic people are no longer leading herds of camels and goats as they seek the most

Language Learning 60:Suppl. 1, September 2010, pp. 25–57

recent rain, but they are following economic and cultural opportunities across the globe. (p. 183)

Like Roble and Rutledge, I see Somalis adapting, joining, and contributing to life in Minnesota, but I also see points of struggle. It is particularly difficult for those who arrived well into adolescence or adulthood without the benefit of prior schooling to ease the transition to work or school in a society permeated by text.

The Somali community in Minnesota, as any community anywhere, is diverse in many seen and unseen ways. "Somali-ness" can be a powerful identity constructed in the Diaspora. Somali children are born and grow up here, relatives join family members, and Somalis relocating to Minnesota have lived in other parts of the United States and the world and continue to travel back to these places, including the Horn of Africa. Perspectives and practices change over time within communities, families, and individuals; yet, it is common to find attempts to hold onto things decidedly Somali.

A Somali student named Moxammed[1] can help illustrate this point. A high school senior and already accepted to a state college, Moxammed agreed to come and speak with a group of preservice language teachers on a panel with other high school students from nearby urban high schools. The panel discussion was videotaped and, with consent, was turned into curriculum materials for other teachers via a digital video case format.[2] I quote here in some length what Moxammed said when introducing himself:

> I'm from Somalia, but I never grew up in Somalia. I don't have no idea
> how it looks like. But I was told by my mom always never to forget where
> I'm from. She always keeps reminding that at home while we are at home
> always know how to speak in Somali even though my Somali is not as
> perfect as like the rest of the people who come from Somalia. But I do
> feel—um I do have like a strong culture identity. Because everywhere I go
> today my culture is being represented no matter where. In every country
> I've been I've seen like a lot of people know where my country is—in
> Africa and stuff like that. So basically, by the way I learn my culture was
> just you know to learn from people who come from my country, my
> homeland, where I'm from. So I just take my—I see what they do and then
> try to follow it and try to you know learn from it. And at the same time if I
> do something wrong of course they are there for me and they will tell me
> that's not how things are done up here and I kind of accept it cause I don't
> know how things were dealt with back there so. And I'm still learning

today, everyday. Every day that goes by I see a new person I learn
something. So, so that's how it is for me basically.

Moxammed chose to share a number of personal facts in his introduction
that seem telling and possibly contradictory. He is from Somalia but does not
know what it looks like. He speaks Somali, but not as perfectly as people who
come from Somalia. Moxammed is guided by others who "know how things
were dealt with back there" but is "still learning today, everyday." Moxammed
dispels an important myth about being Somali; namely, that national and ethnic
identities can be chosen and cultivated. Being Somali is not necessarily *only* a
fact of birthplace.

Moxammed's self-introduction suggests that he is highly invested in being
Somali, and learning to speak and act Somali is part of this. Speaking and
acting Somali seem to have great symbolic power in who he wants to be(come).
Moxammed's membership goes beyond only a personal or family association,
but it reaches out across the world to others whom he wishes to emulate. Likewise, being "Somali" does not necessarily require firsthand experiences of life
in Somalia. Someone else's memories about Somalia may suffice and transfer
to him. Furthermore, a person can learn how to speak and be Somali from
others who are doing it *and this is possible to do in Minnesota.*[3] Moxammed
reminds us that there are many narratives among immigrant communities about
who they are—some are based on nationality, some ethnicity, and perhaps some
draw upon profoundly idealized or nostalgic memories that encompass specific
ways of acting and speaking.[4] Moxammed's sense of belonging comes from
"back there" and extends to "here." Benedict Anderson (1983) and later Stuart
Hall (1990) have framed this feeling or sense of being as *imagined community*
through the creation of new practices and self-representations that are discursively imagined. Moxammed includes himself in a local Somali community
as well as in a transnational community that extends or transcends place and
nationality. His community is at once local and global, an idea explicated by
Sarroub's (2008) discussion of the "glocal" in immigrant youth literacies and
transnationalism. Somali culture and language have meaning for him and seem
to be facets of being Somali in his family and being Somali in his local community in Minnesota. It also seems that Moxammed's mother influences his
desire to speak Somali and "never to forget" where he is from. Perhaps she also
engages in an imagined community that is glocal.

Some of the questions that arise from Moxammed's text are the following: How is a person's potential for imagining shaped by contrary or more

powerful imaginations? Is one's own imagining powerful enough? Does it matter whether identity is legitimized by others? Moxammed's introduction of himself affirms the relevance of speaking the home language and the reality in Minnesota that native language maintenance and development will probably be cultivated outside of school. Is language shift inevitable and permanent for the 1.5-generation[5] teen like Moxammed? Being Somali for Moxammed means knowing how to speak Somali as well as how to act Somali, and he is embracing the symbolism of language and culture to cultivate and validate his claim to being Somali. The way Moxammed lives in the Minnesota Somali Diaspora is sure to be different from other Somali youth. It depends on many factors that all influence identity construction, such as the length of time in the United States, age of arrival, and community investment.

This chapter will explore how youth like Moxammed came to live in Minnesota by retracing briefly some of the premigration circumstances common to many in the Somali community and the cause for limited formal schooling and low levels of print literacy. The demographics of the local community will be outlined for the purpose of placing the subsequent research in a context. Then a discussion of the meaning of orality to traditional and contemporary Somali cultures will be explored. Finally, an overview of research on what all of these cultural, political, and historical facts and circumstances may mean for schooling and English language learning in Minnesota will be given.

Demographics of Displacement

In order to understand the vastness of the human toll caused by the Somali civil war that began in 1991 and has continued with varying levels of political unrest until today, it is important to outline some of the facts related to the initial displacement. The United Nations High Commission on Refugees reported that the conflict had initially caused the displacement of 50,000 Somali to Mombasa, Kenya, 150,000 to the North Eastern Province of Kenya, and 400,000 to eastern Ethiopia. In 2008, there were approximately 100,000 refugees and asylum seekers who had fled violence and persecution at home and live in or around Nairobi. At least 270,000 additional refugees now live in Kenya's refugee camps: Dadaab, near the Somali border, and Kakuma camp, near Sudan's border (Chanoff, 2008). As of January 2009, the Dadaab refugee population had grown to approximately 240,000 people and had exceeded its capacity by 270%.[6] The UNHCR (Integrated Regional Information Networks, 2009) mounts periodic attempts to repatriate Somalis, but these have not been very successful. Armed clashes among clan militia in southern Somalia have prevented their return. Furthermore, their chances of going to other countries are slim. Although resettlement applications to third countries (such as the United States and Australia) have been made, very few have been accepted. According to one Web site, "it seems that, for the future, life will be bound by the live fencing that surrounds the Dadaab camps."[7] These camps were and continue to be places of inhumanity, disease, and violence, with violence against women high. The camps within Somalia for internally displaced persons are no better.

In addition to fleeing to neighboring countries in the region, Somalis have settled in massive numbers in Europe, the Middle East, and the United States, creating numerous cultural and linguistic contact zones throughout the world. Thus, Minnesota is only one among many places where Somalis have settled. For instance, the Somali community in London dates as far back as 1914, when Somalis fought alongside the British in World War I. Like Minnesota, the United Kingdom welcomed tens of thousands of Somali refugees in the 1990s and today is considered to be one of the largest Somali communities outside of East Africa.[8] Nevertheless, Somali communities in Minnesota are distinct and important, and the Twin Cities rivals Toronto for claims to the largest North American Somali community.

Although not everyone who identifies as Somali in Minnesota was a refugee or lived in a refugee camp, many Somalis in Minnesota do share the experience of civil war, loss, and displacement, followed by many long years in refugee camps, and the new challenges of resettlement. Most of those who have moved to Minnesota have arrived since 1997. There are also numerous smaller communities of refugees in Minnesota, including those from Liberia, Ethiopia, and, most recently, Burma and Bhutan.

Somalis are now a visible presence in Minnesota. There are large numbers of Somali children in the schools, adult basic education, and literacy classes. Some estimate the population to be as high as 50,000. However, the precise size of the Somali population here and in other cities is difficult to calculate because it changes dramatically every year due to different refugee policies and constant migration from other states to and from Minnesota. Furthermore, official census figures are often inaccurate because families living in rental properties are likely to report the number of residents allowed on the lease, not the actual number living in the dwelling.[9] However, Somalis make up the third largest foreign-born group in the state, after Latinos, who are the largest group (approximately 175,000), and Hmong (approximately 60,000), the second largest group.[10] The Minnesota Department of Education figures show that 9,583 children in the 2006–2007 academic year reported speaking Somali as their primary home language. In the same year, 32,239 children were reported as having Spanish and 22,665 children were reported as having Hmong as their primary home language.

Race, Religion, and Xenophobia

To understand the meaning of the large migration of Somali refugees to a Midwestern American region, it is important to understand the larger racial and ethnic picture of Minnesota. The total population of the state of Minnesota, according to the 2006 Census, is 5,167,101.[11] Statewide, 87.8% of the population said they were White; if cities and urban areas are considered separately, the diversity increases somewhat. Thus, in the city of Minneapolis, 68.5% said they were White, 19.3% said they spoke a language other than English at home, and 14.8% were foreign born. In the city of St. Paul, 65.8% of the population said they were White, 22.9% said they spoke a language other than English at home, and 13.8% of the population was foreign born (for more demographic detail, see Tarone et al., 2009).

The year when this research began, 2004, is suggestive of certain facts among Somalis living throughout the Diaspora as well as in the Horn of Africa. Officially, between 1997 and 2004 there had been 7,211 Somali refugees resettled in Minnesota and, again, approximately the same number of additional resettlements between 2004 and 2007.[12] Thousands more arrived to Minnesota from other U.S. cities. Somali businesses and nonprofits serving the community started appearing and the workforce included a large number Somalis. At this time, schools were learning and relearning how to welcome large numbers of refugees. The Hmong, who are the first and largest group of refugees, were resettled in large numbers in Minnesota beginning in the 1970s. There were differences, however, because the Somali community was Muslim, whereas many Hmong refugees practice shamanism, animism, and ancestor worship. Public schools were new to seeing women and girls with veils and were asked to accommodate these and other religious and cultural practices. Schools and other institutions are still in the process of learning about Islam and our East African communities.

The media have tried to introduce Somali refugees to the dominant society in educational and generally positive ways. For example, *Star Tribune* reporter Tom Horgen (2007) wrote about dining out during Ramadan. This piece focused on the Muslims in the Twin Cities. It explained the religious practice of Ramadan as well as places Muslims go to break their daily fasts. It offered descriptions of busy Somali coffee shops and mentioned that some young Somali women go to mainstream chain restaurants during Ramadan. The newspaper article nicely blended the traditional and contemporary ways of being a Muslim in Minnesota. In another newspaper article, David La Vaque (2008) captured some of the feelings that adolescent Muslims may have playing sports in Minnesota schools during Ramadan. He quoted a cross-country runner who was worried about how his teammates perceive him: "I don't want to be thought of as selfish [because of fasting], as someone whose religion is hurting the team. The pressure comes more from myself because I know what my coaches and teammates expect." The Somali runner was portrayed as a star athlete and a respected team player. The fact that he runs while fasting shows the strength of his beliefs and makes him seem all the more admirable because he continues to win races. Both of these stories are instances of positive representation of Somali Muslims in the local media.

There have also been expressions of hatred toward Somalis in the media. Anderson, a reporter for the *Minnesota Daily*, justifiably critiqued the lumping of all East Africans as Somalis but went on to say that there is "a unique and particularly potent brand of racism" against Somalis who suffer "backlash from the locals" as they navigate their religious practices in a secular society (Anderson, 2009). Many instances of violence against Somalis coincided with the events following the terrorist attacks of 9/11. The following recent statement was from an article written by John Gibson (2007) of Fox News, a major cable news network with a reputation for conservative commentary:

Minnesota: America's First Somali-Muslim State?

Somalis coming to Minnesota are not assimilating. They are bringing the Muslim culture of that desert country to Minnesota's snowy woods. They may have to wear warmer clothing, but the Somalis want Islamic law just like back home. And they want the same illegal drug [khat] they had back home, too.

Minnesota is famously liberal and now all eyes are on the state to see how voters there react to this onslaught against their culture and law . . . . What Minnesotans must say is this is America. We already have law here, and if the Somalis wanted to live under Koran law, Sharia, they could have stayed in Somalia.

These expressions of righteous outrage and hostility are some of the most explicit ways Somalis specifically living in Minnesota experience minoritization and public Othering. Sometimes the media is more subtle. For example, in a *New York Times* article about the unusual rise in the incidence of Somali children with autism in Minnesota, the author associated the headscarf with living outside of mainstream society in the following quote: "The city is welcoming and social benefits are generous, but many live a life apart as conservative Muslims, the women in head scarves and long dresses" (McNeil, 2009). It is unfortunate that the hijab is interpreted to signal separation from mainstream society when this is clearly not the case. Many Somali women simultaneously wear a veil and hold professional and blue collar jobs, pursue higher education, and are contributing members of society within and beyond their own co-ethnic communities.

The international media also expose abuses from all places where the Somali Diaspora resides in large numbers. It seems, however, that Malta and South Africa rival each other for becoming the most notorious for their massive anti-Somali public outcry and violent oppression. In Malta, Somali refugees, including minors, are often detained in miserable conditions. Unbridled xenophobia from the Maltese is common and even physical attacks against immigrants have occurred (Walker-Leigh, 2006). South Africa has created refugee camps in an effort to protect Somali refugees against violence that claimed up to 60 lives in 2008 (Allie, 2006; Mabandu, 2009). The media must continue to cover these stories to put pressure on governments to improve the conditions of immigrants and refugees within their borders.

Low Print Literacy and Interrupted Schooling

In addition to death, injury, and witnessing immense human tragedy, the struggle for survival followed by long waits in refugee camps also results in a high incidence of low print literacy and limited formal schooling among many recently arrived Somali adolescents. Although refugee camps sometimes offer schooling, classes typically have few materials and are large. It is nearly impossible for most families to afford to send children to school in the camp because of the requirement to buy books, uniforms, and so forth. Furthermore, the culture of the camps makes it more and more dangerous for girls to persist with schooling. In her visits to Dadaab, Cawa Abdi (2007) found that in one particular year, only 69 of 675 high school students were girls. Abdi explained that one reason for this is that as they reach marriageable age, they are at higher risk of sexual violence. Therefore, families keep their girls home.

Limited formal schooling is also the result of coming from rural backgrounds where there was little access to formal schooling. Three fifths of the Somali population was comprised of pastoralist nomadic people, living off of their herds and the harsh terrain (Kahin, 1997). Of course, there are many Somalis who come from towns and large urban areas with more opportunity

Figure 2.1 Map of Somalia drawn by Ayan Hudle, a Somali high school student from Ogadeneia. Reprinted with permission © Ayan Hudle 2010.

for formal education. In the past, the nation's capital and largest city of Mogadishu was alive with commerce, had two large universities, and a large sports stadium. Therefore, there are dramatic differences in attitudes about and experiences with education among pastoralists and urbanites as well as between those who were of school age during times of peace versus war and unrest (i.e., those who were young children prior to 1991).

Figure 2.1 shows a map of Somalia within the Horn of Africa, along with neighboring Ethiopia, Kenya, Djibouti, and Eritrea. This map was drawn by Ayan Hudle, a Somali high school student from Ogadenia.

After consulting the maps I gave her for reference, finding her own references, and discussing the map with her parents and her friends' parents, Ayan made a number of important decisions about how to draw her map of Somalia. She drew dotted lines along the border between Somalia and Ogadenia because this is a contested political border. She said that many people from Ogadenia would prefer to be part of Somalia, not Ethiopia. She also chose to distinguish Oromia within Ethiopia because she wished to honor their wish for independence. The portions of Ethiopia that are not labeled are, as Ayan told me, "just Ethiopia," or the unmarked, overarching geographical area within which Oromia and Ogadenia lie. She labeled the political and tribal divisions in Somalia as opposed to the smaller regions. Other people from her region may contest this and other choices Ayan made, saying that it reifies clan-based social structures that have contributed to conflict and war there. Ayan chose spellings of place names in the region that cross multiple languages in which various spellings are widely used (e.g., Djibuti and Djabuti; Galgadud and Galguduud). Ayan chose Somali spellings for her map. We discussed adding the major refugee camps in the region (e.g., Dadaab and Kakuma), but Ayan argued that these are places of transition and pain and that she did not think they should be part of a map of the area. It is possible that by the time this map is in print, the political context of the region will have changed and Ayan would draw it differently. It is certain that other individuals from the region and the Diaspora would both embrace and dispute her decisions on how to represent the political divisions within the Horn of Africa. Maps are not always neutral artifacts of peacefully agreed upon geographic boundaries, especially in postcolonial Africa. I chose to include Ayan's depiction of the region because I wish to privilege the perspective of a teenage member of the Somali Diaspora.

Somalia gained independence in the early 1960s and was under civilian rule from 1960 to 1969. In 1969, Siad Barre's military overthrew the government in a coup d'ètat and brought forth a number of ambitious programs, including the choice of "scientific socialism" as the country's guiding ideology (Abdi, 1998). He remained in power for 22 years, until 1991, at which point the state collapsed due to power struggles among clans.

The British and Italian colonial powers of the 19th century instituted formal schooling to replace traditional pastoralist ways of educating children focusing on pastoralist survival skills and study of the Qur'an. Some Arab countries also supported schools in Somalia where Arabic was the medium of instruction. For instance, between 1960 and 1991, there had been schooling available to a small number of Somalis in English and Italian. The Egyptian government sponsored schools that used Arabic as well (Abdi, 1998). Nevertheless, widespread literacy in the Somali language is a relatively recent phenomenon. In 1972, and after much debate, Siad Barre's government determined unilaterally that Somali

would be written using the Roman script (Warsame, 2001). This event, which
Biber and Hared (1991) characterized as monumental and transformative, was
accompanied by a massive nationwide literacy campaign. It is claimed that
through this initiative, basic literacy went from 5% to over 50% for Somalis
over 15 years of age (UNICEF, n.d.). However, this progress was thwarted by
the Ogaden War in 1977–1978 so that by the late 1980s, the formal education
system had few resources, and schools were shut down due to low enrollment
and the loss of teachers to better paying jobs. The Ogaden War caused a massive
influx of Somalis who had been living in eastern Ethiopia, resulting in many
large refugee camps in Somalia. This was a time of building chaos, and by 1990,
of a population of approximately 7–8 million people, there were only about
150,000 children enrolled in school, one of the lowest school enrollment rates
in the world. When the civil war broke out in 1991, about 90% of the schools
in Somalia were destroyed and massive displacement occurred. As of 2008,
Somalia's literacy rate has fallen to 37.8% (49.7% male; 25.8% female).[13] Abdi
(1998) spoke to the magnitude of the situation when he said: "The country's
children are now, for all observable intentions, 'aspiring' illiterates in today's
interdependent, technologically advanced and global economy-oriented world"
(p. 328).

Many Somali youth have parents or grandparents who have had formal
schooling in Somalia or abroad. Nevertheless, it seems clear that although
there had been few Somalis in school before 1990, after 1990 there were even
fewer. Additionally although some children were able to attend school as they
awaited resettlement, the consistency and quality of the schooling was often
poor. As large numbers of Somalis had to spend more and more time in refugee
camps or otherwise displaced within Somalia, large numbers had to be resettled
with little or severely interrupted formal schooling.

Language: Orality and Literacy in Everyday Tradition and Culture

It seems that one of the most important cultural artifacts of Somalis in the
Diaspora is their ongoing and exuberant sense of orality. Oral language in
the form of stories, dramas, jokes, riddles, proverbs, and poems are centuries
old and this love of the spoken word has transferred to English and reaches
through all means of communicating through today's technology. I will never
forget when I was asked to be a judge at a poetry recitation competition at
a charter high school that tends to enroll East African Muslim students. The
poems to choose from were mainly written by famous American or British poets
and about 15 students had been selected from the advanced ESL and English
classes to perform. When I arrived, students were bringing out rugs to cover the

gymnasium floor for the entire study body to attend. When students began to file in, they had made posters to support their friends and eagerly awaited the event. Each time that a poet approached the microphone, there was loud cheering, and when they finished their poem, there was great applause and more cheering. Favorite poems chosen by multiple students were Langston Hughes' "I, too" and "Theme for English B" and Maya Angelou's "Phenomenal Woman" (Angelou, 1978). When the results were announced moments after the performances, the two winning boys, both of Somali descent, were spontaneously lifted to the shoulders of their friends and carried around the gymnasium like star athletes. East African orality was alive and well in this high school in Minnesota. It was an English teacher's dream.

There are numerous venues for spoken word poetry in the Twin Cities that are attended by Somali teens and adults. Somali Web sites have forums for poets to post their poems, including rap-style poems. Poems are written mainly in English and Somali or blends of the two. These forums offer often separate sections for proverbs, riddles, jokes, and stories that also reflect the multilingual community (e.g., http://www.somalilife.com/vbforum/). Poetry is still improvised for Somali weddings in Minnesota (Abukar Ali, personal communication, April 7, 2009). Teachers, also, frequently comment on the highly interactive spirit of their Somali students, and cultural liaisons and educational assistants working with Somali families know that the best way to communicate with parents and guardians is by phone or face-to-face, not via written memos home. The Minneapolis International Middle School, an East African charter school, uses automated phone trees to contact parents and guardians for parent-teacher conferences. Abdirashid Warsami, its director, told me that parents are contacted five to six times to remind them about the events, and this results in percentage rates of parent attendance in the high 90s (personal communication, November, 24, 2009). In books about how to teach Somali youth in the United Kingdom (Kahin, 1997) and the United States (Farid & McMahan, 2004) there is always mention of the importance of orality to the Somali culture.

Secular Oral Texts

In Somalia, poets are deeply respected and poetry is used for a range of purposes from influencing current public affairs (Andrzejewski, 1988) to entertainment. Ali Jimale Ahmed (n.d.) wrote that still "orality is the preferred medium used for cultural representation" (p. 1) in the Somali context. Ahmed explained that the Somali oral tradition "extols the virtues of memory" and relies on "the existence of a pool of memorizers" and "a constant repetition of the 'word' for its survival":

In oral cultures, children are taught about their tradition by word of mouth. Each generation in the process selectively preserves its wisdom and that of preceding generations for posterity. Oral literatures, therefore, apart from their aesthetic quality and the experiential wisdom inherent in them, ensured the survival of tradition in the minds of the young. (pp. 1–2)

Ahmed explained that stories in Somali culture "depict the tasks, the preoccupations and contradictions that Somali society grapples with, and attempts to explain to its members" (p. 7). As such, there are poems about traditional topics as well as contemporary dilemmas. Jama (1994) explained that poetry also plays a significant role in politics, particularly among women during times of conflict. She said,

[P]oets adopt the position of journalists, spokespersons, and politicians rolled into one. Poets from different sides of the conflict exchange poetry that is performed at assemblies and traditional courts. These poetic compositions are also passed to different settlements and communities by word of mouth through the professional memorizers and reciters. Proverbs are used in everyday verbal exchanges in both rural and urban societies. Riddles are more commonly used by nomads, who continue to test each other's knowledge and intelligence by presenting complicated oral puzzles to one another. (p. 185)

K'Naan, whose verse served to open this chapter, is an excellent example of a contemporary Somali Diaspora poet (and popular rapper). He was born in Somalia but grew up in Canada. He is popular among Diaspora youth and plays at mainstream music venues in Minnesota. The language is English and the messages are about current problems of racism and injustice, but his role and his craft seem timeless and squarely set within Somali oral traditions. The spoken word for Somalis has had great richness and importance historically and in the present day. It is used to mobilize public opinion as well as agitate for different causes. K'Naan embodied this fact. K'Naan attributed his art to his grandfather, who was a poet, and his aunt, who was a singer (Persson, 2009). K'Naan often offered social commentary in his songs, such as the following verse from "Wavin' Flag":

So many wars, settling scores,
Bringing us promises, leaving us poor,
I heard them say, love is the way,
Love is the answer, that's what they say,

But look how they treat us, Make us believers,
We fight their battles, then they deceive us,
Try to control us, they couldn't hold us,
Cause we just move forward like Buffalo Soldiers. (from "Troubadour,"
2009)

He made allusions to Somalia, but his message was easily embraced internationally, which is likely why this song was chosen as the anthem for the World Cup in South Africa in 2010.

The role of traditional oral texts in the everyday lives of adolescent Somalis is often apparent. It is impossible to refute that primarily oral cultures "can produce amazingly complex and intelligent and beautiful organizations of thought and experience" (Ong, 1982, p. 57). They compose and perform poetry at school and in community settings. Even Somali children who are English-dominant enjoy reading and telling long Somali folktales and jokes in English. A team of educators from Lyndale Community School in Minneapolis has compiled numerous Somali folktales that reportedly inspire many culturally relevant teaching lessons and intergenerational dialogue around text. It is called The Somali Folktale Project/Sheekooyin Carrureed (http://www3.mpls.k12.mn.us/schools/elementary/lyndale/somali/index.html). These secular oral texts are often part of collective memories and stories of survival. This is seen in the story that two teenage sisters, participants in my research, told about their time in a refugee camp. They described to me how their mother entertained them and their siblings with interesting and funny stories. They lived in the refugee camp for 7 years, and although they recall the camp as a very dangerous place, they have fond memories of their mother telling folktales at night. The sisters said they missed those days in the camp when they were together and felt so close. For this family, storytelling was a literacy practice located in a particular time and place, which took on the added function of supporting a sense of family unity and safety in very dangerous times. Reflecting on their new lives in the United States, the sisters lament that the television takes up that time in the evening. This particular way of using traditional texts changed, but (as we will see in chapter 3) this genre remained relevant to the children as they acquired English at school.

Qur'anic Schools (Dugsi) and Religious Texts
Although the Somali language was not encoded in the Roman alphabet until 1972, Somalis have had a long relationship with text, particularly religious texts. Islam is pervasive in the daily lives of many Somalis and the Islamic holy book, the Qur'an, is central to religious schooling and to an Islam life(style). Qur'anic

texts as memorized oral texts as well as written texts are an important part of the lives of many adolescent Somalis because they are part of daily prayers and central to Qur'anic schooling—referred to as "Dugsi" among Somalis I know. In my research, teens often met with me for interviews before or after going to Dugsi on Saturdays. Most teens are happy to talk about their progress in memorizing the Qur'an and I recall one young man who was very proud to say that he was no longer attending Dugsi because he had finished memorizing the Qur'an, a fact that brought him respect among his peers. Qur'anic schooling is part of Somali oral tradition because of the value placed on being able to recite from the Qur'an. I have often been surprised to see which young person is in charge of leading the prayers at formal gatherings —which reminds me of my position as being outside the community. The person charged with reciting the Qur'an, usually male, is not necessarily the one who seems most conservative, most religious, or the best student.

Recitation of Qur'anic text does not necessarily include comprehension of the text but fulfills the primary purpose of going to Qur'anic school, which is to adopt Muslim values and a Muslim identity. This process plays out all over the world and is well documented in Leslie Moore's research among the Fulbe in Cameroon (Moore, 2006). In Somalia, and in the Diaspora, Qur'anic schools are community owned and the teachers are respected within society. The community pays the teachers and maintains the schools. Historically, not all of the children in a family were able to go to Qur'anic school, and male children often received preferential treatment (Abdi, 1998). This fact helps explain why many Somali refugees across all ages seem to have no experience with print literacy. Qur'anic schools have remained in Somali during times of unrest while the deliberate destruction of other institutions of learning have been rampant (Abdi, 1998). Mr. Abdi Farah Saeed "Juxaa," the Minister of Education of Puntland, a self-governed region in Somalia, said that he is grateful to the Qur'anic schools in Somalia because they have taught basic literacy and numeracy to children during times when there were few other educational opportunities. They were a major source of elementary education in times of crises (personal communication, April 6, 2009).

Educators often wonder what aspects of Qur'anic schools transfer to formal school settings. Potential points of transfer may involve literacy learning processes as well as the deeper meaning of going to Dugsi. In Qur'anic schools, children must learn the Arabic alphabet and how to pronounce the text of the Qur'an. This does not mean that children learn to understand Arabic print in this process, but they do learn that text corresponds to sounds that make up words which carry meaning—in this case, sacred meaning. In other words, if children are learning to pronounce Arabic through Qur'anic text, they are learning basic alphabetics (e.g., word boundaries, directionality of text). On the other hand, Qur'anic schooling and public schooling may not be mutually beneficial. Moore (2006) cited educators and researchers who argue that "Qur'anic schooling interferes with students' social, cognitive, and linguistic development by teaching children a passive, non-analytic learning style" (p. 114). Likewise, her research reveals the belief of many Muslims that "public schooling ... interfere[s] with the social, moral, and spiritual development of their children" (p. 114). In her examination of language socialization in both contexts, Moore found that the two schooling traditions in Cameroon—Qur'anic schooling in Arabic and public schooling in Fulbe and French—share the same basic sequential structure in the core language-centered activities (modeling, imitation, rehearsal, and performance) with an expert supervising and assisting the novice in each phase. This guided repetition, however, unfolded differently across the two settings in terms of how novices were linguistically socialized within Islamic and French colonialist ideologies. Moore's data show how the disciplinary regime of Qur'anic school taught Fulbe children to "love the sound of the Qur'an" (p. 121). Likewise, French-language socialization through dialogues offered preferred affective responses to social situations such as the first day of school. These experiences helped the child learn to use the texts that, in turn, engaged the child in communities of practice relevant to society. One of my research participants theorized similarly: She said that students who have gone to Dugsi will be good students because Dugsi helps them be better people and thus more dedicated and serious students.

Literacy and Religion

Sacred texts—oral and written—can be a source of great strength during times of crisis. Two research participants, Sufia and her sister, recalled to me that although the family had always been religious, the civil war caused them to become more religious, a common phenomenon among Somalis. The sisters believed that their strong faith helped the family cope during their drawn-out migration experience. Their connection to their Islamic texts and practices helped them survive and remain united through times of great danger and difficult. In this sense, the sacred texts they evoked protected them emotionally from the trauma of the camp.

Many have written about how and why many Somali communities have become more religious in the past two decades (Abdi, 2007; Berns McGown, 1999; De Voe, 2002; Forman, 2001). For example, Forman reasoned that

Islamic tenets provide a cohesive force in the Somali community, and it is often the adherence to practices of the Muslim faith that binds Somali teens together in their new cultural environments, including the school. As some have said, in a world where so much has been taken from them, where all that was once certain has been rent apart, Islam provides the single most stable force in their daily lives. (2001, p. 37)

Other researchers (Berns McGown, 1999; De Voe, 2002) also recognized this explanation for why Somalis turn to religion in times of crises. Abo-Zena, Salhi, and Tobias-Hahi (2009) have analyzed essays by Muslim youth, including Somali youth, as they respond to anti-Muslim sentiment and discrimination. Many of the essays powerfully show how their faith helps Muslim youth withstand stereotyping and hostility at school and in their communities.

However, Cawo Abdi, in the most scholarly exploration I have found about the phenomenon of how Somali women dress (Abdi, 2007), explained that a citizenry left economically and politically vulnerable creates a particularly ripe context for the rise of religion and therefore more conservative dress codes. Religious leaders evoked Sharia law, or an Islamic way of life based on the Qur'an, to keep peace, and this resulted in women's dress becoming more conservative in the camps to allow them to move about refugee camps with more security. Abdi (2007) reported that this reimagined Somali woman is now "permanently inscribed in textbooks produced for elementary children in Somalia" (p. 203). For example, textbooks produced by UNESCO depict Somali girls "as young as four or five all wearing the *jalaabiib*" (p. 203). These religious and cultural practices continue into Diaspora communities. Abdi found that, in Minneapolis, women veil in many ways; however, it is common to see Somali women and girls in very conservative attire. Abdi has interviewed women in Minnesota who believe that the change in dress is tied to more women participating in religious education. Women in the Diaspora may be going further in their study of the Qur'an than they were able to go in Somalia, particularly in large Somali communities where there are ample numbers of mosques and religious tutors. Contrary to the belief of many that the veil is always other-imposed, this finding shows that changes in Somali female dress may originate from within an ethnic Diaspora community and among women. Other researchers have explored shifts in dress of women in Arab countries as well. For example, Abu Odeh (1997) explained, from an Arab feminist perspective, that veiling for some women can be an empowering and liberating practice that addresses sexual harassment in the street while not denying women educational or employment opportunities. It can be a sort of backlash to Western-imposed views of how dress reflects women's liberty. With these examples, we see that the point is that veiling or not veiling is not divorced from dialogue with sociopolitical events or larger discourses, including those informed by feminist ideologies.

Second Language Learning and Limited Formal Schooling

It is clear from the previous discussion that Somali language learners in the Diaspora bring many specific cultural and religious characteristics to their schooling experiences. For example, many youth arrive with various and strong oral language traditions, as well as formal Qur'anic schooling. I have found many Somalis to have great appreciation for the beauty and power of language, and many Somali youth possess the talent to create and reproduce oral texts. Many bring prior language learning experiences (e.g., in Swahili, Amharic) and have parents who have done their formal schooling in, for example, English, Italian, or Arabic. Nevertheless, the high incidence of limited formal schooling seems to cause these assets to go unnoticed in the eyes of many educators and the types of educational programming that are offered. One way that lack of prior schooling is foregrounded in Western educational settings is by constant comparison to their to same-age, U.S.-born peers as well as other immigrant youth who have not missed any schooling. Practically speaking, a low level of formal schooling is often, but not always, synonymous with low levels of print literacy, which has serious implications for learning academic content through traditional means.

The assumption in secondary schools is that students can and do learn academic content through reading and producing academic texts. The other assumption is that students begin schooling with a certain amount of background knowledge and experience with academic content. Unfortunately, educators typically know very little about the implications of limited formal schooling and low literacy and are often overwhelmed by the learning needs of their students with limited formal schooling. Teachers' professional preparation may not have included methods for teaching adolescent and adult learners to become literate for the first time, particularly when the learners' first experience with literacy is in a language that they are only just beginning to learn. Likewise, teaching students who may learn language and content best through oral language is new to teachers. It is very difficult for many to imagine classroom learning that is not intricately and essentially tied to written text. Although some teachers may recall how it felt to be monolingual and then learn a second language, it is practically impossible for teachers to imagine what it felt like to lack print literacy and then become literate. I have never met a language teacher who has gone through this process as an adult. Despite limited formal schooling and low print literacy, adolescents and adults do become fluent in additional languages. Multilingualism and illiteracy naturally coexist in many places in the world. For example, consider countries such as Burkina Faso, where literacy rates in the population age 15 and over is only 21.8% (www.cia.gov) yet there are 68 living languages (www.ethnologue.com). It is not far-fetched to infer that the population of Burkina Faso is multilingual and that Somalis arriving to the United States and elsewhere without print literacy will learn to communicate in English or the language(s) of the new country. Helping students acquire the academic skills and language to complete secondary school in a truncated amount of time is the challenge school systems face.

Unfortunately, when educators turn to the field of SLA, there is little research that addresses the language and learning of individuals with little or no alphabetic literacy. The knowledge produced in mainstream SLA research shows little recognition that individuals become multilingual without literacy. Little is reported in the professional literature about what the typical language learning or educational trajectory is for adolescent and adult language learners who have not been to school. Typical pedagogies of language teaching and learning tend to rely heavily on written texts and traditional scripts of how learning in school settings is done. However, prior schooling and print literacy are *major* ways in which learners can vary, and these variables have been largely ignored in SLA research. For example, accounts of individual difference in the SLA research literature typically include such factors as personality, aptitude, motivation, learning styles, and learning strategies (Dörnyei, 2005). However, if thinking is shaped by literacy and schooling to the degree that the relevant research suggests (e.g., Olson, 2002; Ong, 1982), then it is problematic for the field of SLA to leave the individual difference of literacy level out of most, if not all, research programs in SLA. It is impossible to attempt to generalize the findings of SLA research to all human learners when a large segment of language learners is entirely left out of the inquiry. This gap in the research was acknowledged by Green and Reder (1986):

> Despite the growing interest in adult SLA, most of the research to date has been of only minimal utility to individuals who teach English to recent immigrants and refugees . . . . In part, this is due to the still limited number of studies which focus on adults. However, the major barrier to applying the research is the disparity between the characteristics of the adult subjects of most studies and the backgrounds of the many adults who have arrived . . . in the last five years. In general, researchers have examined the

acquisition of a host country language by foreign students or educated foreigners (such as Americans living abroad). Such individuals have been highly educated in their own countries and enter at a high level into the educational system in the country in which they are studying. (p. 300)

Almost 20 years later, Bigelow and Tarone (2004) made the identical observation. It is difficult to comprehend, given the fascinating and robust research available regarding orality and literacy, why more SLA researchers have not taken up the many questions that pertain to the second language learning processes of learners without print literacy.

Research With Monolingual Adults Without Alphabetic Print Literacy

In the field of cognitive science, illiterate monolingual learners' phonemic awareness has been explored (Adrian, Alegria, & Morais, 1995; Loureiro, et al., 2004; Morais, Bertelson, Cary, & Alegria, 1986; Morais, Cary, Alegria, & Bertelson, 1979; Reis, Guerreiro, & Petersson, 2003). This research, however, focused on phonological and phonemic awareness in relation to low or no alphabetic print literacy. These researchers found that normally functioning literate and illiterate adults performed the same on some kinds of oral language tasks, but very differently from one another on oral tasks requiring phonemic awareness.

Research by teams of cognitive scientists (Morais, et al., 1979; Morais, Content, Bertelson, & Cary, 1988; Morais & Kolinsky, 2002; Reis & Castro-Caldas, 1997; Reis, Faísca, Mendonça, Ingvar, & Petersson, 2007) offers a solid base upon which to develop a basic SLA research agenda on the relationships between literacy and orality. These researchers found that literate and illiterate monolingual adults performed similarly on tasks for which they were asked to identify words that rhyme (e.g., *bird* and *word*). They did equally well on identifying words that began with the same or different sound (e.g., *pen/pig* vs. *pen/Ken*). They performed similarly in oral tasks focusing on meaning, such as naming words in a semantic category (e.g., name all of the animals you can think of). Repeating real words was also equally easy for both literate and illiterate adults in these studies. These findings are useful because initial literacy instruction often focuses on these sorts of skills and it is quite likely that English language learners without print literacy will do well with games and activities that tap into these strengths.

On the other hand, the illiterate adults in these studies did significantly worse, compared to their literate counterparts, on tasks that required an ability to manipulate linguistic segments. The following tasks were harder for participants without print literacy: phoneme deletion (e.g., take the /s/ off "stan" or "slide" → "tan" or "lide"); phoneme reversal (e.g., what is /los/ backward? /sol/); syllable deletion (e.g., if you take /ka/ off /kade/, what do you have? /de/); syllable reversal (e.g., what is /kade/ backwards? /deka/); listing all of the words that begin with a specific sound (e.g., /b/); repeating nonwords (e.g., skriltch) (Adrian et al., 1995; Castro-Caldas, Petersson, Reis, Stone-Elander, & Ingvar, 1998; Reis & Castro-Caldas, 1997). In sum, illiterate adults performed significantly worse than their literate counterparts on tasks requiring manipulation of linguistic forms.

Is this phenomenon related to literacy in any script, or is there something about being able to decode an alphabetic script that produces this effect? In order to begin to address this question, Charles Read and his colleagues (Read, Zhang, Nie, & Ding, 1986) replicated some aspects of the studies reported previously with monolingual adults in China. Their participants were two groups of adults who were equally well educated: one group that could read only logographic characters and another group that could read characters as well as an alphabetic script called Hanyun Pinyin. Remarkably, Read and his research team found the same results as the researchers who studied literate and illiterate adults: Those who could read the alphabetic script significantly outperformed those who could not on the kinds of oral form-focused tasks just described. These results suggest that it is not reading per se that matters in participants' ability to do certain types of phonological manipulation tasks. It is reading an alphabetic script that improves performance on these kinds of oral tasks. It seems that the ability to represent a phoneme with a visual symbol gives a person clear cognitive advantages in performing tasks involving the manipulation of language segments such as phonemes and syllables. This is a very interesting and important assertion because most researchers (Sawyer & Fox, 1991) who focus on native-speaking children learning to read say that phonological awareness *results in literacy*, not the reverse, as Read et al.'s study suggests.

If an individual is able to perceive a linguistic segment in the oral input, alphabetic literacy seems to help individuals visualize linguistic segments and manipulate them mentally. Alphabetically literate individuals have available to them a strategy in which visual-graphic meaning is given to units that are smaller than words, units with no semantic value. These segments are introduced sequentially in a working memory system in the form of visual experience (Baddeley, 1986). Then it is possible to manipulate those written symbols, each mapped to a sound. As Reis and Castro-Caldas (1997) surmised: "Therefore, learning to read and write introduces in the system qualitatively new strategies for dealing with oral language: that is, conscious phonological processing, visual formal lexical representations and all the associations that these strategies allow" (p. 445). Visual representations offer a language processing strategy to people who have alphabetic print literacy, but not to people who do not. Having this strategy of visualizing and manipulating phonemes may make certain types of input more easily noticed and therefore more easily incorporated into the learner's interlanguage system.

The relationship people have to the scripts they learn may go beyond cognitive processing and include physical representations of how they become literate. Richard Young offers an example of this phenomenon through a Vygotskyan (or Lurian) sociohistorical lens, in addition to a cognitive one:

> When people visualize things they are mediating their cognitive processes and because they can actively engage with a visualization (just like with language) they can modify higher order mental processes like memory, planning, and attention. The nature of the tool that they use for mediation is of course culturally and historically determined. So if you're Chinese your visualizations are located in the culture and history of your upbringing. Just like alphabetical representations are culturally embedded in our culture. Chinese certainly envision logographs (i.e., Chinese characters) because the form of the character is encoded not only visually but also in bodily movement of their hands. (You've seen how a Chinese person writes invisible characters on their palms when the person is explaining the character to another Chinese.) (personal communication, March 11, 2009)

In Young's description, processing oral language with the tool of logographic literacy helps to moderate cognitive processes (e.g., memory) in very particular ways; those ways of structuring memory are different from those imported by the tool of alphabetic literacy. The processes people use to store and retrieve oral language in memory are closely associated with, and even developed through, the types of script in which we become literate.

Research With Adolescent and Adult L2 Learners Without Alphabetic Print Literacy

It should be cautioned that the research just cited with monolingual adults who have not learned alphabetic print literacy does not imply anything about the intelligence, the linguistic aptitude, or the humanity of those individuals. It does, however, help develop a theoretical argument for how alphabetic print literacy may change the way a *second* language learner may process oral input in a new language. The researchers studying monolingual adults cited previously concluded that the ability to represent a phoneme with a visual symbol gives clear cognitive advantages in performing phonological awareness tasks. The ability to represent phonemes with graphemes promotes an individual's ability to segment the sound stream and then to visualize it as a series of linguistic segments. That series of segments can then be stored in memory, available for mental manipulation of the sort we have just seen in phonological awareness tasks.

Given how simple these phonological awareness tasks of deleting or adding a phoneme, inverting syllables, and so on seem to them, educators may think that all English language learners with low print literacy need is a few months of high-quality, balanced literacy instruction to become similar to other beginners learning English as a second language. However, the research I have conducted with colleagues (Bigelow, delMas, Hansen, & Tarone, 2006; Tarone & Bigelow, 2007; Tarone, Swierzbin, & Bigelow, 2006), which was published in a volume entitled *Literacy and Second Language Oracy* (Tarone et al., 2009), suggests that differences persist in the processing of second language input, even when learners have acquired some alphabetic print literacy. The research question that framed our series of studies was: How do low levels of alphabetic print literacy influence L2 oral language processing?

To explore this question, my colleagues and I chose a partial replication and extension of Jenefer Philp's (2003) study of recasts with highly literate college students. Recasts are targetlike reformulations of the participants' nontargetlike utterance, as in the following example:

Participant Trigger:	*Why he is very unhappy?*
Researcher Recast:	*Why is he very unhappy?*
Participant Recall:	*Yeah why is very unhappy?* (Philp, 2003, p. 108)

Philp's study fits into a robust line of SLA research in the area of recasts in second language oral interaction (Long, Inagaki, & Ortega, 1998; Lyster, 1998a, 1998b; Lyster & Ranta, 1997; Mohan & Beckett, 2001; Nabei, 2003). Philp explored whether and how her participants noticed her oral recasts of their nontarget utterances. Following Philp, we also analyzed the types of recasts offered to participants, in terms of length and the number of changes to the participants' utterances, and then carried out a complete analysis of the types of errors the participants made. Philp explored whether their stage of acquisition in English question formation (Pienemann & Johnston, 1987; Pienemann, Johnston, & Brindley, 1988) would be related to how well participants were able to perceive and repeat the recasts they received. In our study, however, all of our participants were at the same stage in the acquisition. The variable we added to our replication of her study was level of alphabetic literacy—something that had not been previously examined in studies of adolescent/adult oral SLA. Bringing low literate adolescents and adults into the SLA literature through replication of Philp's study allowed for comparison, albeit broad, with her literate and schooled participants. Replication studies are important for the field and this research was also a response to the call from many SLA researchers (e.g., Polio & Gass, 1997; Santos, 1989) for more replication of SLA research. Philp's study was a useful choice for partial replication because it used research methods that were entirely oral. The tasks were easily explained and modeled and required use of no printed text.

The participants in our study were all Somali refugees who had fled the civil war in Somalia. Most of them had spent time in refugee camps before resettling. In individual sessions, we assessed their literacy levels in Somali and English using a screening device. Based on that assessment, we formed two comparison groups of learners: one with low measured literacy and one with moderate literacy. We compared the performance of these two groups in three types of oral tasks designed to elicit their question formation in English, but we used the data to analyze participants' language production on other forms in addition to questions.

In the first analysis, the following question was addressed: Is accuracy of recall of a recast related to the literacy level of the learner, the length of the recast, or the number of changes made by the recast? Results showed that literacy level was significantly related to the ability to recall oral recasts in correct or modified form (i.e., when participant recalls of the recasts were scored as perfectly correct or partially correct). An exact permutation analysis showed that the moderate literacy group performed better overall than the low literacy group ($p = .043$). The ability to recall an oral recast was not related to the length of the recasts for either group; there were no statistically significant differences in recall based on recast length between the two literacy level groups or the participant group as a whole. In other words, participants in the two literacy groups responded similarly to long and short recasts, unlike Philp's (2003) participants, who found longer recasts harder to recall than shorter ones. Regarding the complexity of the recasts, the moderate literate group recalled more complex recasts (i.e., those with two or more changes from the original trigger utterance) significantly more accurately than did the low literate group ($p = .014$). Thus, a relatively higher level of alphabetic literacy significantly improved the accuracy with which these second language learners recalled oral recasts of their nontargetlike English questions.

The second portion of the study involved a close examination of one participant: Abukar. This analysis is reported in greater depth in Tarone and Bigelow

(2007). The goal was to explore how one participant with low print literacy processed oral recasts on questions in English. Abukar was 15 years old at the time of the study. He was very fluent, but his literacy level was quite low. He had spent 4 years in a refugee camp during some of his school-age years. His common challenges in English question formation included not doing subject/auxiliary inversion (e.g., "... what, what he is looking"), and failing to use do-support (e.g., "... why he come this room?"). He seemed to find it particularly difficult to repeat targetlike inversion in recasts accurately, as in the examples below:

1	Abukar:	What he sit on, what he SIT on, or whatever?
2	MB:	What is he sitting on?
3	Abukar:	Mhm.
4	MB:	What is he sitting on? Again. Repeat.
5	Abukar:	What he sitting on?
6	MB:	What IS he sitting on?
7	Abukar:	Oh. What he sitting on?
8	MB:	What IS he sitting on?
9	Abukar:	What IS he sitting on?

We documented a similar difficulty many turns later:

1	Abukar:	Oh. What he try to write down?
2	MB:	What IS he trying to write down?
3	Abukar:	What he's, he's try to write down?
4	MB:	What IS he trying
5	Abukar:	What he is t, try to, write down?

Later in the protocol, it appears that what Abukar first noticed in the recast was stress placement on the second syllable/word rather than a change in word order:

1	Abukar:	Why he is mad? Why [he], he is mad?
2	MB:	[yeah]
3	MB:	Why IS he mad?
4	Abukar:	Why HE is mad? Why
5	MB:	Why IS he mad?
6	Abukar:	Why IS he mad? Why is, [is he]...

On the other hand, Abukar had no apparent difficulty noticing oral recasts focused on vocabulary and incorporated these into his subsequent speaking turns right away. His skill in focusing on meaning (vocabulary) but not on linguistic form (word order) resonates with the research results discussed earlier where adults with little literacy are very skillful at processing language semantically but not in terms of linguistic form.

Another analysis of the data compared the way participants responded to an oral elicited imitation task versus the recast task just discussed. The research questions were the following: (a) Is the ability to recall target sentences in an elicited imitation task related to the literacy level of the learner? (b) Is there a difference in accuracy of recall of utterances in the elicited imitation task and the recast recall task? Results showed that literacy level was related to accuracy on both the elicited imitation and the recast tasks. The difference between literacy groups in recast recall accuracy was significant. For both literacy groups, accuracy of recast recalls was significantly better than for elicited imitation recalls, for reasons we explore in Tarone et al. (2009) and Hansen (2005).

The last analysis in this set of studies explores the impact of literacy level on the interlanguage, or the set of second language (L2) grammar forms acquired and used by these learners. This analysis involved a comparison of the grammatical forms used by the two literacy groups of learners in producing the same oral narrative. The exploration focused on the following question: Does literacy level correspond to the grammatical forms participants use in retelling story completion tasks in narrative form? Specifically, would the low literacy learner group use fewer semantically redundant grammatical morphemes (e.g. plural –s, third-person singular, past tense –ed) than the moderate literacy group? Would their sentence complexity be lower than that of the moderate literacy group? Because this analysis focused on grammatical forms produced in meaningful communication in a comparatively small study, inferential statistical analyses were not carried out, but rather a descriptive linguistic analysis was used to identify patterns that will have to be evaluated more rigorously in future studies. We compared the two groups' production in their oral narratives of semantically redundant grammatical morphemes, including bare verbs (verbs with no morphological marking) versus verbs with morphological marking (–ed, or third-person singular –s), the use or deletion of auxiliary *be*, and the use of bare nouns versus nouns with plural –s marking in referring to plural entitites. To compare sentence complexity we examined differences between the two groups in their use of relative clauses, noun clauses, and clauses with *because, so,* and *since*.

The grammatical forms that had been acquired and produced by the moderate and low literacy groups did appear to be different. The moderate literacy group provided more morphemes for verbs than the low literacy group, which produced more bare verbs. The following examples show how participants from the two groups used morphemes with verbs in their story retells:

1   1 Her mom *says*, "Come in now, in a car." (Faadumo, moderate)
2   Her mother they *say*, "We going right now . . . " (Najma, low)
3   So, she *called* him. (Khalid, moderate)
4   Somebody *call* him. (Fawzia, low)

The difference between the two groups in their marking of verbs was not categorical: The two groups' performances overlapped. However, the low literacy group marked a much lower percentage of verbs than did the moderately literate group.

With regard to plural noun marking, the database was smaller and individual performances in the two groups overlapped, so caution in interpreting these findings is important. However, there seemed to be a greater tendency for the low literacy group to leave off the plural –s on plural nouns, producing more bare nouns in obligatory contexts than the moderate literacy group, sometimes substituting quantifiers as in the following examples:

1   *A lot of monkey* they take his hat_. (Ubax, low literacy group)
2   *The monkeys* took all his hats. (Khalid, moderate literacy group)

These findings, although not statistically verifiable, are in the anticipated direction and are consistent with the idea that alphabetic literacy level may affect not just learners' ability to notice linguistic features of oral L2 input, but as a consequence, the linguistic features of the L2 that they acquire and use in their speech production. It seems that the findings are consistent with claims of Ravid and Tolchinsky (2002) that children do not acquire more complex syntactic forms of the native language until they are literate; literacy broadens genres of use and accompanying structures. However, more and larger studies are needed to examine this phenomenon. The findings of the present study fall in the predicted direction and are consistent with studies in related fields, and they set out a clear agenda for next steps of research.

Certainly, Tarone et al. (2009)'s findings suggest that literacy level is significantly related to the ability to recall oral recasts that make multiple changes to the learners' nontarget questions. This finding is consistent with Reis and Castro-Caldas's (1997) assertion that literacy has a positive impact on working memory for oral language. The participants in the low literacy group seemed to have fewer phonological awareness skills to help them hold the recast in working memory, compare it in working memory to their original utterance in terms of its linguistic segment, and then produce a reformulation of that original utterance that incorporates the differing segments provided in the recast. Whether a person is noticing the endings of words in a recast (Bigelow et al., 2006), or producing semantically redundant morphemes (e.g., past tense –ed) in an oral narrative (Tarone et al., 2006), or repeating a sentence crafted by the researcher (Hansen, 2005), the same cognitive processes appear to be involved. The grapho-phonemic strategy that results in the ability to visualize the orthography of a word and then produce the linguistic segments represented by that orthography appears to be connected with a person's experience with alphabetic literacy.

Philp's (2003) study, the initial inspiration for these studies, showed that her highly literate adult learners did not do as well with long or complex recasts as they did with short recasts that make few changes to their original utterance. The participants in the present studies, on the other hand, differed from Philp's participants in that they did not find length of a recast to affect recall difficulty. This is an interesting and perhaps unsurprising finding for a community with many strong oral language traditions. Perhaps speakers who are not alphabetically literate have developed other skills for processing oral language that enable them to hold language in mind more easily than participants who are literate. For both Philp's participants and the participants in the current studies, the more changes made by an oral recast, the harder recall was. Perhaps the more complex recast changed the intended meaning to the degree that it became incomprehensible to the participant. Perhaps, as was the case with Philp's more literate participants, it was too difficult to hold so many changes in working memory long enough to recall the original nontarget utterance and compare it to the recast in such grammatical detail. Complexity of the recasts seemed to matter more for the participants in the low literacy group, whether this was because they lacked the metalinguistic tool to visualize the corrections to English question syntax and make an accurate comparison from a mental picture in their minds or because they were simply more focused on meaning than on form.

The research reported in this section is promising but has limitations and needs to be replicated. The data were produced by a small number of participants and even though exact permutation analysis can be used with a small N, future studies should include more participants and different statistical measures capable of more carefully pinpointing individual differences across participants. Another limitation is the literacy measure used. Although it was far more precise than anything previously used in SLA research, this measure was not fine-grained enough. More precise measures of difference in literacy level at the low end of the continuum are needed; future studies could more carefully measure participants' levels of phonemic awareness, for example.

One of the most important findings of this research is that L2 oral language processing is likely to be affected by alphabetic literacy level in important ways in the adolescent and young adult population studied. This means that teachers may need to find alternative means of teaching some of the grammatical forms of the language while learners are becoming literate. Level of alphabetic print literacy may influence the noticeability of some morphemes and word orders in oral input and the ability of learners to acquire these features in oral interaction. Another key finding is that one cannot assume that current SLA findings, all based on data from literate L2 learners, apply to illiterate or low literate adolescent and adult populations. The results show that participants with low literacy processed oral L2 input differently from participants with moderate literacy and differently from Philp's (2003) highly literate college students. Until more research is done, it is impossible to make assumptions about what it is like to learn to speak a new language when learners do not have strong literacy skills. In this spirit, scholars must not even dismiss the possibility that some aspects of L2 oral language learning may in fact be easier among learners with low literacy than among literate learners. These and many more questions remain with regard to the role of literacy in L2 oral language learning.

Conclusion: The Abyss Between Experiences of Orality and Literacy

The importance of oral language cannot be undermined in the Somali ethos. It may be very difficult for people from print-focused cultures, like most in the West, to grasp the relationship Somalis have to the spoken genres, traditional and contemporary, that are still in use. It also may be difficult to understand that even as Somalis adapt to highly literate societies and become highly literate themselves, they still may have preferences for the oral. Consider the following email I recently received from a community collaborator:

> Hallow Martha
> I did not hear from you for Ten days, are you feeling well. Please write to me or call me and keep in mind I am from oral society.

His direct reference to orality brings this fundamental difference between our cultures to light. The distance between individuals from these different traditions is vast.

There is a rich body of linguistic and anthropological inquiries into the differences between societies grounded in orality as compared to those grounded in literacy. For example, Alexander R. Luria (1976), a student of Lev Vygotsky, advocated for an exploration of language use through an analysis of sociohistorical influences. This approach to understanding human cognition is currently known as cultural-historical psychology. In his work in the early 1920s–1930s, Luria studied individuals with differing degrees of literacy ranging from none to functional to more academic in Uzbekistan and Kirghizia. He explored the consequences of literacy through conversations with adults in locations like tea houses (Ong, 1982). One of the various things Luria would ask his participants was to give definitions of concrete objects (e.g., a tree). He reported that this was met with resistance, because, he argued, a real-life experience with a tree is more satisfactory than a description of something everyone knows about. Ong (1982) wrote that it is impossible to refute this world view, "all you can do is walk away from it into literacy" (p. 53):

> There is hardly an oral culture or predominantly oral culture left in the world today that is not somehow aware of the vast complex of powers that is forever inaccessible without literacy. This awareness is agony for persons rooted in primary orality, who want literacy passionately but who also know very well that moving into the exciting world of literacy means leaving behind much that is exciting and deeply loved in the earlier oral world. We have to die [in orality] to continue living [in literacy]. (p. 15)

Ong's words are a good reminder of the emotional and even spiritual difficulty an individual or society may experience in a transition to literacy. The differences in ways of being in the world are profound. Jill Watson (2010) framed these differences between societies and cultures based in orality versus literacy as *an abyss*. This metaphor serves researchers and educators well because it elucidates the overwhelmingly different lived experiences of an individual steeped in orality versus one steeped in literacy. Watson also echoed Ong as she noted that the process of becoming literate proceeds in one direction. In other words, it is impossible for a person who is literate to return to a primarily oral way of life (Watson, 2010) just as it is difficult to imagine returning to an era without electronic communication (McCluhan, 1994). This is not to say that a highly oral culture turns entirely away from orality upon embracing literacy or that orality does not influence the way print literacies are used in everyday life, including those that are digital or electronic. However, it does mean the end of cultural values based on utter embeddedness in an encompassing oral worldview. Orality does not just denote communicating through listening, speaking, orating, and reading poetry; in the deepest sense, it refers to a way of life entirely organically fashioned on face-to-face human relations.

Bigelow and Watson (in press) explored some of the issues and questions that arise from the presence and dilemmas of the abyss between ways of being that are highly oral and those that are hyperliterate. There are many opportunities for more investigation into the role of educational level in learning across modalities. If lower levels of literacy make it more difficult to acquire some grammatical features of the L2 in the oral modes (Tarone et al., 2009), what other linguistic domains are affected by low literacy? What conditions are necessary for learners with limited formal schooling to acquire sufficient fluency and automaticity in L2 literacy to move from decoding letters to comprehension of texts relevant to their lives? These questions lead to more questions about the limits and possibilities in educational programming for L2 learners with limited formal schooling. How can schools create alternative paths toward program completion, diplomas, and degrees? How can students' assets and strengths become points of access to other skills that help them reach self-determined goals? How do educators of students with limited formal schooling see themselves in the broader historical and geopolitical landscape of transnational migration, and what special responsibilities and opportunities do they have? These and so many more issues need to be explored through interdisciplinary lenses. We argue:

> Some of the most important dimensions of the issue of educational level and L2 learning may be those hardest for educators and researchers on the hyperliterate side of the abyss to articulate and to face. A true reckoning would remind us that the attitude of global supremacy which underwrote imperialism in times past—with its gruesome legacy of cultural distortion and destruction—marches on still in the neoliberal agenda pursued under a banner of globalization . . . . It is not difficult to see that the presence of L2 learners in the classrooms of industrialized countries is a direct consequence of the exercise of political and military might, coupled with a sense of messianic right. It may be less obvious, however, that the western approach to academic schooling is also an exercise in privileging certain kinds of learning and knowing over others. (Bigelow & Watson, in press)

We worry that as we welcome unschooled immigrants into the institutions of our society, we inevitably participate in the extinction of a way of life that is based on orality, relationality, memory, and context. This is a particular risk in our current educational environment of standardized tests and tight codification of factual knowledge, a trend that enacts the abstract opposite of contextually constructed oral knowledge, amounting to a kind of embalming of subject matter and student heuristic consciousness (Watson, 2010). The possibility of proceeding in a more culturally reciprocal way would be a true departure in the how immigrant education is done in the United States. This possibility, however, would require beginning to understand different ways of being in the world. The following chapters attempt to create, grow, and complicate understandings of Somali immigrant youth in ways that can inform educational practice, research and public policy.

Notes

1 This is a Somali language spelling because it uses an "x" not an "h." The pronunciation is basically the same as the more commonly spelled "Mohammad."

2 The digital video case can be accessed via the Web site http://www.cehd.umn.edu/CI/faculty/projects/bigelow/multic.html

3 A much more controversial side of this phenomenon of "becoming" Somali in Minnesota was portrayed in a newspaper article about recent discoveries that Somali youth in Minnesota have been recruited to terrorist groups. Diaz (2009) quoted a Somali spokesperson saying, "these kids have no perception of Somalia except the one that was formed in their minds by their teachers at the Abu-Bakar Center [Mosque]" (p. A8).

4 There are members of Diaspora communities who identify as Somali (perhaps among other identities) but are citizens of Djibouti, Kenya, or Ethiopia. This is because Somalis historically have lived throughout the Horn of Africa before colonists divided the region into the countries now seen on maps.

5 "1.5 generation" is typically used to describe immigrants who arrive to a new country as children or teens and 1.25 and 1.75 generations are added derivatives of the category. This term is problematized by Matsuda and Matsuda (2009) because of how it has effectively lumped individuals of many different backgrounds into one group with presumed rather than defined characteristics. It is a problematic term because it confounds immigration history with language use. In other words, the immigration of English speakers is not considered, nor the possibility that learners may not have immigrated but are English language learners.

6 Integrated Regional Information Networks (IRIN) (2009, February 6), Kenya: Camp resources stretched by influx of Somali refugees. Retrieved June 25, 2010, from http://www.unhcr.org/refworld/docid/498fed1a1d.html

7 This quote was found on the Web site named Hii Dunia: http://www.hiidunia.org/ 2007/03/in-pictures-dadaab-refugee-camps-kenya.html.

8 See Hopkins (2006) for information about the large number of Somali community organizations in London and Toronto and see the following Web site for information about Somalis in London: http://www.bbc.co.uk/london/content/

articles/2004/08/11/communities_somali_feature.shtml. See http://webhome. idirect.com~siao/background.html for more information about Somalis in Toronto.

9 See http://www.macalester.edu/anthropology/ref_imm/somali_main.html for more demographic information about Somalis in Minnesota.

10 These estimates come from the Minnesota Office of Geographic and Demographic Analysis and are derived from the combination of new enrollment data from the Department of Education, data from the Minnesota Department of Health Office of Refugee Health and Vital Statistics, the U.S. Department of Homeland Security's Immigration Statistics, and the 2000 Census. Data were retrieved on March 20, 2008, from http://www.mnplan.state.mn.us/resource.html?Id=7193.

11 See http://factfinder.census.gov for state demographic data.

12 These figures came from the Minnesota State Demographic Center: http://www.demography.state.mn.us/documents/Immigrants2007.csv.

13 See https://www.cia.gov/library/publications/the-world-factbook/geos/so.html# People

Language Learning   ISSN 0023-8333

CHAPTER 3

Multilingualism and Multiliteracy Among Somali Adolescent Girls

*I can make thousand
stories.
no one can stop me*

*I am student
ready to learn
new things.*

From untitled poem by Fadumo

Introduction

Fadumo, a Somali teenage girl, was a participant in the qualitative research that is the focus of this chapter. The lines that open my recounting of this research come from a poem she wrote and that readers will encounter in full later in this chapter. They offer only a glimpse of her immense poetic skill. She also makes two important identity statements: She is a limitless storyteller and a student who is ready to learn. One of the things I hope to show in this chapter is that the cultural and oral roots of her first statement can and should link to her second statement in emotional and pedagogical ways; that is, her linguistic strengths as a storyteller have great potential for Fadumo's learning at school. Like so many newcomers, Fadumo arrives "ready to learn" and trusts that her school will offer opportunities to learn. Connections between and among literacy, orality, and culture are at the heart of implications for pedagogies that support the Somali newcomers who readers will meet in this chapter.

The research took place as four newcomer Somali adolescent girls were in the midst of navigating the social and academic world of their urban high schools. The primary purpose was to learn about the girls' language and literacy practices in English and Somali as well as the successes and challenges

they faced as they strove to complete high school graduation requirements before they reached the age of 22, when they would no longer be able to attend
traditional high schools, according to state law in Minnesota. Although their
experiences are highly individual and contextualized, they offer a deep understanding of the social and cultural aspects of multilingualism and multiliteracy.

Many kinds of literacies are used by and among adolescents in any society,
even adolescents with low first language (L1) print literacy. These literacies are
enacted in certain moments, in certain spaces, and my assumption is that they are
mediated by issues of identity, agency, and power, which, in turn, afford or limit
learning opportunities (Lewis & del Valle, 2009). For example, just a few of the
many conditions that may be needed for an adolescent to participate in a literacy
activity are the following: (a) There are opportunities to find a way to contribute
one's knowledge and skills to the task; (b) participation throughout the process
of the task is supported by teacher and peers, not marginalized due to difference;
and (c) the adolescent must believe that doing the task does not threaten cultural
or linguistic status in the classroom community. Learning and enacting literacies
at school may be social, multimodal (Jewitt, 2008), and highly contextualized
within the classroom context. Of course, and like other adolescents, immigrant
and refugee youth produce a range of texts that include and are influenced by the
genres from their home language(s) as well as other languages they may have
learned during the process of migration. Furthermore, they may use text with
other bilinguals or multilinguals, which gives them contexts for multimodal
codeswitching. Funds of knowledge (González, 2005)—that is, skills, talents,
and knowledge that reside within families and communities—may include
particular ways of creating and reproducing oral or written texts. Yet, teaching
and research on language learning and literacy for immigrant youth is often
approached from monolingual, dominant culture instructional perspectives,
where the focus is on second language (L2) functional oral and print skills
and where prior print literacy is taken for granted (Bigelow & Tarone, 2004;
Ferdman & Weber, 1994) and literacy practices that tie to cultural practices are
unknown.

An example of how literacy and culture are connected is documented in
Sarroub's (2001, 2005) ethnography of Yemeni American Muslim high school
girls. Sarroub found that, among adolescents who are religious, the ability to
quote from or memorize sacred texts often receives praise, whereas certain
songs or magazines may be prohibited. Yemeni American girls negotiated
cultural spaces that were "in-between" Yemeni and U.S. culture and this was
often accomplished through secular and religious oral and written texts that
depended greatly on the textual, social, cultural, and physical surroundings.

Sarroub framed her analysis using Scribner's (1984) metaphors for literacy: literacy as adaptation, literacy as power, and literacy as a state of grace. As with the Yemeni students in Sarroub's research, the Somali girls in this study use their multiple oral and print literacies across the different secular and religious spaces in which they live.

Research and schooling practices must include a broader range of cultural practices as contexts for the development of first and subsequent language literacy (Reder, 1994) across modalities. The links and overlay of oral and written literacies are not unidirectional, with oral language always informing written language, but rather are bidirectional and greatly informed by the broad range of cultural activities as contexts for multilingual and multiliteracy development. By knowing how the participants in this study feel about and use their multiple languages and literacies, it is possible to begin to understand both the development and abandonment of such skills. Furthermore, language instruction will be most beneficial "if complemented by expansion [and recognition] of the social and economic opportunities and rewards for all students to acquire societally valued skills and knowledge" (Reder, 1994, p. 66). More needs to be understood about how immigrant and refugee youth from limited formal schooling backgrounds use oral and written texts in and outside of school with the possibility that the texts they produce "represent different system[s] of signification and different kind[s] of meaning" (Hull & Nelson, 2005, p. 28). I conducted the case study reported in this chapter to explore these issues.

The Four Participants

The participants were four Somali high school students who I call Fatima, Magol, Sufia, and Fadumo. Fatima and Magol are cousins. At the time of the study, they were 21 and 18 years old and lived with an aunt who was in her forties. Sufia and Fadumo are sisters. They were 18 and 15 years old at the time of the study and lived with their mother, step-father, and seven siblings. They are the oldest girls in the family and shared many responsibilities for household chores with their oldest brothers. Their mother worked evening shifts when the older children were home and could take care of the younger ones. All four girls identified as Somali and Muslim. Their schooling experiences are summarized in Table 3.1. We were a Saturday tutoring group for 2 years.

As shown in Table 3.1, the girls were between 13 and 17 when they began school in the United States—their first experience with formal education. They all started in ninth grade, with the exception of Fadumo, who began in an urban middle school in seventh grade. Magol and Sufia switched schools during their

Table 3.1 Comparisons among participants regarding U.S. high schools attended

Participant	Years in refugee camp	Age when first enrolled	Year #1 Grade; School type	Year #2 Grade; School type	Year #3 Grade; School type	Year #4 Grade; School type
Magol	8	14	9th Large Urban School #1	10th Afro-Centric Charter	11th Same	12th Same
Sufia	7	14	9th Large Urban School #1	10th Afro-Centric Charter	11th Same	12th Large Urban School #1
Fadumo	7	13	7th Urban Middle School	8th Same	9th Large Urban School #2	10th Large Urban School #2
Fatima	8	17	9th Large Urban School #2	10th Same	11th Same	12th Same

Note. Shaded boxes indicate years that overlap with the research in the Saturday tutoring group.

4 years in secondary school, whereas Fatima did not. Fadumo spent 2 years in a middle school and went on to a high school from which she graduated in 4 years. Of the four girls, only Sufia made her school record available to me.[1] It showed that in ninth grade, she took World History, Pre-Algebra, and Algebra, all in Somali, an opportunity that is possible only when there are enough students of the same L1 to fill content courses taught in that language. She had a grade point average of 3.8 upon graduation. Her sister, Fadumo, told me that she took some content courses in Somali but was quickly placed in sheltered content classes. Her English-as-a-second-language (ESL) classes continued for five more terms. It was only during her senior year that she stopped taking ESL classes. She had a grade point average of 2.9. After a few attempts, Magol, Sufia, and Fadumo passed their state-mandated graduation tests in reading, writing, and mathematics before finishing the other course requirements for graduation. Fatima did not pass these tests before leaving high school, despite repeated attempts. Fatima, the oldest of the four students, still struggled to make herself understood, follow pragmalinguistic and sociopragmatic norms, or comprehend spoken English. During our meetings, she often asked for clarification about what I or the others said, expecting the others to rephrase in Somali.

All four girls directly experienced the civil war in Somalia. They lost loved ones, were separated from family members, and lived in refugee camps in Kenya for 4–6 years before coming to the United States. They did not attend school prior to arriving to the United States. Nevertheless, all of the girls report some study in Qur'anic schools as children, and Fatima, Sufia, and Fadumo were able to slowly decode and encode some Somali texts. They report learning to read Somali from family members, except for Magol, who could not read or write in Somali.[2]

Hopeful Girls

All of the girls told me that they do things that help them succeed at school, such as go to class, show drafts of their papers to their fellow students, get their homework done, and ask their teachers if they can retake tests when they get anything less than an "A." Knowing to engage in these behaviors and how to engage in them is a form of cultural capital (Gibson, 1988; Portes & Rumbaut, 1996; Zhou & Bankston, 1994). However, I worried that much of their academic success was a byproduct of these "good student" behaviors, documented in other studies (e.g., Platt & Troudi, 1997; Rymes & Pash, 2001). Likewise, I feared that these young women, like the participants in Nancy Lopez's (2003a) study, had not been adequately prepared to reach their goals. Similar to the girls in Lopez's study, they hoped to become nurses; yet, the path to become a nurse was academically and financially challenging for them. It was remarkable to me that all of the participants persisted through their overwhelming social transitions to school, which were compounded in difficulty by limited formal schooling and low print literacy.

Context of the Research

My entrée into the neighborhood where I gathered data was through Family Opportunities and Literacy Collaborative (FOLC), a community organization that focused on using existing community resources and adding needed services to support immigrant and refugee families. My role was to work with others to organize and coordinate the various homework help programs in the neighborhood, connect college students with volunteer opportunities in the community, and help provide summer activities for youth.

I met the four girls through the recast research project reported at the end of chapter 2 (Tarone et al., 2009). The group came into being when Magol, after completing the tasks for the SLA study, asked me if I could help her with her reading and writing. I agreed and we decided to meet to work on her English. She suggested that some other girls she knew would like to do that too and the group was formed. She invited Fatima, her cousin, and two sisters, Fadumo and Sufia. We decided to meet every Saturday afternoon for 2–3 hr. This was an ideal time because Fadumo and Sufia lived in a different neighborhood and came to Magol and Fatima's neighborhood to go to the mosque. Saturday afternoons were one of the few times during the week that they were released from childcare and cooking responsibilities. Sometimes it seemed as though the girls' commitment to our meetings was similar to how they viewed their Qur'anic tutoring with their Dugsi (tutor)—it was part of a routine and something they felt was beneficial. We met in the neighborhood or in my office on campus, which was very close by. The first day we met in October 2003, all of us, including me, said what we each wished to gain from and give to the group. They agreed that they wanted to work on their English and get help with their homework. They said they could give reliability, support, and friendship to the group. I said that I wanted to learn about them and their lives and that I was willing to give help with English and homework. After many months of meeting, I asked them if they would be participants in a research study and they agreed. I gathered data between January 2004 and July 2005.

Our meetings always began by chatting about the week and then working on homework or projects. We also read pieces selected jointly or wrote on personal topics for enjoyment if they did not bring homework to do. We sometimes went to culturally appropriate plays and events together, which, in turn, gave the girls topics about which to write. In the last few months together, we worked on college essays and applications and financial aid forms. We visited a couple of local colleges together. I believe that they saw me as a mentor in that they asked me for advice about school-related decisions and periodically asked for my help with things such as getting school pictures or doing online job applications.

Method

The methodology I used was an exploratory case-study design. Case studies have the potential to "investigate a contemporary phenomenon within its real-life context, especially when the boundaries between phenomenon and context are not clearly evident" (Yin, 2003b, p. 13). This design was chosen because it can cope with many variables related to the lives of individuals with unusual and complex backgrounds. It was also chosen because of the need to rely on a number of different types of data sources that converge around the topics of literacy and identity. Although I read widely about literacy in Somalia and interacted with many people from the Somali community, I used the case to anchor literacy, culture, and identity in the contemporary lives of Somali high school girls who are becoming literate in an L2 as they engage in life and academics in the United States. I saw the Saturday tutoring group as the bounded unit and the participants as focal students within the case.

Data Sources

The data for the inquiry came from the following sources over a period of 16 months, including one full academic year:

1. *Participant observation.* I observed participants in our tutoring sessions. Hand-written field notes were taken after the observations took place.

2. *Focused and open-ended interviews.* Participants were interviewed multiple times. Early interviews were used to gather information about the participants' life story, including their immigration process and educational past. Later interview questions focused on specific issues and artifacts (e.g., assignments, relationships with teachers, obligations outside of school, events at school).

3. *Documents related to reading and writing.* These artifacts (e.g., assignments, writing, textbooks) were categorized and analyzed according to genre (e.g., poems, stories, academic essays). These assignments were examined in conjunction with strategies participants used to grapple with reading and writing tasks far beyond their literacy and English language levels.

4. *Reflective researcher notes.* These notes served as a tool for synthesizing intuitions and as a way to track my own learning and reflection about the issues.

These data sources were coded and categorized inductively and deductively (Coffey & Atkinson, 1996). The process was deductive because the coding was informed by the literature review and the research questions (e.g., identity and race, identity and language, identity and literacy). It was inductive because of emerging themes and patterns from the data that dealt with the participants' multilingual and multicultural literacy uses (e.g., Islam in public lives, challenges at school, resources for school, sports, and literacy). It was important to have an inductive approach because there is very little literature specific to Somali youth and I wished to stay open-minded in my analysis of the data. My analysis strategy was explanation building, which presumed sets of causal links (Yin, 2003a) about the phenomenon of being young black Somali Muslim women, refugees, and English language learners with low literacy and limited formal schooling and attending U.S. public schools. Because participants always communicated with each other in Somali and due to the fact that their level of English speaking proficiency ranged from fairly low to high intermediate, Somali was often used in the group. Although I do not speak Somali, I encouraged the girls to reconnect with each other every week in Somali and to use Somali to help each other understand their school work. The tutoring group was one of the few times during the week that they had to socialize and be away from home. Interviews (in English) were carried out individually and in groups of two or four. Somali was used for discussion and clarification during the interviews[3] and information from the interviews often resulted in follow-up interviews.[4]

The study explored the role of literacy as a social artifact on the lives and social identities of the participants, but literacy is also a very fluid and context-bound phenomenon (Egbo, 2004). Through the data, I will reflect on the role of the literacies used by the girls to help them toward other literacies, which will give them opportunities to increase their "life chances" (Egbo, 2004, p. 248) and allow them to reach their goal of getting an education in order to make a living.

Experiencing Schooling for the First Time and in a New Land

School Adaptation and Achievement

The girls all reported both funny and terrifying memories of their first days at school. Sufia laughed about not knowing what bus to get on. Fatima was embarrassed by her first time in the cafeteria when she had only one dollar but took one of all of the kinds of food available only to find out that she did not have enough money for all that food. Magol told about getting beat up on the school bus every day by another girl until a boy defended her by saying "Why do you beat her up? She doesn't even speak English!" Magol laughed about this now, but it must have been terrible at the time. All of the girls nodded in agreement when Sufia said that in class it was "like you were there but you were not there" because nobody paid attention to them and they could not comprehend so many things that were happening. They were often reminded of how hard it is to adjust to school because other newcomers were always beginning in their schools. Making it through this difficult time seemed to have become a narrative of strength and survival for the girls.

The dynamic between recent arrivals and those who came before is described in a number of well-known ethnographies done in high schools (e.g., Olsen, 1998; Sarroub, 2005; Valenzuela, 1999). In Sarroub's study, the newcomers were called "boaters." These Somali teens sometimes call newcomers "flights," after an infamous chartered flight #13 that brought Somali refugees from Kenya to the United States in the early 1990s where everything seemed to go wrong, including the plane getting lost. The girls joked about how the new kids also did not know how to eat their lunches or carry their backpacks. Fadumo laughed about how she received extra points for helping a newcomer learn how to eat her lunch. In addition to a narrative of strength and survival, it is sometimes seemed that their hard-won knowledge about how to act in high school evoked some cruel sentiments toward other newcomers, again well documented in other studies of immigrant adolescents.

Although education held an important place in the girls' lives, they all reported spending vast amounts of their school day in silence, and although they often pointed out that having friends at school may be bad or even dangerous, they sometimes lamented not having more friends. Research suggests that friends can be a source of support, and relationships at school can resemble those of true kinship. Ngo's (2004, 2009) study of Lao immigrant students told of a student who regularly skipped classes but attended all three lunch periods to connect with his friends. Peer relationships for the girls were important but turned out to also be risky.

All of the participants have explained to me that being strongly associated with any particular group of Somali girls can have a range of consequences. Most importantly, friends could distract them from school. Their view was that it was much more important to do well at school than to have friends. Therefore, the girls sought out friends with whom they could study, such as each other. They preferred friends who were more religious as well. (The girls never discussed any male friends or classmates. The clear expectation from their families was that they would not date or have boyfriends.) The girls discussed how "bad friends" could involve them in harmful gossip and possibly fights with Somali or non-Somali girls. It is important not to forget that although immigrant students often face conflict from ethnic groups different from their own, they also face social tensions from within their own ethnic groups.

In addition to the adjustment to schools in the United States, they all experienced failing the state-mandated reading and writing exams many times. These tests are one of the key obstacles for many adolescents who arrive without formal schooling, and the powerful role they play cannot be discounted in teens' schooling experience. These tests are seen by students, parents, and many educators as irrational hurdles because, quite often, students, such as the participants in this study, get very good grades but still cannot pass them. All educators who work with immigrant students know of individuals who have scholarships to attend college but cannot graduate because they have not passed these tests. The reason for failing the tests is rooted in the nature of the assessment. The tests are not valid for English language learners with low levels of language proficiency and are even less valid for students without the academic background to penetrate the format of the test or the knowledge assessed (Menken, 2008). It is certainly true, moreover, that standardized tests are likely to elicit an English language learner's worst performance, compared to authentic process-oriented performance assessments, with which English language learners can do well. Given the gaps that students with limited formal schooling often have in background knowledge, academic language, and standardized test formats, it is no surprise that the Minnesota Basic Skills Test proved challenging for the four girls.

Reframing Parental Involvement in Schooling

The participants' literacy activities in English were not linked to their parents' literacy use in direct ways, because they do not report their parents using any English literacy. Lack of parental or guardian literacy does matter in many ways as the participants navigated new educational and health systems. For example, the college application process for the girls was something they needed to navigate largely on their own. There was also an incident that happened when Magol was hospitalized. While in the care of a nurse, she became unconscious and fell, losing her front teeth. Although the hospital fixed her teeth, this event resulted in a lawsuit that was later dropped. Magol told me that she carried her legal file in her backpack for many months, not knowing what to do with it after the lawyer told her to drop the case. The issue surfaced again much later when the hospital billed her for $10,000.00 for the dental work. This bill was cleared up with the help of a relative who called the hospital for her.

This does not, however, mean that the participants' parents did not offer effective support in their English literacy development or schoolwork in general (Bigelow, 2007; Weinstein, 1986). A common misconception is that immigrant parents with limited formal schooling have little to offer in the schooling of their children. Sufia and Fadumo's mother did a number of concrete things to support their schoolwork. For example, she relieved the girls from household chores and care for the small children when they had schoolwork to do. She redistributed tasks to other members of the family, including the boys. She also allowed them to travel by city bus to a Somali neighborhood where (bilingual) homework help could be obtained. Their mother expressed interest in academic achievement and good attendance at school. She watched who her children socialized with and placed academic achievement above peer relationships. She was even willing to move her children to another school to protect them from a peer group that would get in the way of their learning. When I asked Sufia what her parents did to help her with her homework, she said that when you are in high school, parents should not have to help you do your homework anymore. However, allowing the girls to get extra help elsewhere was indeed "help." Sufia also reported getting help from her younger brothers and sisters, who were often better at English. Sometimes, she admitted that they did her homework, even though they were much younger than she was. These examples show that Sufia and Fadomo's mother drew on funds of knowledge (e.g., ways of sharing chores, bilingual homework help) as she supported her daughters' academic success and that the family had much cultural capital (e.g., knowing the importance of completing homework assignments, younger siblings having English language skills to help the older siblings).

Fatima and Magol were also supported by their aunt, although their home responsibilities were somewhat lighter given that there were no children in the household. Fatima and Magol, however, had much more pressure to send money to family members in Africa. Their aunt also regularly allowed them to attend bilingual neighborhood homework help programs, of which there were at least three. Magol did, however, report once that her aunt did not understand why she needed help, given her high grades. This skepticism about the need for homework help did not result in denial of permission to get help.

In sum, the education of the four participants was an endeavor in which many adults participated, including me. The girls were also working extremely hard to do well in school so that they could graduate and find work to support themselves and their relatives. During this time, I was becoming aware that the graduation policies, the types of programs they attended, and the social climate of the school did not do enough to meet the girls halfway.

Contexts of Use of English Language Literacy and Orality

Over the 16 months of the study, I learned about the girls' native language literacies and about their English language literacies. In presenting the data, I hope to acknowledge and show that there is significant overlap across cultural activities and that their communicative practices draw on speech and writing as they are enacted (Gee, 1986). Although the girls were likely constructed as preliterate or emergent readers in their schools, I found that they had multiple oral and print-based literacies.

The participants used their English language oral skills mainly to communicate with other English language learners in school. They reported that their teachers (including me) were the only fluent English speakers they typically spoke with, except for Sufia and Fadumo's younger siblings. The lack of interaction with highly proficient speakers of the target language is a phenomenon that has been noted in the literature (e.g., Valdés, 2001; Wong Fillmore, 1991). Magol got a job at a large department store the second half of her senior year and was able to interact at work in English, but she reported that her boss and most of her co-workers were Mexican and spoke Spanish all the time. She proudly displayed to me the new words she had learned in Spanish (e.g., she would say "*once*" when she was in the elevator to tell someone she was going to the 11th floor of the building). Magol reported fewer opportunities to interact in English at work than she did when she was in school. As school was the only English domain that the girls experienced, this could explain their lack of confidence to use English in some settings. This lack of English language fluency presented a challenge for the girls when they looked for work, when they had to do presentations at school, and when they needed to help their families with the daily trials of getting things done in an L2.

English language print was ubiquitous in the lives of the participants, albeit not always comprehensible. They engaged with English language print in all of their classes as well as for enjoyment. Although their literacy levels in English were not high, they eagerly attempted to read a number of genres such as poetry, fiction, nonfiction, and newspapers. In the following sections, I will describe the sorts of English language texts with which each of the girls engaged.

Sufia Becomes a Writer and a Reader

Sufia read her school newspaper. One day she was very upset about an article written by an African American girl entitled "Somali and Black students find new light." The point of the article was to show how far the two groups had come in learning to understand and appreciate each other. The part of the article that bothered Sufia was the following:

> From my own perspective, I've seen a lot of resentment when the Somali students seem to be imitating the Black students' style and clothing, which makes the Black students feel like Somali students don't have their own sense of self. But I think it's just the Somali students trying to fit in, and at first that was what the Black students didn't understand.

Sufia thought that it was ridiculous that the African American students believed that Somalis were imitating them. She explained to me that Somalis were merely shopping at the same places they shopped, just as the African Americans would if they lived in Somalia. She said, "People will act the way we act. They will act that way because they going to our classes, they going to our stores, so they have to buy the clothes." For Sufia, dressing in hip-hop-style clothes had nothing to do with imitating African American students. I wondered if part of her anger toward being accused of copying African Americans was her resistance to being racialized through the symbolic and stereotypic meaning that hip-hop styles take on in mainstream media and society. Sufia's reaction may reflect a loss of agency in reading the article as well as a loss of agency in terms of her group and individual identities. Identities such as this are often imposed by others and simultaneously taken up by teens themselves (Guerra, 2004).

With limited literacy skills, Sufia contested the opinion expressed in the newspaper. Her strong reaction and analysis of the opinion of the author showed me how Sufia was using English texts in ways that were meaningful and important to her. She was engaging with English text in ways an educated user of the language would—by reacting to meaning, by critiquing. In this act, Sufia contested how students like her are often characterized by educators as unable to engage in higher order thinking and analysis or that newcomers have to learn English before being challenged with academic learning opportunities.

The homework the girls were asked to do for school was extremely challenging for them. It often seemed that the girls were given assignments involving very dense texts with little knowledge of how to access them and no background knowledge on the topics addressed. I saw the girls employ very few strategies such as using the index of the textbook to find the answers to the chapter questions or using the headings or pictures to determine where to look for the answers. In Sufia's poetry class, it seemed that the assigned poetry often contained so much nuanced cultural information and abstract use of language that the meaning of the text was practically impenetrable. However, although at the beginning of the term this poetry class was one in which Sufia constantly expressed frustration, it soon became one of her favorite classes. She realized that she could do well in the class if she merely attempted the assignments, which were typically answering questions about poems or writing poems using an established form (e.g., limerick, diamonte). Sufia observed that few of the students attempted these assignments and her teacher was always pleased that she at least tried to complete them and she earned an "A" in the class. This is an example of a poem Sufia wrote:

I Am Poem[5]

1) I am a live today, and
   I am a girl.
   I wonder when I see a dead body
   I hear this of friends out lunch today
   I see in the dark a light coming
   to my eyes
   I want to go to school next year
   I am alive today and
   I am a girl

2) I pretend I am a famus model
   I feel I am flying on the sky everynight.
   I touch when the air going too fast.
   I worry about when I am slower then the other
   student in the class
   I cry about when I see my friends died bodies
   I am alive today and
   I am a girl.

3) I understand when I cause
   problem with my family
   I say when I'm sure that story is realy true.
   I dream of being a famuse person in my future
   I try to be always strong women
   like my mom.
   I hope I get a wonderful daughter never let me alone.
   I am alive today and
   I am a girl.

The poem is both admirable and interesting. Sufia followed the pattern of the assigned poem, including keeping the first two words of each line, despite the fact that they signaled present tense when other tenses are intended. Sufia offered brief flashes of past violence, dreams for the future, and the role of family in her life. She seemed to reach into the past twice, and both times involve mention of death: "I wonder when I see a dead body" and "I cry about when I see my friends died bodies." The fact that both lines are written in present tense, because of the pattern, suggests to the reader that the events are still somewhat fresh. This piece is a window into Sufia's hopes for the future, as well as a comment on her role in society as a female and as a daughter. Her poem suggests the primacy of gender for her with the refrain "I am alive today and I am a girl" and by weaving in mention of "strong women, like my mom" and the wish to have a "wonderful doughter" some day. The assignment offered her an opportunity to express herself in ways that more academic writing cannot. She can use first person and she is free to experiment with language and free to celebrate her life.

Sufia wrote other poems and essays in our time together—some for classes she was taking and some for enjoyment. She compiled her poems into a collection entitled *Poetic Girl: Personality, Joy, Anger, Nervouss, Peaseful*. Her "I Am" poem was the first in the collection of 50 poems. The following essay is an example of academic writing produced for the purpose of applying for a scholarship from her high school.

> I am going to study nursing in college. An important part of my life is helping people. Nursing is challenge that helps different people of different ages, and I look forward to undertaking.
>
> Assistant nursing will be my higher education degree that I seek to obtain. Since in my nineth grade I have planned to be an assistant nurse. I have seen a lot of people being an assistant nurse. I spoke to them and they told me of the benefits and joys of nursing.
>
> I always have good study habits. I finish my homework quickly as much as I can. I also have perfect attendance in school. I never have been absent. I feel I have an excellent attitude to go on to school. I do have responsibilities in my work. For example, I take care of babies always feeding, clothing and entertaining them. These babies are my relatives and I care for and love them deeply.
>
> I feel I deserve this scholarship. I exiel in education and have a lot of experience caring for others. This scholarship will help pay for my schooling as I do not have a lot of money. I guarantee that I will make [*Urban High School #1*] a proud organization by putting this scholarship to better myself.

This piece of writing shows her understanding of audience and giving evidence to support why she would be a good choice for this scholarship (e.g., qualified to be a nursing assistant, good student, monetary need). She demonstrated control over sentence and paragraph structures. This essay, however, does not have the sophistication or daring use of language and emotion that the poem has. The limited skill in crafting the particular type of writing seems to impede noting the multiple ways Sufia shows she deserves the scholarship (e.g., "I never have been absent," "I do have responsibilities in my work") and the ways the scholarship will help her (e.g., financially) and the school (e.g., make them proud). She is working very hard to negotiate a voice within this academic genre and discourse of self-promotion. Sufia takes risks, and these may be the places where her voice comes through the strongest when she writes, "These babies are my relatives and I care for and love them deeply" and later when she writes, "I do not have a lot of money." Revealing this personal information, although done in unconventional ways, is persuasive and perhaps a way to generate sympathy from and awareness of the audience, the latter being an essential quality in academic writing.

Given the fact that Sufia is only in her fourth year of formal education, both the poem and this essay are examples of the magnitude of her accomplishments in English literacy development. However, as a poet, she is much more at ease in her subject position compared to the scholarship essay in which she is trying to find herself in a less comfortable discourse. As such, I am reminded how "the self is shaped by multiple discourses . . . , and composed of multiple subjectivities deriving from heterogeneous codes, registers, and discourses found in society" (Canagarajah, 2004, p. 267). Sufia seems to be negotiating the subject positions with greater or lesser success across these two discursive and material contexts.

Toward the end of our time together, I gave Sufia a book entitled *Aman: The Story of a Somali girl,* by Virginia Lee Barnes and Janice Boddy (1994). This is a novel geared toward an adult audience. Nevertheless, the week after I gave Sufia the book, I picked her up and she was silent. I looked in the rearview mirror and she was reading the book. When I asked her how she liked it, she said she loved it. When I asked her what page she was on, she said, "page 167." In 1 week, she had finished almost half the book. When I asked her what the book was about (I planned to read it too, but was not as fast as she was), she said it was sad. She said that the woman had been through terrible things, that she was crazy because of the things that she did, and that the woman was married to an old man. The weeks we discussed *Aman* were exciting because Sufia told the other girls what the book was about. The discussions were animated and the girls asked many questions about the book. They discussed the issues that were brought up in the book, making many links to their own lives.

I believe that part of the success of this novel for Sufia was that it was a first-person narrative set in a cultural context that Sufia found familiar, albeit more similar to the life of her grandmother than someone her age. She told me that it was the first time she had ever seen a Somali woman's life in a book and she loved it. The high interest and cultural relevance of the text seemed to trump reading level (O'Brien, 1998) and resulted in comprehension of the text. Later, Sufia told about how she lent this and other books to girls at her school who were hungry to read something about a Somali woman. Recently, Sufia told me that this book marked a turning point in her life. It seemed that this book came to symbolize Sufia's new identity as a reader and this identity gave her status among her peers as someone who both read and owned good books.

Magol's Use of Orality, Literacy, and Digital Communication

Sufia and Magol were good friends. At one point, they attended the same school and they enjoyed catching up each week. A routine that became established over the many weeks that we met was to pick up the Saturday's newspaper left outside the building where my office was located and look at the sports pages. Magol and Sufia were basketball fans and avidly followed the men's and women's professional and college teams in the state. By reading the newspaper, they interpreted, for example, how likely the women's college basketball team was to win the final four tournament by calculating the percentage of games won by each of the four coaches. (The newspaper presented only the number of games won out of total games played, not percentages.) Magol and Sufia also enjoyed reading about many personal facts about the players in the newspaper. Magol told me about the first time she went to see a game. Her most salient memory was not being able to locate their seats, something that required a number of literacy skills including but not limited to interpreting what part of the ticket indicated the seat and finding the section, row, and seat, in that order. Magol also said she liked to watch the games on television, a fact that caused her to be teased by an uncle who said her tastes were like those of a boy. A couple of years later, when she moved to another state, Magol made a point of mentioning to me how good the men's professional basketball team was. Evidently, she had looked them up and was preparing to root for a new team.

Magol and Sufia began using email during the time I worked with them. This resulted in another opportunity to use English. I helped them set up their email accounts and they checked their accounts at school. (To this day, they use the same accounts.) At first, Sufia did not reply to me, but when I saw her, she always said she received my messages. Magol also regularly checked her messages. The following messages from Magol were the most common types of early messages I received from her, and they typically dealt with our meeting:

1 "Hi marta this is Magol am hope if we can see tomorrow. and Sufia to if you have time to meet with us. thank you"
2 "Hi martha, it is Magol Imissed youon saturday but I want see you this week tuesday or any time that you are available."
3 "Hi martha it is Magol me and Sufia wanted to see you Tomorrow and friday we both deciede that two day to see you if you have time. Have a greater day."
4 "Hi it is Magol martha am sure if i can see Sufia to day because she don;t call me but i will be there today. Thank you"

These messages read similarly to the voice mail messages Magol left me on the same topic. What she knew about the voice mail speech act (e.g., "This is Magol.") informed how she composed her email communications on similar topics, evidencing the ways literacy and orality were linked for her in this speech act.

Once I received the following message regarding being "exited" from her school. The director of Magol's charter school gave her the alarming and worrisome news that she could not return to school the second semester of her senior year because she had already met all of her graduation requirements. The following message was a reply to my suggestion that she ask for individualized classes, in the unlikely event that she had taken all of the classes offered by the school:

"Hi martha I see what you said and I always like totake your advise My personal I like to learn as much as I can I don.t see anything better than Education if even I find a Job the part line is my school is important to me. I talk to all my teacher and ask them if can finished the schol rest of the year but they said you already take your courses. and I wast happen what they said but finally I found school on st. paul which is Esl. am think I will start next month
Thank you martha. And I will call you today . . . ."

This message is different in that it elaborates more on a particular issue. It serves a different purpose than the messages above, which work much like a voice mail message would. Magol is able to communicate with me in a way that is appropriate, given my age and role in her life.

This event is perplexing because Magol had only been attending formal schooling for 3.5 academic years. She had passed her graduation tests, which is an enormous accomplishment, and apparently had enough credits to graduate from high school. It is unthinkable that she would not benefit from more content classes at higher levels and certainly more opportunities to develop her academic English. She stayed on for some time at this school, but in the end, she switched to an adult ESL program to continue developing her academic English skills. She graduated from this high school and attended the graduation ceremony. The Saturday tutoring group witnessed the remarkable event together.

School is the participants' principal English domain, but, more importantly, school held a place of supreme importance in their lives. These young women, like many adolescents, saw high school as their opportunity to go to college and later get good jobs. The sisters, Sufia and Fadumo, cared about this because they want to be independent one day. Their motivation to finish high school seemed typical to many students. Magol and Fatima, on the other hand, felt tremendous pressure to send money to their mothers, who still lived in Kenya and Ethiopia, respectively. This pressure is illustrated in one particular critical incident. Magol's mother asked her to quit school in order to send her $100.00 a month, which Magol's father, who lives on the West Coast, had stopped sending her. Magol was ready to do this, but this decision caused her great emotional turmoil. However, she came to realize that her mother did not understand how important it was for her to graduate from high school for her own well-being as well as her ability to help her family more. This was particularly difficult for Magol because although education was her highest priority, she realized that her mother was willing to sacrifice this for a momentary need. Luckily, Magol came to understand that it was possible to send this amount of money to her mother and stay in school, which she was able to do within 3 months when she obtained part-time employment.

Magol asked her teachers for help. She often showed them drafts of her assignments in order to receive feedback before they were graded. This was a strategy that improved her work and won her praise from her teachers, who noted how diligent she was about her school work. One would assume that academic English language literacies are crucial for success in U.S. high schools. I saw, however, that a range of academic work, and presumably academic literacies, may be carried out with a low level of English language proficiency. This was a fact for three of the four participants who were still developing their skills in English but were having academic success. Admittedly, their academic success may also be due to a high level of strategic awareness in terms of good student display behavior (Platt & Troudi, 1997). These "good student" behaviors, which were similar to Sufia's, seemed in line with how Magol was outside of school, where I frequently saw her figure out strategies for coping with problems on her own. For example, she was able to get a job and obtained a driver's permit on her own. I saw her as fearless in her ability to interact on the telephone and with strangers and to use her emerging literacy to solve everyday problems.

Magol wrote a number of essays in our time together. Her writing style was to talk about her ideas and then simply sit down and write furiously. She did not hesitate over spelling or word choice decisions. The following essay is an example of an essay she wrote as a reaction to a play we went to see together called *Snapshop Silhouette*, which was commissioned by The Children's Theatre Company in Minneapolis to explore the immigration experience of Somalis. The girls could relate to many of the issues in the play, including the worry Najma (the main character in the play) had that her mother, who was still in Somali, did not have enough to eat and that her younger sister died because of not having enough to eat. The essay below touches on these issues as well as the issue cultural differences between Najma and the African American family who was fostering her:

Between African American and Somalia

1 They both are black and they have a lot of
2 common things. We know that African America
3 came from some area of African and we
4 believe that African America was part of African
5 but it's hard to communicate with African American
6 Najma live family which is African America
7 When she came to America we know that Najm did
8 not have family in America and she left her family
9 from Somalia so she live this family unit her
10 family came to America. We don't know how long
11 they take to come to America but Najm live
12 one of the best which is Africa America family. This family
13 had young girl. I think she was 12 year old
14 like same age of Najm this two young girls
15 they cannot communicate with any way They went
16 although mother of young Africa America girls was
17 best mom and she help both girls the best
18 way and also the mother help Najm because

19 she is very smart young gril but her [illegible]
20 and Najm had some physical [student drew line here]. Sometime
21 and its hard to find out what is going on between
22 Najm and Tay when mother left home They both
23 had some physical talk between them. Sometime was
24 when Najm went to pray the African America play
25 with her because her pray different Them one
26 They have so she made her pray with fun.
27 Although everybody have their own religion so may
28 be Najm get angry when she play with her
29 pray. But that is not the point between two girls
30 Najm had young sister but died so may
31 she have a felt about her sister and also
32 her family who behind in Somalia although Somalia
33 war is going on that time and Najma left in
34 Somalia when they had big war because that time
35 so many Somalia family loss each other
36 and also I knew that a lot of parent died many
37 way so I think Najm was very smart
38 young girls and she was hard work about
39 herself because she know that all her family
40 behind in Somalia and she supposed do a lot of
41 things if she can.

This essay is an excellent example of the emergence of Magol's academic writing. In this piece, and according to her title, she chose cultural difference as the main focus. She begins in lines 1–4 with how African Americans and Somalis are both black and come from Africa. In line 5 she introduces some of the conflict in the play by saying "but it's hard to communicate with African American." Lines 7–14 give necessary background about the play to a reader who has not seen the play. This is an important aspect of academic writing. Line 15 returns to the communication problems between the Somali and the African American girls. Magol gives the example of the fight the girls had when Najma was trying to pray. Then, in line 29, Magol explains that the fight "is not the point" because Najma is sad because her sister died and her family is still in Somalia (lines 30–36). Line 36 includes Magol's validation of Najma's worry when she shifts to first person and writes, "I knew that a lot of parent died." I also see that Magol related to Najma because of the pressure she feels to "do a lot of things if she can" in order to help herself and her family still in Africa. Like Sufia's connection to the book *Aman*, this play offered topics and issues about which the girls could comment and relate. Their English literacy skills are illuminated through these culturally relevant literacy texts.

Fadumo and Folktales

One advantage that language learners who are literate in their native language have is that they can use native language resources, such as dictionaries, to learn the L2. The youngest member of the group, Fadumo, who had some print literacy in Somali, was the only one who reported using such resources. She even brought to our meetings an English-Somali bilingual dictionary and a bilingually written grammar book designed for Somalis to learn English. She said that she obtained these resources from the public library near her house. She told me that the book was a way that I could learn Somali, showing her belief that native language resources were valuable as learning tools. Once I showed her a book of Somali poetry in English, and she said she had seen it at the library.

Fadumo was passionate about folktales. She wrote a number of folktales during our time together. The following text is one example. It is an excerpt (the first third) of Fadumo's narrative of "Arawela," a Somali folktale. Fadumo has given the folktale her own title (line 1), but most Somalis would recognize the tale and know the name Arawela:

```
1                    Woman Hates Men
2
3        Once Upon a time there was a girl Her name was
4   Arawela. She lived in East Somalia. She was Born in March
5   1903, her Family were very rich in the Whole City. Arawela
6   didn't have Brothers and sisters. When she was only seven
7   years old her mother was died, then her Father used to take her
8   to school. She was very Smart girl in her Class. Every day her
9   teacher used to give her good thinks. Because she used to get
10  A+ every Semester. Her Father was a President of Country.
11  She wanted to be President in her Future. Only men have a
12  Power. But Women never get Power. The only things that they
13  do is cook and clean houses.
14       Arawela used to ask her Father why only men become
15  president? Her father was mad because he didn't like to talk
```

16 about President. Arawela she ask again same question. and he
17 said Women are good at cooking and care about children. so
18 Arawela doesn't want to be like the other ladies. to work at
19 home. But she wants to be a president like her father.
20   After seven years she finished Middle school. so she
21 went to High school. so when she Start the high school. she
22 was very smart girl and every boy in the school use to like her.
23 She went to the school only. Because she get her Diploma so
24 fast. then after that she went to college in there in the college
25 for three years. After she finish college she was a Nurse.
26   And she get married. to a men that she used to like
27 when she was in high school. they had a baby girl after one
28 year. Arawela try to take Power from the men. She tolk the
29 men give the ladies to Power one month. And men should stay
30 home cook and clean. men said No because the Women they
31 didn't know how to make President Arawela said did you guys
32 saw Women doing that things? they said no. Arawela said if
33 you guys want know what is Women are give one month of
34 Power. and ladies give you back.

Fadumo's retelling of this famous folktale has many elements of the narrative genre (e.g., "once upon a time," the inclusion of dialogue). Fadumo introduces Arawela in lines 3–10 in ways that develop Arawela's character as a rich, smart girl. Lines 11–13 directly pose the problem for Arawela: "Women never get Power. The only things that they do is cook and clean houses." This piece is an example of how the strong oral tradition in Somali informed Fadumo's writing choices in English. She reports what her characters say and even uses English slang when, in lines 31–32, she says "you guys saw Women doing that things?" She gives many details and develops her tale into an entertaining fable with a moral. Fadumo was concerned that her stories had too many errors in English and she was very interested in revising them so that an English speaker could enjoy them as much as she did. If folktales had been part of Fadumo's language arts curriculum, they would have been ideal texts for her to revise for linguistic accuracy.

Fadumo was also a poet. She immensely enjoyed poetry by women. One of the poems she most loved was "Phonemenal Woman," by Maya Angelou. She encountered this poem in her English class and brought it to the group to read and reread. Fadumo then wrote her own poem that evoked Angelou's voice.

Phenomenal Woman (last verse)	Untitled
Now you understand	I'm a book
Just why my head's not bowed	with full of stories.
I don't shout or jump about	when you open me up
Or have to talk real loud	you keep on reading me
When you see me passing	because I never stop
It ought to make you proud.	telling tales.
I say	I'm resemble quiet,
It's in the click of my heels	but I'm talkative with jokes
The bend of my hair	I can make thousand
The palm of my hand	stories.
The need for my care.	no one can stop me
'Cause I'm a woman	
Phenomenally	I am student
Phenomenal woman	ready to learn
That's me	new things.
By Maya Angelou (1978)	By Fadumo

Fadumo mirrors Angelou's celebratory voice of the beauty of the individual through first-person statements of self. Like Angelou, Fadumo does not follow a rhyme or pattern. She does describe herself, as Angelou does, and she breaks the last stanza off into three poignant lines, as Angelou does.

Fadumo's interest in literature seemed to center on female writers and stories that included strong female characters, like Arawela. Fadumo, even as a middle school student, was at work developing her understanding of gender roles and ways of being female in her social worlds. She drew from both traditional texts, such as folktales, as well as contemporary American poets, such as Maya Angelou.

I was unable to collect an example of Fadumo's academic writing. She used the Saturday group to do what she most enjoyed: write poems and folktales. Nevertheless, these texts can be bridges into English language acquisition and academic writing. I believe that what Fadumo is learning about control over English language text may be transferred to other genres, with some assistance.

Fatima and Learning to Read With Difficult Texts

Fatima's English literacy use was typically within the realm of the required. She often seemed frustrated and overwhelmed with her homework, but she diligently attempted all of her assignments. One day, however, Fatima wanted to talk with me alone as the other girls chatted. During that time she showed me a small, ragged book that she found in her ESL classes about immigrant adults. The book had stories of one or two paragraphs followed by simple comprehension questions. She highly recommended this book to me. This was a moment in which I saw the level of English Fatima was able to comprehend comfortably and I realized what a huge distance there was between this text and the dense writing of, for example, her Economics textbook. Fatima rarely showed me any writing that she did independently. When she brought writing assignments to our sessions to work on, it took much effort to work through the outlining of ideas and drafting of simple sentences into paragraphs. Fatima's reading and writing skills in English were by far the lowest of the four.

The following is an essay Fatima wrote for an assignment in her ESL class:

1 School the good and the bad.
2 Why school is haid.
3 I was come to American in 4/19/2001 and I did not anything because I
4 am new. Then I go to high school. And this is my first year I take many
5 claeses and I have bad garyet [grade] store because all my cleases is
6 every haid. After that I go to Libry and I stry my homework. Then my lo
7 garyt. I am anderte [understand] more because everyday I stary reading
8 and writing. Then my 11 year I Vel [very] good because I am anderten
9 more. Always I helped my teachers because and my friends me and my
10 friends always, we sturte [study] same libry. Then I nevery forget my
11 teachers and my friend because I helped me because before I come to
12 American did not anything and I helped my teachers. And I say all my
13 teacher things [thanks] for helhed [helping] me.[6]

In lines 1–2, Fatima states her title and focus: "School the good and the bad. Why school is haid." Then she offers some background about why school is hard for her: She was new, she had many classes, and she had bad grades because her classes were so hard (lines 4–6). Nevertheless, she tells a narrative of hard work and support from teachers and friends. Fatima's control over the English orthography is much less developed compared to the other girls. Fatima was a little older than the other girls when she arrived and learning English seemed harder and slower for her. She often was overwhelmed with her schoolwork and placed in classes that seemed to minimally meet her language and literacy needs. Nevertheless, the essay above shows that she is developing paragraph-length text and is able to communicate her ideas with the literacy skills she possesses.

I witnessed Fatima work with graphic organizers provided by her ESL teachers to generate ideas for academic writing. This was an excellent tool for engaging with Fatima about her ideas and discussing which examples worked best to support her topic sentences. Although it was challenging for Fatima to turn the phrases and words from the graphic organizer into paragraphs of an essay, this technique was the one that seemed to help Fatima grasp key concepts about academic writing. Although it seemed that the other girls would have benefited from programs with different features, Fatima needed a dramatically different program that taught literacy in more scaffolded, gradual ways, with text that was accessible and plenty of bilingual instruction to build background knowledge in the content areas.

Somali Print in the Minnesotan Linguistic Landscape

On the surface, it seemed that the use of native language literacies played a minor role in the participants' lives. All four of the young women reported seeing Somali newspapers in their homes from time to time, which Magol said she tried to read with little success. All of the participants reported seeing some public signs in Somali (e.g., at the train stations) but that they did not understand why they were there, given the fact that so many Somalis could not read them. Similarly, they reported having seen pamphlets and flyers produced by health agencies or school personnel that were in Somali. Perhaps city officials are attempting to make the city welcoming to Somali speakers or at least acknowledge their presence, yet their approach, possibly mirroring how they have welcomed other immigrant groups, did not take into account the fact that the new community may not use text to obtain information. The existence of Somali text in public places is based on mainstream frames and ideologies of a highly literate society and optimistically promotes the notion of a multilingual society.

The participants could not think of any time when they used written Somali to communicate with each other or anyone in their family that was still abroad. An example of the everyday implications of no print literacy occurred when I was given tickets to a women's college basketball game and invited Magol to go with me. Because she had little prior notice and was unable to get permission from her aunt to go, she asked me to leave her aunt a message saying that Magol was with me. She said that her aunt may need to verify that she was with me. In the end, Magol's aunt did not call to confirm that we were together, but this story illustrates a minor inconvenience of not having the possibility of leaving a note about one's whereabouts.

Complete lack of Somali print literacy, however, is somewhat impossible if a person is literate in English and speaks Somali. Somali uses the Roman alphabet and is orthographically shallow because of a one-to-one correspondence between graphemes and phonemes (much like Spanish) and can be "read" by someone like me who does not comprehend the language but can pronounce the text accurately enough for it to be minimally comprehensible to a Somali speaker who is listening. Magol did not, however, think it was possible for her to read Somali. So, on one of our Saturday sessions, I presented her with a Somali folktale written in Somali.[7] I suggested that the other girls could show Magol how to read it. They eagerly tackled this task and indeed succeeded in helping Magol use her English skills to decode the Somali text. They pointed out the key differences in the script, such as the fact that "x" is pronounced /ħ/, a voiceless pharyngeal fricative (similar to how one would pronounce the "h" in Mohammad but further back in the throat) and "c" is pronounced /ħ/, the voiced version of the pharyngeal fricative, which monolingual English speakers have great difficulty producing. The success of this task surprised Magol and thrilled me. This was the first time I had witnessed firsthand Cummins's (1981b) interdependence principle, which points out that increased skills in one language (in this case, the new language) can promote increased skills in the other language (in this case, the native language).

Whereas older, highly educated Somalis I know went to great pains to bring some of their books from their homes to the refugee camps and then to the United States, the participants in this study appeared to have little connection to written Somali, beyond the symbolic (Gardner-Chloros, 1997) meaning of language as part of a historical fact of Somali ethnicity. Due to the high numbers of Somalis without print literacy in Somali and the fact that few texts are currently produced in Somali worldwide, the ability to read and write in Somali seems to be of little value in the workforce for Somalis in Minnesota. The investment (Norton Peirce, 1995) to maintain or develop Somali literacy is low because so many Somali speakers prioritize becoming literate in English. For the four participants in this study, there were few domains in which print-based Somali was used or needed, and the investment in developing Somali literacy was generally very low. That said, Sufia and Fadumo were proud that they could read Somali and Sufia enjoyed showing other Somali girls her age how to read Somali. She thought that it was important to be able to read Somali, even if the only rationale is that you are Somali. For the other girls, however, speaking Somali was enough.

Somali language *oral* texts and skills were very useful to the girls. As described in chapter 2, oral traditions in Somali society are much more highly valued than written traditions. One of the key ways that the participants were able to express their national and ethnic backgrounds was through Somali oral language use. They used Somali in their everyday lives: for social, familial, and academic purposes. They used Somali constantly with other Somali youth and elders and with Somali teachers. In these ways, the participants were full members of the Somali speech communities (Dorian, 1982), in that they were completely comfortable using Somali with other Somalis.

The girls' shared Somali identity was expressed through codeswitching—that is, using a "we-code" (Gumperz, 1982, p. 66) in which they were fluent. This "we-code" was the way they blended English and Somali in a way comprehensible to them (not me) to suit their communicative needs. In fact, the girls' Somali conversation was often so peppered with English that I could follow the topic threads, knowing virtually no Somali. Among the group members, Magol was the one who used the most English when she spoke Somali, and Fatima, her cousin, and the oldest member of the group used the least amount English in moments when codeswitching was possible. Although the sisters, Sufia and Fadumo, were fully fluent in Somali, I discovered that their younger siblings (ages approximately 3–10) would be considered more marginal members of many Somali speech communities because they were quickly becoming English-dominant. Sufia said that her mother was learning English but that she still spoke only in Somali. She also said that her mother was concerned about the younger children not learning Somali, showing that she believed Somali still had either functional or symbolic use for them. The cousins, Magol and Fatima, spoke exclusively in Somali at home with their aunt, who spoke very little English. I was unable to detect any codeswitching between Somali and English when they interacted with her.

Poetry recitation and storytelling are forms of entertainment and a way of instructing children in clan values, genealogy, and history (Arthur, 2000). Arthur indicated that "the interpersonal exchange of news retains its salience as a social practice in rural and urban Somali-speaking communities, both in Somalia and elsewhere" (p. 262). I was told by the participants and others in the community that poetry recitation and invention are still quite common. For instance, it is typical for a well-known poet in the community, or even someone hired from another city, to collect personal information from a couple to be married and use this to craft long and often funny poems at the wedding reception. In these varied ways, ancient poems are still recited in the Diaspora and new poems are constantly being composed that incorporate the experiences and news of life in the United States.

Oral Somali was also useful for religious study as texts were discussed and instruction was given. The girls' meetings with their Dugsi was an important way they could connect with other Somali adults and interact in Somali. As part of these sessions, Magol reported listening to tapes in Arabic of the Qur'an that she memorized via the oral mode. It was understandable that there were tapes in Arabic, given that low print literacy in Somali was likely to include low print literacy in Arabic as well.

Somali was also spoken at school when the girls first arrived because there were sufficient numbers of Somali teens to warrant some bilingual classes. Therefore, students could use Somali to learn content in school, and for many, this was their first foray into formal education. The participants in this study were no longer in any bilingual classes when I began to follow them, but they told of seeking out neighborhood help from two well-regarded Somali teachers who volunteered their tutoring services in Mathematics and Science, thus continuing their schooling in Somali, albeit informally out of school. They reported feeling as though they learned much more with these teachers because of the obvious fact that they could learn in Somali.

Conclusion: Language Use Among Multilinguals in the Diaspora

At the time of this study, Somali oral language use was useful, if not necessary, in this large Somali community, whereas Somali literacy—framed purely in terms of embodied print—seemed to be of little use for the participants, despite the fact that it was part of the linguistic landscape of the urban areas where the girls lived.[8]

Will print literacy in Somali persist or increase for Somalis who have come to the United States in their teens? I believe that it is unlikely for Somali literacy to grow in this community, given that none of the schools I know of supports additive bilingualism. Subtractive bilingualism through schooling produces a situation in which potentially bilingual or multilingual children and youth gradually become monolingual (Cummins, 1994; Goldstein, 2003; Lambert, 1975; Valdés, 2001; Valenzuela, 1999). For communities experiencing language shift because of forced migration, native language maintenance may be a last priority (Romaine, 1995).

Heritage language learners of Somali have some opportunities to recover or develop Somali language skills, but these opportunities are exceeded by the numbers of youth seeking them. All-English programs quickly show teens that their native language is no longer valued or relevant in their schooling. This message is exacerbated by the fact that most teens have limited past experience using Somali for academic learning. Stable patterns of multiliteracy of minority groups depend on using the written language in noncompeting and complementary social functions, such as Hebrew literacy for religious purposes and English literacy for academic purposes (Fishman, Riedler-Berger, Koling, & Steele, 1985). In order to maintain multiliteracies, the literacies must occupy different spheres in society with different purposes. If written Somali were used more widely, and within realms that do not compete with English, there may be more hope for its survival and development among youth.

In addition, although teens like Magol could become fluent readers and users of Somali print by using their literacy skills acquired through English, the status of Somali print is likely the more important barrier. Sufia, Fadumo, and Fatima will likely find it difficult to continue to develop their literacy skills in Somali because of the challenge of finding texts to read and reasons to use them. It is possible that teaching Somali literacy at school or in community programs could make youth feel that their language and culture are more valued as well as give them status among Somali elders. Jo Arthur (2003) studied the language values and practices of Somali Diaspora girls through a Somali literacy class in the United Kingdom. She found that the course fostered debate within the Somali-speaking community over the role of Somali literacy in cultural expression. It also fostered empowerment, in that the course "contributed to [the students'] knowledge about their cultural inheritance and gave them a positive experience of the communicative use of Somali" (p. 264–265). This study suggested the potential for home or heritage language use in community settings throughout the Diaspora. Perhaps such use could occur in culturally specific schools with high numbers of speakers of Somali.

It may be that new uses of Somali print will maintain Somali in Diaspora communities. Perhaps Internet spaces are where Somali text is most likely to be used and reproduced because of its potential for attracting authentic uses and audiences that include other multilinguals. For example, there are electronic and digitized ways of reading and writing Somali that include a combination of Somali text with other languages such as Swahili, Arabic, and English (Bigelow, 2009a). Perhaps Diaspora communities will be the largest producers and distributors of printed materials in Somali.[9]

Somali oral literacies and language use, on the other hand, may persist longer, given their high value and widespread use among speakers, particularly those who live in a large and relatively new Somali Diaspora community. Spoken Somali in Diaspora communities will have different styles that involve, for example, codeswitching. The oral genres that are part of the Somali oral tradition are sure to include new topics relevant to life in the United States. Knowing about these genres and the power they have in the lives of youth would be relevant to educators who wish to build English literacies. Finding bridges between the native language oral strengths and English is likely a key underpinning to sound pedagogy for Somali teens with limited formal schooling. The examples offered in the chapter are suggestive of some pedagogies that may be effective, such as the following:

1. Poetry and folktales can be enjoyed aesthetically across students' languages and through oral and written modes. They can include students' home language(s) and culture(s) and allow for hybrid uses of language and cultural expressions. The creation of poetic and narrative texts can include prewriting and postwriting pedagogies involving oral discussion and performance. The production and use of these texts can include memorization, which is culturally familiar to many Somali youth who have studied the Qur'an.
2. Creating academic texts can also involve oral language interaction, co-construction, and negotiation in the language(s) the student chooses to use. Familiar topics can be mapped onto graphic organizers using words and short phrases, which, in turn, help students see the organization of the text. Culturally relevant texts (film, books, newspaper articles, theatrical productions, songs) can serve as appropriate avenues into academic writing tasks involving much oral language. Kinesthetic and three-dimensional activities may help to concretize academic texts.
3. Writing assignments can include audiences beyond the teacher. The writing that youth do in their out-of-school lives merits examination in terms of what is possible in the classroom. Writing may include register or codeswitching across the languages the students use with multilingual peers and adults beyond the classroom (Bigelow, 2009a).

From research with monolingual children (Dyson, 1993, 2003), we know that communicative practices draw jointly on all of the linguistic resources the learner uses, across oral and written modalities. This phenomenon has been explored less among adolescent multilinguals who are learning English without the tools of print literacy or formal schooling.

Diaspora youth in contexts such as Minnesota are much more likely to invest in English print literacy because of their perception of its use. However, what are their opportunities to learn the literacies they need to reach their goals to finish high school, go to college, and obtain a profession that will allow them to support themselves and others? Returning to Lewis and del Valle's (2009) assertion that literacy is mediated by issues of identity, agency, and power, it is possible to examine some of the ways English literacy may be problematic for Magol, Sufia, Fadumo, and Fatima.

First, it is very difficult to create an identity of reader and student when one comes to school without prior schooling. However, Fadumo and Sufia were able to create these identities through texts that closely related to some of their familiar cultural practices of poetry reciting and composing and sharing folktales. Sufia actually became a reader for the first time when she read *Aman*, a book about a Somali girl. Fatima struggled more to see herself as a successful student because of all the ways her schooling did not meet her need to slow down, comprehend text, build background concepts for understanding academic texts, and develop confidence as a reader and writer through successful experiences. Magol came to English literacy—which is the only literacy she claims—through determination and hard work. She was relentless in how much she was willing to do to achieve and please her teachers. Magol found topics to write on that she felt passionate about, such as the relationship between African American and Somali culture. Her agency came through as activist and organizer for the group. She was a good friend to the others and supported others' learning. The agency the girls had seemed to be supported by family and community encouragement to do well in school. The home lives of the girls facilitated learning and the bilingual homework help they were able to get was often crucial. As the girls were enacting identities of students, they were also faced with an educational system not designed for them. In this sense, their opportunities to learn were limited by their schools as enforcers of policies such as graduation test requirements and a 22-year age limit for high school students. Schools as powerful and normative institutions did much to discourage the girls as they worked so hard to be good students.

What is it that allowed Magol, Sufia, Fadumo, and Fatima to create a space for hope and possibility, given the intense challenges they faced at school? They persisted through many demoralizing failures—for example, the failure of the state graduation tests. They survived early struggles in their mainstream classes. One explanation is that they invested in what Kanno and Norton (2003) termed "possible worlds" (p. 248) and what I would like to call "future worlds" that may reward their persistence and effort. Kanno and Norton posited that imagined communities, which are not immediately tangible and accessible, "enable us to relate to learners' visions of the future to their prevailing actions and identities" (p. 248). Participants in this study were, as Fadumo said in her poem, "ready to learn." I ponder if we are "ready to teach" them. This is the point in which researchers must consider an advocacy role. Do educators know enough about their how and why they engage with text across multiple domains? Will this engagement offer them opportunities to gain the education to support themselves and others in the future? How does educational level intersect with investment (Norton Peirce, 1995) and identity? I believe that there is still much to learn and the following chapter explores how schooling can fail students like the girls described in this chapter.

Notes

1 Sufia seemed to be the strongest student and also very proud of her good attendance record and high grade point average. It is possible that the other girls did not want to share their transcripts for fear of losing face with me or each other. Likewise, I had asked to shadow the girls at their schools and was never able to obtain permission from them to do this, possibly for the same reason. The girls had developed a "face" during the Saturday study group meetings that may not coincide with how they were in other settings.

2 This knowledge came from having administered the Native Language Literacy Measure (n.d.) in a prior study for which all four participants volunteered (Tarone et al., 2009).

3 Early in the research I considered involving an interpreter who was Somali and female; however, as the group's rapport and trust developed, it seemed that bringing in an outsider would change the group dynamics and thus the quality of data gathered. Furthermore, the presence of an older Somali adult woman would likely influence how the girls chose to present themselves to me (and her) and limit conversations about such things as dating and marriage.

4 Member checks (Lincoln & Guba, 1985) with the four focal students were done by presenting, in English, simplified sections of the syntheses, orally and in writing, to the participants for verification and with the option of removing anything the participants wished, as per their informed consent.

5 This poem follows the format available on the Web site http://ettcweb.lr.k12.nj.us/forms/iampoem.htm.

6 Because this essay was handwritten, I had to approximate Fatima's capitalization and word spacing in this transcription.

7 This collection was referenced in chapter 2 and is available at the following Web site: http://ultra.mpls.k12.mn.us/lyndale/somali/.

8 In 2009, the University of Minnesota began offering a Somali language course for heritage speakers and literacy is a component of this course, which offers a small amount of hope for another context of use for Somali print.

9 An example of a Diaspora community assuming a leadership role in distributing books in Somali is a book fair in Stockholm, Sweden, advertised together with other literacy events on the Web site: http://www.redsea-online.com/modules.php?name=News&file=article&sid=456.

Language Learning   ISSN 0023-8333

CHAPTER 4

The Co-Construction of Racialized Identity Among Somali Youth

You bring out the Somali in me.
The prayers of fayr. The awaiting school.
. . .
You bring out the prayer of "Duhr" in me the whole yummy food of my Mom.
. . .
You bring out the soccer in me.
My crazy friends and neighborhood. The daily arguments of world-class teams. You bring out the "madrassa" in me. My dear Qur'an and the prayer of "asr" in me.
. . .
You bring out the tasty dinners of my sisters.
The "maghrib" prayers which I love.
The family meeting every night. The free time with my brother. You bring out my brother in me.
. . .
You bring out the prayer of isha in me, the freshly bought milk afterward.
My comfortable bed as I sleep.
You bring out the dreams in me.

From poem entitled "You Bring out the Somali in Me" by seventh-grade student, Ahmed Suleiman[1]

Introduction

The inquiry described thus far in this book began to crescendo politically as issues of education and language coalesced around race, racialized identity, and religious identity. Simultaneously, the dialectic between me as researcher and the young people who I was researching underwent a tangible change. After working for many months with the Saturday tutoring group, I decided to engage in more systematic work with Somali elders, boys, and youth who had been in the United States longer. Conversations with Somali youth in focus group settings and interviews with Somali adults became another comprehensive education for me as they explained and theorized about their experiences in Minnesota.

When asked to name their greatest worry about Somali teens, respected community and religious leaders focused on identity. Below are two representative quotes:

> *Abdul (Somali, Muslim, male):* I would say the greatest . . . challenge or concern [for Somali teens] is identity of who they are versus where they came from versus what they are in the United States. So they do struggle with that a lot. Religion is very important in the identity. I've seen some of those students who learn the Qur'an and who try to say their prayers and generally they tend . . . to be more well behaved than a lot of teens.

> *Said (Somali, Muslim, male):* They become torn between these two cultures. There's the point. The new culture is driving them forcefully. And the other culture is driving them on the other part. Basically they are in the middle between two different worlds and that's the dilemma. That's the struggle. Should I be a Somali, an African, and a Muslim . . . or more Americanized and do what any American teenager does?

These quotes explicitly acknowledge the metaphorical in-between cultural spaces youth occupy and the complicated decisions youth face, as Abdul says, "who they are versus where they came from versus what they are in the United States." According to Abdul, youth are struggling between some core self, a self grounded in a previous place, and a self grounded in the United States. Abdul recognizes religion as central to Somali youth identity and says he has observed that youth who practice Islam behave better. In the second quote, Said says that youth are "in the middle"—in a place that is either Somali, African, and Muslim *or* American. This quote gives meaning to the image of being "torn between these two cultures" and suggests that he views these two cultures in opposition to each other. However, it seems that being in the middle is like being nowhere because the middle is neither Somali nor American. Again, what is going on in the middle? It seems to be a place of struggle.

If the choice is binary, it is easy to see how the metaphor of being "torn" between the two would arise. The values of one culture are competing with the values of another under the assumption that the cultures do not have overlapping practices or perspectives. This negative conceptualization of cultural adaptation easily fits with other common metaphors of the experience of encountering a new culture, such as "culture clash," or the experience of having a dual cultural frame as a mental illness. For example, Gaspar de Alba (1995) used the term *cultural schizophrenia* to describe the mistaken identity that comes from the cognitive disorientation resulting from oppression by a dominant culture. Schizophrenia is a hyperbolic metaphor, and the characterization of the experience as a mental illness makes it seem that the process of adapting to a new culture is abnormal and unhealthy. On the contrary, migration is a personal as well as a social process that is entirely normal and quite common worldwide, and it need not be characterized as mental ill health.

Most Somali adults acknowledge the identity dilemmas or struggles youth may face, but they are not always accepting of the identity choices they make as they navigate life in Minnesota. This is exemplified in the following excerpt of an interview with a parent:

Ali (Somali, Muslim, male): Yes I know a lot of students, even high school students, who work and send their money back to their relatives. So a lot of them are just doing very nicely. They know what they can take from American culture and what not. That part is the positive part. A lot of Somali students also they just take the other side. Like you know, from African American youth. Always listen to music, wear loose pants, sometimes even like making their hair like woman. In Somali culture, men's hair is always like this [referring to his own hair]. Short. But when you make, what do you call this?

Martha: Braids?

Ali: Braids. That's totally not in our culture. Not focusing more about their education. Not coming to mosques . . . more important are music and sports.

It seems that it is possible to be "doing very nicely" by retaining a "Somali" identity and selectively choosing what to take from "American culture" such that it does not include signs of what this parent perceives as "African American youth" culture. Ali's quote shows how easily the way youth look determines an assumed identity, which, in turn, is accompanied by assumed behaviors that are not aligned with what it means to be ethnically Somali. "Loose pants" is the most frequently cited way Somali boys irritate and worry their elders. It is the most typical example given by adults that seems to suggest to them any number of concerns: They are getting into trouble, leaving Islam, becoming American.

Ali's quote also shows how natural it is to draw lines around what is and is not Somali culture, as if culture were a static entity. As seen in the quotes from Said and Ali, research of the kind I report in this book has the challenge of coping with data that essentialize African American culture as commodified hip-hop fashion, music, and Black-stylized vernacular English. Very harmful stereotypes of African American youth in the data include not doing well in school and getting involved with crime and gangs. At the same time, Somali youth are making sense of how they may embrace or reject being racialized as "Black" and lumped together with African Americans in ways that include these essentializing, stereotyping cultural views from many directions—peers, Somali adults, teachers, and the police. In other words, Somali youth are simultaneously making sense of (Blackledge, 2005) Black racialized identities while they are learning about cultural differences among and between the African American peers they interact with in their schools and communities.

In the present chapter, I will share data that speak to imposed, assumed, and negotiated identities across a range of settings, including school, and will describe other ways that identity and mistaken identity unfolded for Somali youth. The research will explore the ways in which students are negotiating and recreating what it means to be "Somali" and how their identity announcements may or may not conform to popular understandings or images of "Somali" or "refugee" or "urban." This work aims to begin recounting the experiences of Somali youth as they define and redefine themselves in this particular society in the Midwest. Consider how "acting Black" may mean becoming a minority and "acting White" may mean social marginalization from one's peer group. Fronting a Muslim identity rather than a racial one may mean that some may imagine Somali youth as "threatening" or "foreign." Somali youth choose across all of these socially constructed realities as they locate themselves and are located by others in U.S. society. They are "doing" identity as they speak and dress and act among peers and at home with family members. They also "do" identity as they interact with institutions, including the criminal justice system. Youth are the receivers of ethnic labels and stereotypes, which mingle with the agency that youth need to evoke, contest, or embrace other-imposed identities.

This work of knowing and understanding Somali youth as they make choices about who they are, and who others think they are, has at its core the desire to be informed and inform others about how to support and advocate for minoritized immigrant youth as they adjust to life and school in Eurocentric, Judeo-Christian societies. Another not less important goal is to contribute to theories that connect social identity and inform the complex and dynamic process of cultural adaptation by exploring the following overarching question: How do Somali immigrant youth construct and negotiate identities in a U.S. cultural setting where there is much racial and religious bias?

Context of the Research

The main data source for this chapter came from six focus groups, four of them totaling 23 male Somali high school and college students and two more totaling 10 female Somali high school and college students. Additional secondary data were also collected via (a) five semistructured interviews with adults (Somali and non-Somali) who interacted closely with Somali teens, (b) a video produced by local Somali teens, (c) newspaper articles, and (d) data from the case-study research reported in chapter 3. I personally gathered all of the data, with the exception of five of the interviews with Somali male community members, which were collected by Mustafa Ibrahim, a graduate student at the University of Minnesota.

The focus groups were approximately 1.5 hr in length each and were co-facilitated by Ladan Bashir Yusuf, mentioned previously in chapter 1. Groups were separated by gender, age, and amount of time in the United States in order to facilitate the sharing of common experiences. The focus groups typically included participants who knew each other. The participants referred to each other by name and referenced each other's experiences. There were moments of respectful silence as participants shared sad memories, sometimes crying. There were times when participants nodded in solidarity when someone angrily told about interactions with authorities—typically police officers, guards at school, and sometimes even educators. They laughed too, in a way that seemed to suggest astonishment at the stories told. The young people who participated theorized, co-theorized, and reflected about the events and the topics discussed. The group format served to produce synergistic conversations among the participants and it seemed that they were creating knowledge about identity as well as affirming or contesting each other's comments. This dynamic interaction, or "magic," of the focus group conversations allowed for the participants to speculate and, in so many ways, "trouble" the status quo in their communities and at their schools. The topic of identity was intensely engaging for the participants and the conversations were animated and thoughtful. The group interviews often took the shape of narratives used to exemplify points. The narratives were often co-created and re-created among the participants such that it is nearly impossible to attribute any one quotation to a single participant, even if he or she was the one to produce it. As Labov (1982) pointed out, "Ownership is also diffused by narrative collaboration. Storytelling unfolds in relation to others, who more or less collaborate in giving a story its shape and substance" (p. 179).

Likewise, Ladan and I were not simply "narrative depositories or passive receptors" (Gubrium & Holstein, 1998, p. 181) as we elicited the data. Rather, we reacted to sad or tragic stories and supported the telling of the stories by asking questions and saying that we thought what they experienced was wrong. My being White likely influenced the telling of the stories too. For example, participants would sometimes talk about "White" people and turn to me and say, "no offense." Our age differences (Ladan and I being adults interviewing youth) also undoubtedly influenced the narratives and the tone of the meetings. For example, participants often thanked us for our interest in their opinions and experiences and for exploring the difficult issues of racism and Islamophobia in their lives.

One might worry that talking with adolescents about topics related to difficult issues of race and religion is intrusive or even hurtful. I recall a presentation I gave on these data at another university in 2009. An audience member asked me why researchers bothered immigrant kids with questions about who they were and how they identified themselves. She said, "Isn't it better to just leave them alone?" This is an excellent question; however, the interview data from this study would suggest the opposite. Somali youth were eager to talk about and process their experiences with us and the other participants. Our conversations always lasted much longer than planned and participants thanked us for our interest in hearing about things that had happened to them. Those who stayed in touch with us were pleased that the data resulted in action. Conversely, in an informal lunchtime presentation I gave at my home university on these data, a number of Somali students attended and contributed approvingly. They felt the issues related to race and Somali youth needed to come to light.

As in the research presented in chapter 3, the analysis sought to connect how Somali teens' identities may be constructed and co-constructed by others in this particular urban setting. The data were coded and categorized inductively and deductively (Coffey & Atkinson, 1996). The process was deductive because the coding was informed by the literature review and the research questions (e.g., identity and race, identity and gender, identity and religion). It was inductive because emerging themes and patterns from the data dealt with the participants' schooling experiences (e.g., Islam in public life, Islam in private life). The analysis strategy was explanation building, which presumed a set of causal links about the phenomenon (Yin, 2003a or 2003b) of being, for example, young, Black, Somali, Muslim, refugee and engaging with U.S. institutions such as schools and law enforcement.

Ethnic and Racial Identities

Thinking about identities as *imposed, assumed*, and *negotiable* (Blackledge, 2005; Pavlenko & Blackledge, 2004) is helpful for the discussion of the data presented in this chapter. *Imposed* identities are those that are not negotiated. A common imposed identity is that of refugee—an identity that may be assumed given the history of Somali migration to Minnesota. Identity is imposed if the person identified does not have the opportunity to contest this categorization. For instance, a teen born in the United States of Somali parents may be inaccurately assumed to be a refugee by educators and actually never have the opportunity to negotiate this imposed identity. An *assumed* identity is one that is also not negotiated, but unlike an imposed identity, it is accepted by the individual thus positioned. An example of an assumed identity is when a girl born in Kenya, where many Somalis live, is identified as female and Somali by peers or teachers and she accepts this identification. *Negotiable* identities are those that are contested or challenged by individuals or groups. For example, a girl of Somali descent may contest assumptions many people make about Muslim women as being oppressed by wearing a hijab and fronting a highly educated and politically progressive identity.

Determining whether a particular event exemplifies imposed, assumed, or negotiated identity requires situating the event in a particular sociohistorical context. As Blackledge (2005) pointed out,

> Options that are acceptable for and not negotiated by some groups and individuals may be imposed on others, or even on the same group at a different point in time. Alternatively, assumed identity options that are not negotiated by one group of individuals, may become a battleground for another group that approaches them as negotiable. (p. 36)

As already stated, "race" does not exist in any biological way, but *racism* is a powerful social process that excludes, lumps, and stereotypes people based on assumptions about how they look. This social process of giving meaning to something that does not scientifically exist is at once evident in the experiences of Somali youth while obfuscated by metaphors and categories standing in for race as a basis of group differentiation (Blackledge, 2005; Schmidt, 2002). As Blackledge argued, race is created among individuals, and racial groups are "as much 'imagined communities' as are linguistic [or national] groups" (2005,

p. 47). Blackledge went on to point out that the boundaries and meanings of racial groups "are subject to on-going change and re-definition" (p. 47) just like the boundaries of linguistic or national groups. Nevertheless, Mica Pollock (2004) has observed that as complex as racial identities may be, racial identification is shockingly simple and determined in a brief moment. This moment of judgment is what may be termed racism. The following definition of racism places the social process of identifying groups of people within a power structure:

> Racism is based on the hierarchising construction of groups of persons which are characterized as communities of descent and which are attributed specific collective, naturalized or biologised traits that are considered to be almost invariable. These traits are primarily related to biological features, appearance, cultural practices, customs, traditions, language or socially stigmatized ancestors. They are—explicitly or implicitly, directly or indirectly—evaluated negatively, and this judgment is more or less in accord with hegemonic views. (Reisigl & Wodak, 2000, p. 275)

Reisigl and Wodak's (2000) definition encompasses the many ways racism can occur, including the more insidious ways individuals can be "Othered" and "lowered" through the construction of social hierarchies. Therefore, racial and ethnic labels have consequence in the lives of adolescent Somalis as they do with other ethnic groups (see Chhuon, 2009, on Khmer youth).

Racialization is a social process that is not neutral and "whose point is inequality" (Schmidt, 2002, p. 158). It is a process in which race becomes a key way of defining oneself or being defined by others. Racialization may occur when one group of people is categorically or relationally in contrast to another and this process can occur within and between socially constructed races (Omi & Winant, 1994). Racialization as a process is damaging to agentive identity work, because it objectifies and imposes identities or forces potentially painful negotiations. As a research frame, racialization it is very useful because it helps deconstruct and explain many power issues that are otherwise invisible or naturalized and hidden from inspection.

Racialization at School

In the public lives of visible ethnics, they are defined by their racial or ethnic heritage—or rather, by people's perceptions and stereotypes of their heritage. As visible ethnics, Somali immigrants have different experiences with identity than White, U.S.-born Americans or White immigrants. Somali immigrants typically come to countries such as the United States with an ethnic, religious, or national identity, and over time, they develop a *racial* identity in countries where they are minoritized. This is due, in large part, to the ways that race and racism undergird U.S. social institutions (Bell, 1992; Crenshaw et al., 1995; Omi & Winant, 1994) and inform the national discourse on identity (Feagin, 2000).

When Somalis first arrive, they often talk about how they are surprised at how diverse this society is. In a focus group of young male Somalis who were newcomers, some shared that although they had heard about racism and the police treating Black people badly, they had not yet experienced it themselves. They talk about being happy to live peacefully and glad that they had the opportunity to become educated, finally. The Somali youth who had been in the United States longer, on the other hand, were adept at articulating issues of racism and had many experiences with Black-White racial discourses. There is evidence in the study that adolescent Somalis are entering into the "acting White" (Ogbu, 1988) discourse, where doing homework or being a good student may mean being ostracized from the peer group. In a newspaper story about a Somali college student who grew up in the suburbs, the student reported that she sometimes clashes with Somalis from urban areas (Mathur, 2005). According to the student, the other Somali students told her, "You must be from the suburbs because of the way you talk and the way you dress." They told her that she seems "more White." Similarly, Magol, a newcomer teenage refugee introduced in chapter 3, became acquainted with the term "acting White" at school when a White classmate in her class said that she "acted White" because she read a lot. This caused Magol to laugh because she never thought that reading was something that could be "White." She thought that was ridiculous. In data from Bigelow and Basford (2008), a girl also made mention of acting White as a way that seemed to position Somali girls who had been in the United States longer against those who were newcomers:

> I felt the Somali girls rejected me. They spoke English really well and wouldn't speak to me in Somali. They acted better than me. They dressed [Americanized] and had the habits of their White friends and judged newcomers like me. Back then, I was like, "Oh my God, they're better than you so you should watch out." They had their space. I was mostly quiet.

It is striking that speaking English and dressing and acting White seemed to cause a newcomer to feel smaller and quieter.

All of the focus group participants wished to discuss issues of race and their African American peers. The 10 high school girls who participated in the two female focus groups had much to say about the racial dynamics of their schools and their friends:

> My school like, the Somali and African Americans, they don't get along. And we're two separate—like one side is the Somalis and one side is the Black side, 'cause they don't get along, you know what I'm saying?

> The reason, the reason why is that because, like, you, there, there there's some students that like it's there are schools—like our school is immigrant school. That's what I see it as, you know, it's that students who need to learn English, who need help with like the language, you know, and everything, who need help, like, with math and stuff like that, you know? And there's like, a lot of kids, like, kids that just, people that just came from Africa, like two years ago go to that school, you know? And when the African American students see them, you know, sometimes they might make fun of the way that they dress or the way that they act, you know? Or the language that they're talking, you know?

The girls, although they are quick to recognize intercultural misunderstandings and tensions, also told about having African American friends as well as friends who were Hmong and Latino. A participant in this same conversation told about how she felt going to an all-White elementary school where her classmates thought she was African American:

> Elementary, I went to an all-white school, and then like, every time February came around, and they talk about Black history, and, like, I'm not African American. It's not my history. So they'd be like, they talk about slavery and they'll come at me, and they'd be like, 'How do you feel about slavery?'

> Yeah

> I'm like um, um, um. I'm like you guys. I wasn't a slave . . .
> [laughter]

> So I'm not sure how I feel about it. I wasn't slave, I wasn't. I'm not African American, and they'd be like, 'But you're', they like, they always like, act like the whole class is like, using me as like a prop or something.[laughs] It bothers me!

Using a student "like a prop" is problematic in a number of ways. The individual is used to represent a group of people, defined and delimited in some way by the teacher. The student is made to serve, or self-offer, as an explanation or illustration that supports some (essentialized) understanding of the more powerful members of the class. The student is, in the moment of being "used as a prop," frozen in time and space and objectified in a public way. The teacher, as Ellsworth said, "does not play the role of disinterested mediator on the side of the oppressed group" (1989, p. 309) but rather interweaves his or her own interests into the poignant moment of Othering.

Racialized discourses were overt in Magol's school, which is primarily African American and Somali. At her graduation, in a speech directed at the graduates who were all African American or Somali, the African American speaker said, "You will be treated differently for no other reason than because of the color of your skin." This statement warns graduates that society will lump all those with "black" skin together, regardless of ethnicity. Here, a racialized identity predominates and ethnic, religious, or other identity labels are secondary. When I asked Magol what she thought about this statement, she brushed it off saying, "that's how they [African Americans] always are." Magol clearly did not see herself as racialized in the same way as some African Americans do. She did not identify with the racialized discourse of the speaker at her graduation. However, this could be due to the fact that she had not been in the United States very long.

Harmful racialization can occur as youth interact with their teachers and guidance counselors. A female high school student said this about her perceptions of one of her teachers:

> I'm not gonna lie—um, our school, some teachers are racists, even the teachers say that some teachers are racist. They're racist, like they, they don't help you. I have this class, and then, she was the, she was, I think she was a racist people I ever met in my life. The comments she makes about Muslims. I didn't like that. I used to hate that class and then, and then, it was required, so I had to take it, and I couldn't like—"Oh, man" and I couldn't wait that class. They won't help you with nothing. They, they be like, "Oh," you, if you miss a class or something, and you be like, "Can I make it up? Can I make up the work?" They be like, "No." (Bigelow, 2008, p. 29)

This quote shows how the speaker views Islamophobia as a form of racism. In addition to struggles with teachers, Somali Muslim youth experience tensions with other ethnic groups. The experience of being racialized also occurs outside of school, as seen in the next section.

Racialization Through Contact With Local Law Enforcement

Many Somali students who were interviewed expressed being judged and mis-judged around racial identity by peers, elders, and teachers. However, some of the most serious and hurtful ways Somali youth are racialized emerged in the conversations about their interactions with police officers.[2] These stories arose mainly in focus groups when participants were asked if they had ever been mistaken for someone they are not. This seemingly simple question inspired many sad and angry accounts of adolescents being mistreated by police officers. Many of the male participants recalled an incident in the summer of 2006 when a robbery and murder occurred in a neighborhood in Minneapolis. Initially, the report suggested that the suspects were Somali (the convicted killer was not Somali). This resulted in massive searching, questioning, and incarceration of young male Somalis. High-school- and college-age students had personal stories about this event that they understand as racist. This massive level of profiling teaches Somali youth to mistrust institutions.

Boys said that bodily searches of male adolescents were common when they were found on the street in their neighborhood. Disturbingly, many youth reported that male adolescents who were found doing something "suspicious" were transported (read kidnapped) by police officers in police cars to an African American neighborhood and left. Youth said this was "common practice" in their neighborhoods. They realize that this practice was meant to intimidate them because they perceived African American neighborhoods to be life-threatening to them. Sadly, this police action, or threat of this action, served to further pit ethnicities against each other. When police chiefs were told of these stories, they were surprised and outraged, saying that it was absolutely illegal for officers to do this.

Ironically, although this police practice pitted Somali youth against African American youth, many other accounts in the data show that Somali youth feel that they are lumped together with African Americans, therefore making Somali youth learn that it is their race that matters most in this society. Consider the following excerpt from one of the focus groups:

> (*The high school male participant reports the following event occurring when he was waiting for a bus to go to class at an evening alternative high school.*)
> "He had the uniform on. The dude, he had no right to come at me the first time, you know what I mean? 'Cause I'm all grown. I don't think I look like a little kid, you know what I mean, that you come and talk to anytime. Actually, when he took me to the side and he start cussing at me, you

know. *[laughter among focus group]* Like verbally, he start cussing, then I kind of apologized, you know what I mean, so I could get out that little spot I was in, but I look at, I look at that as racism, though. The dude just came at me, and just started, he just kind of used a lot of profanity words, you know what I mean? That was the first racism thing I ever experienced in my life, you know, and I look, you know, some people say, you know cops is this and that, I kind of believe 'em now, you know what I mean? 'Cause I've dealt with something like that."

(*High school male student*) . . . You know, like they [police] see us, they see us culture-wise and then the cops see us color-wise. 'Cause old Somali people try to separate themselves from black people, but the cop, he sees you as a black person and he's gonna do whatever he will do to another black person.

(*High school male student*) They get a call saying there's this black guy who just robbed a store, and you mistakenly, you walk by and you [are ?] black man, because African, Somali, Kenyan, Congoan—we all the same—we black men. Have the skin of black.

[several others laughing and talking during this]

You got small nose, big ears. It doesn't matter. We all Africans and we all the same. So police doesn't know the difference.

Many of the college-age male participants theorized about their interactions with the police. One young man said that he not only has learned that the police mistreat members of his community—male and female—but that they also do not offer the community the type of protection they need. He wondered aloud what his taxes were supposed to pay for. Another young man believed that these interactions with police officers promoted criminality among middle and high school students. He said that it does not matter if a person is innocent or guilty, because the police would arrest you for something. This phenomenon is similar to "stereotype threat" where individuals who are expected to perform in ways that conform to a stereotype in fact live out those expectations (Steele, 1997; Ward, 2004). The police recognized that there were poor relations between them and the Somali community (Condon, 2009). They also complained about having little cooperation from the community in solving crimes. Clearly, it is very difficult to police a community that will not communicate with police officers, despite there being many witnesses to crimes, but this dynamic has developed through negative interactions with the police.

Racial Identity: Youth Agency and Adult Worries
Many urban teens of all ethnicities are drawn to the aesthetics of hip-hop culture, including clothing and hair styles, music tastes, as well as a way of talking that seems to have features of African American vernacular English, or what many locally refer to as an urban vernacular, due to its widespread use among youth.[3] Because most Somalis have a Black racial phenotype, embracing the hip-hop culture is a decision loaded with significance and tension. Part of this tension comes from many parents' desire for their children to be distinguishable from what they understand to be African American youth, which is typically a stereotype. To Somali elders, acting African American is alarming and may signal to them not only a departure from Somali culture but also a departure from Islam. In this sense, some Somali youth engage in difficult identity work to place themselves in peer groups and at the same time respond to messages they may hear from Somali adults in the community. The way elders see youth adopt contemporary youth culture has inspired community actions such as the creation of East African charter schools and decisions in families to send youth back to Africa. The way their youth look and talk is a common topic of discussion and worry.

In 1972, Bryce-Laporte proclaimed that African immigrants' "identity, loyalty, accent, and traditions have melted rapidly in the *black pots* and *white pots* of America leaving only slight residues" (p. 51, emphasis original). Although the "melting pot" metaphor for integration is old-fashioned, Bryce-Laporte's (1972) words are wise as the racialization of Somali immigrant teens and their co-constructed identities is explored. Some Somalis navigate this terrain by choosing to "become Black" (Ibrahim, 1999) or "act White" (Ogbu, 1988). Others find their place in the "in-between" (Bhabha, 1994). Their concurrent distancing and identification with African Americans seems contradictory, but it is an expected byproduct of the U.S. society (Vickerman, 1999).

Identification and Distancing From African American Peers
The data produced numerous examples of identification with and distancing from African American peers. For example, Magol told about a Somali boy in her school who was well known to be very good at improvising and writing rap poems. This skill brought him status at their largely Somali and African American school, which I was able to witness when he performed in a talent show. It was common for many Somali boys in the neighborhood in which the research was conducted to dress in hip-hop fashion and use urban vernacular slang. However, these practices do not mean that the youth have resigned a Muslim or Somali identity—these identities may simply not be readable on the

surface to an outsider of Somali Muslim adolescent signs and symbols (Hersch, 1998). Nevertheless, "acting Black" are exactly the behaviors that frighten Somali parents and elders. They see "Blackness" (Lee, 2005) as negative, as "bad." For instance, Magol told me that Somalis who act "Black" "have to go back to Somalia because they cause a lot of problems. Some of them are boys. They follow African Americans." At the same time, Magol was not charitable toward African Americans. She stated, "I always scared of [them], I don't know, somehow I scared of them. Especially the girls." She reported being insulted frequently by African American girls at school. The reality is, as a refugee with limited formal schooling, Magol was often placed in the poorest urban schools with American students, many of whom were low achieving and special needs African American students. These experiences seem to have informed her opinions of African Americans as a whole, despite the fact that she has had limited exposure to the diversity among African Americans. She has, therefore, essentialized what it means to be African American.

The violence between Somalis and African Americans in particular has received much attention in the local media. According to one newspaper editorial, the tension is based on miscommunication (Maynard, 2002). Maynard quoted Fabian, an African American student, as saying,

> I see Somalis as Black people but some people don't. They just see them
> as foreigners who came here and don't understand our history. They don't
> know the hardships of slavery. They don't respect what we've been
> through, so they don't get the respect of being Black.

Maynard reported that Somali teens reply to this argument with the fact that their families have suffered too. She quotes Sadia, a Somali teen: "Kids here were watching Rugrats and Barney while we were running for our lives." Maynard stated, "Though they [Somalis] empathize, the way slavery still impacts their Black American classmates is as lost on them as it is on most Americans. That happened a long time ago, they say." Somalis are not the first Africans to come to the United States after slavery and this research resonates with findings from previous research with Black immigrant groups (e.g.,Traoré & Lukens, 2006; Waters, 1994, 1999).

The interethnic tensions documented in the Maynard article also surfaced in the data from the four teenage girl participants presented in chapter 3. They reported feeling that having friends at school was a risky enterprise because any interethnic or intraethnic alliance with girls associated with a particular group could lead to a physical confrontation, at worst, or could be a distraction from study, which was the participants' sole reason for attending school. The participants in the Saturday tutoring group did not see school as a place to find nurturing relationships or support (cf. Ngo, 2004, on kinship relations among Lao students). This is a belief that may be coming from the girls' families. Fadumo said that if her younger brothers started having "bad" friends at school, her mother moved them to another school so that they would be able to focus on their studies.

These data show how Somali teens are racialized in U.S. society, but how teens also make choices that locate them within as well as outside a Black-White dichotomized discourse, as observed by Bryce-Laporte (1972) more than three decades ago. Although they may seem to others to be "becoming Black" (Ibrahim, 1999), they are maintaining alternate and unexpected identities related to religion, gender, and ethnicity and in their own way contesting popular notions of what it means to be an African immigrant in the United States. My data show, over and over again, through narratives about interactions with authority figures, that Somali adolescents' often imposed racialized identity can have the power to subordinate other identities such as the preferred religious or ethnic identities. My data also show that youth contest or embrace racialized identities in both gendered and personal ways.

Religious Identity and Islamophobia

Adjusting to life in the United States can be an unsettling process for newly arrived Somalis because most are not accustomed to having a minority status in their society along racial or religious lines. Neither race nor religion was a primary marker of difference prior to their emigration from Somalia, because most Somalis tend to see themselves as belonging to the same ethnicity (Somali) and religion (Sunni Muslims). A primary societal demarcation is perceived clan differences (Ajrouch & Kusow, 2007), which align with regional identities. However, racial and religious identities typically gain primacy in the United States due to entrenched societal structures of racism and Islamophobia. The adjustment experience that newcomers have to the new ways they may be minoritized can spur a host of feelings ranging from surprise, to resistance, to anger. Furthermore, the combination of discrimination based on both religion and race leads to what can be seen as the development of a "new racism" (Rich & Troudi, 2006, p. 617), which is used to marginalize and exclude those who are both religious and racial minorities.

The mismatch between some fairly unquestioned identity markers from the home country and the biases of their new society place Somali youth in a cultural "in-between" or "third space" (Bhabha, 1994) where youth are trying to navigate new peer groups. Critical to this notion of a "hybrid" cultural, emotional, linguistic, and social place, which is unlike both the home country and the new host country, is that identity is always changing (e.g., Gilroy, 1993; Hall, 1989). Identity is a site of struggle and sometimes contradiction; it is constantly transforming across time and space and related to the desire for affiliation, recognition, and security (Norton Peirce, 1997). The experiences Muslim immigrant adolescents bring to and have at school and in their communities contribute to their new and constantly changing identities, which, in turn, influence their opportunities, investments, and dreams.

National Identity as Religious Identity

My data coincides with other studies that show overwhelmingly that Somali youth tend to have a strong national or ethnic Somali identity, regardless of their official citizenship and even whether they have any recollections of Somalia (e.g., Ajrouch & Kusow, 2007; Berns McGown, 1999). When asked to describe themselves, the majority of youth I interviewed said they were Somali. Some said they were Black, fewer said they were Somali-African, and once in a while they said they were African American. These findings also coincide with other research showing that Black immigrants choose to identify themselves in terms of nationality rather than racial categories (e.g., Lopez, 2003a). Although their answers seemed to vary somewhat according to when they arrived (e.g., newcomers were much more likely to identify as Somali or Muslim than participants who had been in the United States most of their lives), I assume that how the participants identified themselves in the focus groups was also influenced by the context of the focus groups and how they may have tried to gain approval from or position themselves against other participants in the focus groups. However, it is uncommon in my data to find clear distinctions articulated by the participants between what it means to be Somali and what it means to be Muslim. It seems that a national or ethnic identity is often intertwined with religion among Somali youth.

The following quote is from Nusaybah, a female participant in Basford's (2008) dissertation who is identified as Somali American and a high school junior. This quote suggests that national identity can cause some ambivalence among teens who do not have firsthand recollections of life in Somalia or about, as she says, "Somali heritage or background."

> Being Somali in America is so different. I'm Somali, yes, but I don't know
> much about my own Somali heritage or background. Yes, I know a lot
> about American history. I got an A+ in American literature, but that's not
> who I am. That's not where my heritage or family roots go back to. I don't

feel like I fit in either. So I just say I'm a Muslim. I'm more into my
religion, that's what I understand. I don't call myself an American. I don't
label myself a Somali. I'm a Muslim. (p. 90)

Nusaybah says "I'm a Muslim" two times in this quote. It seems that she feels
comfortable with the label of Muslim but does not think she knows enough
about being "Somali" to claim that ethnic label. One might wonder what it
means to be Somali for Nusaybah and why she does not feel entitled to claiming
that identity. Saying "I'm a Muslim" is choosing a religious identity but may
also be akin to and serve as a panethnic identity marker. Being Muslim may
work for her similarly as labels such as "Arab," "Asian American," or "Native
American" work for people with ancestry from a multitude of nations. The
most interesting aspect of this quote is pondering what Nusayba would gain or
lose by embracing a Muslim identity while denying a Somali identity. What are
the perceived benefits and consequences of identifying as Muslim rather than
Somali in her multiple social worlds?

Gender, Religion, and Identity

The girls who participated in the focus groups said they would identify themselves as Somali, but they also said they were aware of others seeing them
as Somali, which was something that the boys did not mention. This suggests
a gendered quality to how identity is co-constructed among Somali teens in
Minnesota. This may be because in Somali societies, following an Islamic
lifestyle often includes wearing a hijab. Somali adolescents, as well as other
African immigrant males and females who are not Muslim, do not typically
wear a religious garb as conspicuous as the hijab. So, in Minnesota, because
most Muslims are Somali, girls who veil are able to assert a national or ethnic
identity by doing so. Therefore, girls who wear the hijab have the opportunity,
in the eyes of many, to remain "Somali," whereas the boys' other-imposed
identities may be along racial rather than national or religious lines. In other
words, many will see the veil as a marker of not only religion but also Somali
national/ethnic origin. In fact, it is possible that by asserting or announcing a
religious identity, Somali girls are able to override other-imposed identities. In
certain contexts, however, this choice has unexpected consequences.

For example, these issues are explored in a qualitative study of middle
and high school Somali girls in a St. Louis school by De Voe (2002), who
found that African Americans sometimes resented Somali girls for veiling,
because it signaled the rejection of the Black American identity. De Voe also
found that although African American students and teachers in the schools did
not differentiate between race and ethnicity (i.e., all were lumped together as

Black), the immigrant youth she studied do "differentiate among and between their group and other groups regardless of race. The main criteria they use are religion, nation-state, language, and sub-ethnic group" (p. 237). Similar phenomena were found in Sorenson's (1991) research with Ethiopian immigrants to Canada. Sorenson's participants, like many Somalis (who may also be from Ethiopia) did not embrace a Black identity. Sorenson found that this rejection of a Black identity was resented by Canadians who were both Black and White. These participants in these studies indicated that non-Muslims in the United States and Canada not only fail to understand the multiple religious, personal, social, and economic reasons for veiling, but they also seem to take veiling as a way to wear an identity that does not include race.

Misidentification can occur among Somali youth as well. To illustrate, one participant told me about a classmate who she did not know was Somali because she did not wear a hijab. She said, "I thought she was Black, but then she could speak Somali. She was Somali." This is an example of how religion, race, and ethnicity intersect among and between Somali youth. The hijab serves to distinguish Somali youth in terms of nationality and ethnicity, even among themselves. Without the hijab, Somali girls and women may be misidentified as African American, whether or not this is an identity they willingly embrace.

A group of Somali teenage girls in Minnesota tried to explain their manner of dress in a video entitled "What's up with the Hijab?" The video targets a non-Muslim audience and features many interviews with Somali girls. Regarding the hijab, one girl explained:

> Some people ask us like it's because we don't have hair. I have hair ok, I'm not bald headed. We just normal person the only thing different is that we cover our hair and the reason we cover our hair is we have respect for our religion.

Basford (2008) captured a similar sentiment from Nusaybah, quoted above, who said:

> You feel like an outsider, cause you're the only one wearing the hijab and everyone's always asking you about it and teasing you about it. So your main concern is I wanna fit in with the group. I don't wanna be isolated. I don't want everyone to think I'm weird just because I'm here wearing a hijab and covered up. I want to be seen as a normal girl. (pp. 100–101)

These quotes illustrate how Somali Muslim girls practice their faith but at the same time worry about fitting in with the dominant society, or Somali girls who do not wear a hijab.

For some Somali girls, however, the decision to wear the hijab is complex and closely tied to trying to accommodate their multiple peer groups and social circles. This is illustrated in the quote from another young woman in the video:

I sometimes wear it but I've been living here for like 11 years. I feel like I've been Americanized, but really I'm not. It's just I've been trying to fit in and I just caught up with them and I kinda stopped wearing it. I sometimes wear it though to fit in with everybody else that's Muslim, all the other Somali girls. I feel like I shouldn't do that because I feel like I should just follow my heart and do what I think I should, even though it's against my religion.

This quote suggests the ambivalence of the in-between (Ngo, 2009, 2010). She asserted that she was Americanized, perhaps referring to her appearance, but then also noting that she is still Muslim. She expressed a desire to fit in with "Americans" but also with other Somali girls. To accommodate these disparate desires, she wore a hijab at certain times. Yet, she ultimately shared that she should *not* wear a hijab to be true to herself even though this would be against her religion. In other words, she still thought of herself as a Muslim, but to be true to herself, she did not feel that she should wear the hijab. Apparent in this statement may be great indecision and the "in-betweenness" of her Somali American identity, but she may also be showing agency as she moves between worlds and chooses identities as needed and according to the social setting.

Somalis, like other Muslims in the Diaspora, choose to wear the hijab for a range of reasons, including being very religious and wanting to feel close to God. Other possibilities may include what Khan (2002) found among her participants. She reports that Manal never wore a hijab in Egypt but felt that she needed to wear it in Canada to visibly identify herself as Muslim in order to try to counteract media representations of Muslims as "fanatics, fundamentalists, and terrorists" (p. 107) and women as "oppressed" (p. 108), using herself as an example to the contrary. Although this reason for veiling did not appear in my data, it is something to explore as Somalis accumulate more time in the United States.

Identity Intersections and Discrimination
These intersections among race, religion, nationality, and gender, therefore, create a dynamic hybrid space where youth may negotiate, assert, and contest other's assumptions of who they are. Negotiating imposed identities is particularly difficult because youth must carry the weight of representing a stereotyped and even feared religion while fighting against these views (Basford, 2008;

Yon, 2000). In particular, Muslim youth are Othered in ways that seem to be purely based on religious bias and discrimination. This discrimination is sometimes difficult to separate from racism. For example, when authorities do identify them as Somali, they also experience religious slurs. Accounts from both current high school students and college students said that it was common practice for police officers to use slurs such as "terrorists," "Bin Ladens," and "Mogadishus" when addressing Somali children and youth. Hassan, a participant in Shepard's (2008) study, reacts this way to classmates who call him Osama Bin Laden:

> I don't care what they call me. I just tell them I am Osama Bin Laden's brother. Yeah. That's what I say. I never say no. They ask me a stupid question; I am going to [give] a stupid answer. I don't care. (p. 70).

Shepard speculated that this name-calling may affirm Hassan's religious identity rather than put it in question. A girl in one of my focus group interviews responded similarly, saying Osama Bin Laden was her uncle:

> One time—when, it was, like, around 9/11, it was like after a week, then one time I was walking, and then this lady came and she was like, "You know some Osama Bin Laden?" She's like, "Do you know Osama Bin Laden?" and I was like "Do I look like I know Osama Bin Laden?" [others laugh]
> And she said, "And why you wearing this?" and then, I'm like, 'Cause I'm a Muslim," and then, she said, um, well, she was an old—she was like 90–80. She didn't know anything about it. She was looking at me like I'm crazy and there was a little—they were making fun of how—of me, even [it wasn't only me, it was five girls?] and then, we like, "Yeah, we are . . . ' and then, the other girl, she was trying to play with her, she was like, I know Osama Bin Laden, and he's my uncle." And then the lady, she actually believed that, she thought it was true.

In the same conversation, another girl said that that Saddam Hussein was her uncle, in response to a stranger commenting on her hijab. In reference to being thought to be Arabs, a girl said, "I guess we're not even considered Black anymore." Her comment suggests that extreme Islamophobia can trump racism as a form of Othering and discrimination.

Religious issues at school typically deal with the following issues: (a) Prayer: Should teens be allowed to take breaks to pray? Where will they pray and wash? (b) Hijab: How to accommodate dress requirements for girls in co-educational physical education classes? How to help other students understand the hijab? (c) Dating: How do Muslim students cope with U.S. dating norms far different from what is allowed by Islam? (d) Food: How to accommodate dietary requirements (i.e., no pork, fasting during Ramadan).[4] Most of the participants had stories about how teachers put them in the difficult position of praying or getting into trouble at school. A high school girl told this story:

> She never let us pray and like, like, one time, like, like, she, she had to let—the principal made her let us, but she really made a big about it. Like, I was running in the hallway one time, and she was like, "Farhiya, don't run in the hallway. Now you're not allowed to pray anymore." I'm like, "I can't pray 'cause I was runnin' in the hallway?" and I'm like, "Wh- I'm gonna go to hell," I said that. I was ju- It was like a joke, so, "I'm gonna go to hell if I don't pray." And she was like, "Well, you're going to go to hell if you run in the hallway, too." That's what she said to me, and she wouldn't let me pray.

Of course, I was not able to obtain the teacher's perspective on this incident. However, whether or not to pray or veil at school are decisions that Muslim youth are confronted with often, because of interactions with non-Muslim teachers and peers. Choosing to stop wearing the hijab may have consequences in the girls' family and community (Basford, 2008; Haw, 1998), but schools could go a long way in making a Muslim identity less challenging for students (for suggestions, see Bigelow, 2008; Haynes, 1998; Parker-Jenkins, 1995; Shah, 2006). Schools do not, however, stand free from powerful discourses in (global) society that instill suspicion and fear of Muslims. Given these complex intersections among national/ethnic identity, religion, and race, Somali Muslim youth face religious dilemmas in school and in their communities. The expectations that peers, teachers, parents, and elders have of them are often in direct conflict.

Conclusion: Identity and Power

Espiritu (1992) reminded us that

> Categorization is intimately bound up with power relations. As such, it characterizes situations in which a more powerful group seeks to dominate another, and, in so doing, imposes upon these people a categorical identity that is defined by reference to their inherent differences from or inferiority to the dominant group. (p. 6)

In considering the construction of identity among Somali immigrants, it is critical to understand the politics and power of identity formation and how individuals experience becoming minoritized and racialized. As a politics of difference that categorizes and essentializes immigrant identities, race seeks to construct immigrants as Other. Simultaneously, race attempts to maintain the status quo—keep everything "the same" and "us" and "them" in "our"/"their" respective places (West, 2002). The data presented in this chapter lend additional evidence to scholarship showing how race is a way for more powerful groups to oppress others. It is also a way that youth experience being mistaken for something or someone they are not. According to Taylor (1994), practices of racialization, where identities are not recognized or misrecognized, can be oppressive and cause harm. Taylor argued that

> [I]dentity is partly shaped by recognition or its absence, often by the misrecognition of others, and so a person or group of people can suffer real damage, real distortion, if the people or society around them mirror back to them a confining or demeaning, or contemptible picture of themselves. Nonrecognition or misrecognition can inflict harm, can be a form of oppression, imprisoning someone in a false, distorted, and reduced mode of being. (p. 74)

Unfortunately, Somali youth experience a great deal of misrecognition.

It is important to note that the present data clearly show how the process of racialization of Somali Muslims is different from that experienced by other immigrant groups, challenging assumptions of a universal experience *within* and *across* groups (Hune, 2000; Lowe, 1996). Somali immigrant youth have a unique set of religious, ethnic, and gendered identities that mediate the constructed and co-constructed processes of racialization. Race is central to this process because, as a societal construct in a normative racial stratification system such as the United States, it tends to override other facets of a person's identity, such as ethnicity (Tuan, 1998, p. 22) or religion. Thus, although the first generation of Somali immigrants may wish to be identified as "Somali" or "Somali American," they are more likely to be identified as "Black" or "African American" by others, as has been the case of other Black immigrants to the United States (e.g., Bryce-Laporte, 1972; Vickerman, 1999; Woldemikael, 1989a, 1989b).

The racialization of students' identities ignores the fluid nature of identity and the ways in which students are actively creating and contesting what it means to be "Somali." The fact that immigrant students' identities are simultaneously constructed by them and by others is of critical importance to understanding that culture and identity are formed through interaction with others. This contested nature of students' identities has implications for educators, police forces, community workers, and parents. We know that immigrants are often lumped together with other groups due to their race (e.g., Oromo immigrant students with Somali immigrant students). This lumping causes tensions and misunderstandings among students, among school staff, and in neighborhoods. The phenomenon is further complicated by students who display multiple identities that may seem contradictory to an outsider (e.g., conservative Muslim beliefs and the ability to compose original rap poems). Furthermore, home and school identities may be at odds with each other (e.g., girls wearing a hijab in the community but not at school).

Because Somali youth experience racism and Islamophobia in a number of settings, it is important to consider what could be done at school to support youth as they make sense of their experiences and find ways to respond to discrimination, bias, and ignorance. Teacher educators, school staff, educators, community organizers, parents, and students should work together to promote welcoming school and community climates for all youth. The following ideas may serve as a concrete list of ways groups could work together for equity and social justice (Bigelow, 2008).

Regarding race
1. Ethnic labels, identity markers, and processes of identity formation can be explored in the professional preparation of all school and community-based educators. Educators could learn about how to foster interethnic and intraethnic understanding through an exploration of common school policies such as how all students need to see clear paths toward participation in the most challenging classes in the school.
2. Race and racism can be a topic in the curricula of many subject areas. Youth could explore how different societies marginalize people. All students would benefit from inquiry about how racialization occurs at schools and in communities.
3. Youth could explore status or identity symbols in a range of youth cultures.
4. All adults could work with youth to gain experience leading conversations about police harassment and profiling.

Regarding Islam
1. School personnel should have the opportunity to critically examine assumptions about how to follow the Establishment Clause of the First Amendment of the United States Constitution (i.e., "Separation of Church and State") in public schools. It is not uncommon for parents, administrators, and teachers to misinterpret the meaning of this law.

2. School personnel can collaborate with Muslim parents and religious leaders to accommodate obligatory religious practices youth wish to follow. Employers can also use this strategy to devise ways to create welcoming work environments for Muslim youth.

3. Teachers can teach non-Muslim students about Islam and the cultural diversity within Islam. In addition to demystifying the hijab, teachers can work against Islamophobia through the curriculum. Islamic arts, history, and politics could be explored across a number of subject areas in ways that would deepen the curriculum and offer a forum for learning how dramatically different Islamic societies are.

4. Local and national media that engenders fear could be analyzed. Likewise, students and teachers can learn to recognize anti-Islamic (and other) bias in textbooks and other course materials. The educational community should actively seek the removal of materials that stereotype or marginalize members of the school or larger community.

The experiences participants described in this chapter were largely framed by complicated readings and misreadings of race and religion. As they were making sense of the things that had happened to them, their analyses ranged in tone from cynical acceptance, to outrage, to bafflement. Being Black and Muslim was not cause for different and discriminatory treatment in Somalia, yet in the United States, these ordinary facts of racial phenotypic appearance and outward religious symbols seemed to be at the root of dramatic and violent experiences in everyday life. The forces of colonialism, globalization, civil war, and migration landed this large immigrant group in this Midwestern context, and race and religion were suddenly "problems." The understanding Somali immigrant youth have come to have about systems of oppression in the United States reflects their experiences of being minoritized as Black and Muslim. Additionally, although their stories may mirror those of others who came before, they say much about U.S. society today.

Notes

1 This poem was written by a Somali boy in a middle school English-as-a-second-language classroom in response to a number of other poems expressing hybrid identities including Sandra Cisneros's (1995) poem "You Bring out the Mexican in Me." For the full text and an analysis of this poem, see Bigelow (2009a).

2 The participants' experiences are mirrored in a study on racial profiling. The Institute on Race and Poverty joined with the Council of Crime and Justice to carry

out an analysis of racial profiling in traffic stops occurring in 2002 with 65 law enforcement jurisdictions (Minnesota Statewide Racial Profiling Report, 2003). They found the following:

> Law enforcement officers stopped Black, Latino, and American Indian drivers at greater rates than White drivers, searched Blacks, Latinos, and American Indians at greater rates than White drivers, and found contraband as a result of searches of Blacks, Latinos, and American Indians at lower rates than in searches of White drivers. Conversely, law enforcement officers stopped and searched White drivers at lower rates than drivers of color and found contraband in searches of White drivers at a greater rate than in searches of drivers of color. (p. 1)

> The largest absolute differences between actual and expected stops and searches for Blacks and Latinos were found in Minneapolis, the largest jurisdiction participating in this study with the highest number of traffic stops. In Minneapolis, Blacks were stopped 152% more often than expected and once stopped, subjected to discretionary searches 52% more often than expected. (p. 2)

3 I know of no research that has attempted to distinguish the linguistic features of what has been documented in the literature on AAVE and this widely used urban vernacular in Minnesota.

4 Similar issues have been documented with Somali youth in Toronto (Zine, 2001) and in Britain (Kahin, 1997).

Language Learning ISSN 0023-8333

CHAPTER 5

The Policies and Politics of Educating Refugee Adolescents

"Everyone has the right to education."
Article 26 of The Universal Declaration of Human Rights

Introduction

Overcoming obstacles to guarantee an education is a matter of human rights. Education is a "multiplier right" because it enhances other human rights such as civil, economic, social, cultural, and linguistic rights (Kalantry, Getgen, & Koh, 2009). Overcoming obstacles to high school graduation is also financially sensible because "[i]mproving educational justice provides substantial returns to taxpayers that exceed the costs" of education (Levin, 2009, p. 5). However, when learners' needs are different, programs must have more agility and educators are called upon to be more creative in efforts to overcome barriers to support their successful learning. Sometimes, unfortunately, the educational system is unable to rise to this challenge and litigation is necessary.

This chapter will recount how 13 East African adolescents and young adults brought a civil rights lawsuit against their alternative school and the organization and district under which the school operated. The lawsuit focused on violations of two federal laws and one state law. The two federal laws were the Equal Educational Opportunity Act of 1974, which requires schools and school districts to make efforts to overcome language barriers faced by students, 20 U.S.C. § 1703(f); and Title VI of the Civil Rights Act of 1964, which prohibits recipients of federal funding from discriminating on the basis of, among other things, national origin, 42 U.S.C. § 2000d. The state law addressed was the Minnesota Human Rights Act, which also bars discrimination based on national origin, Minn. Stat. § 363A.13. The essence of the claim was that the school failed to overcome language barriers to give the plaintiffs access to the district curriculum. The plaintiffs in the case are delimited and defined by their status

as refugee students. In the words of the U.S. District Judge, they are described
in the following way:

> Plaintiffs are thirteen students who attended [the school] between 1999
> and 2006. Nine plaintiffs were born in Somalia, and four in Ethiopia. All
> thirteen plaintiffs fled their native countries and lived for some time in
> Kenyan refugee camps before immigrating to the United States. Most
> plaintiffs were in their mid- to late teens when they immigrated, though
> one ... was as young as fourteen and another ... was as old as twenty. At
> the time of their enrollment at [the school], plaintiffs had varying, but
> generally low-to nonexistent, levels of formal schooling and familiarity
> with the English language. (Patrick J. Schiltz, Summary Judgment,
> p. 4)

A Summary Judgment is a document produced by a court in cases that are
decided by a judge, without a full trial. This description notes the ways the
plaintiffs fall outside the norm in most U.S. secondary schools: born in East
Africa, years in refugee camps, low levels of formal schooling, low English
language skills. Although these descriptors may be unbiased facts, they may
also be converted into deficits, or worse, an explanation for why most of them
did not graduate from high school.

The aim of this chapter is to describe the way the plaintiffs were characterized in a set of documents and through the co-opting of scholarly materials
from the fields of immigrant education and SLA. The theoretical and racist
frames of *structural barriers* and *deficit discourse* were used as a point of
departure in this inquiry. The structural barriers that immigrant youth often
encounter are multiple. However, they are particularly damaging when found
within institutions such as schools and courts (Blank, Dabady, & Forbes Citro,
2004). Also damaging is the way a deficit discourse is used to conceptualize
minoritized youth and families as challenged or lacking, rather than capable
(Auerbach, 1995; Ladson-Billings, 2007). The ways that people are referred
to in discriminatory discourse often represent them in disparaging ways as the
Other. This is done through what Reisigl and Wodak (2001) termed *referential*
and *predicational strategies*. Referential strategies refer to the ways in which
individuals are grouped together using specific characteristics (e.g., ethnicity,
culture, religion, education). Predicational strategies take this a step further
by linguistically assigning qualities to individuals, events, social phenomenon,
and so forth. For instance, traits predicated to "refugees" may be that they are
poor, uneducated, or dependent on social welfare. In the documents examined
for this analysis, referential and predicational linguistic strategies were used to

characterize the plaintiffs in the documents of the lawsuit that served to justify their alleged exclusion from their right to an education.

Limited Formal Schooling: Reviewing the Facts, Reviewing the Discourse
As explained in chapter 2, the most common reason for limited formal schooling and low print literacy among adolescent refugees is the disruption caused by civil unrest. In the Horn of Africa, civil war and subsequent political instability has caused prolonged displacement. Many thousands have lived in refugee camps for years. However, finding shelter in a refugee camp does not guarantee access to schooling, despite the presence of many nongovernmental agencies. In the Dadaab refugee camps in Kenya, youth, who are roughly half of the population, have few opportunities to receive vocational training, skill enhancement, higher education, or employment (Rackley, 2006). Delays in resettlement extend the years of missed schooling anywhere from months, to years, to a lifetime.

It is easy to recognize that these circumstances often (but not always) result in low print literacy and gaps in academic knowledge presumed in most school settings. However, many people ignore the fact that *continued* low levels of print literacy persist *after* resettlement to the United States. This may be the result of poor language learning programs that feature curriculum or instruction that support neither functional literacy development nor academic literacy development. For example, programs at the secondary level, although accustomed to receiving learners with emerging English skills, are often overwhelmed when they receive a newcomer adolescent who has never been to school. This often leads to newcomer student needs being left unaddressed or addressed inappropriately.

Given the ways the learning needs of English language learners with limited formal schooling are ignored and the logical concerns about dropout rates among immigrant adolescents, there is an open debate within immigrant communities as well as among educators about how best to educate adolescents with limited formal schooling. A common response from immigrant parents who are unhappy with the larger, mainstream schools has been alternative and charter school settings focusing on immigrant student needs (Basford, 2008; Basford, Hick, & Bigelow, 2007; Dufresne & Hall, 1997). Sometimes schools create newcomers programs within high schools. Other times, students are placed in sheltered content classes with other language learners and their services depend on the teacher's skill in differentiating content instruction for students with low levels of print literacy.

When refugee youth who previously have not been to school join their peers at school, there are many ways to (un)welcome them (Gitlin, Buendía, Crosland, & Doumbia, 2003). Sometimes district welcome centers seek information about their native language literacy and numeracy skills, in addition to standard procedures for ascertaining background information (e.g., home language survey). Sometimes they are simply placed into the lowest level classes that are age-appropriate offerings. Their very presence in public schools can be met with shock and frustration and described with great drama. Easily found portrayals of these students suggest that their needs are enormous and that programs and teachers struggle to teach them. Consider this description of a class that was widely distributed first by *the Boston Globe* and then through *the Associated Press*:

> Before [the teacher] can teach English to the adult immigrants in his lowest level class, he has to show about a quarter of them how to hold a pencil. "It takes a lot of patience to teach this class," [the teacher] said before his students recited the alphabet and practiced vowel sounds in a recent phonics lesson at the... Community Center. Adult education teachers... are finding themselves starting from scratch as uneducated immigrants and refugees from conflict regions of Africa and rural areas of Mexico and Central America flock to the United States. (Hollingsworth, 2007)

This excerpt highlights several commonly held perceptions about those without formal education. An oft-repeated, dramatic, yet simplistic description of learners without formal schooling typically includes their not being able to hold a pencil, as if this were their one and only distinguishing characteristic. Another perception is that to teach students such as these, one must begin "from scratch" and that the obvious point of departure is letters and sounds just as it would be for monolingual children learning an alphabetic script. Although "bottom-up" aspects of literacy instruction are necessary components to a balanced literacy curriculum (Pressley, 1998), the assumption that the students know nothing because they lack basic literacy skills ignores the reality that these are adolescents and adults who are likely to be parents, workers, and community members. The way refugees with limited formal schooling are often characterized by educators is through this sort of deficit and infantilizing language. However, we know that they may also be survivors of tragic violence and loss and navigators of complex immigration regulations. In the excerpt above, the reference to uneducated immigrants "flocking" to the United States is also common in discourse about this population. It is hyperbolic, creating a sense of crisis.[1] It is within this sort of public and prevailing discourse of difference that the students with limited formal schooling are often placed. Nevertheless, it is the mission of public schooling in the United States to educate all students.

Failing to educate underschooled immigrant youth is typically the result of systemic problems fueled by a complex web of educational policies that unfold in day-to-day practices in classrooms. In addition to large and over-arching federal educational policy initiatives, there are policies that are created by school districts, among teaching staffs, and in individual classrooms (Hargreaves, 1994, 2003; Menken & Garcia, 2010). These policies—legitimate or not—come to bear on the lives and education of adolescent immigrant youth with limited prior schooling. Different ways of sorting students into existing programs, choices in curriculum, decisions about how the home languages are used, procedures for entering and exiting programs with special services, and how to communicate with parents are all among the powerful ways of promoting or obstructing the educational opportunities among adolescents with limited formal schooling.

The phenomenon of being in high school with limited formal school and low literacy is captured in Angela Valenzuela's (1999) ethnographic study of immigrant youth in an urban school in California. In an interview, "Lupita" tells Valenzuela about a math teacher who complained loudly and publically to her principal "that she did not belong in the class" (p. 134). Valenzuela reported discussing this with the teacher who did not recall the incident but said, "When they can't even write their names, makes you wonder why they even come to school at all" (p. 135). It is common to hear these descriptions of students with limited formal schooling in the popular media outlets and among educators. This description, however, magnifies how far outside the norms students with limited formal schooling seem in the eyes of some educators. Lupita reported that she was in the math class for 6 weeks before being removed and that, in the meantime, the teacher "made no effort to teach her anything" (p. 135). Valenzuela quoted Lupita, who said, "A mi me tenían ahí como pendeja, como sorda y muda en esa clase. (They had me in there like an idiot, like a deaf mute in that class)" (p. 135). Finally, Lupita and her friend Carolina, who was in a similar situation, were placed in an English-as-a-second-language (ESL) class with a knowledgeable bilingual teacher who, unfortunately, left the school the following semester, after which both girls dropped out of school. Esteban, another student with limited formal schooling, floundered in programs that were inappropriate for his needs and then switched to an ESL program in which he took ESL courses most of the day. This program isolated him and focused on oral skills rather than literacy skills, resulting in his failing his non-ESL classes.

These examples serve to show that there are ample opportunities for students with limited formal schooling to fail in a range of programs typically offered by public schools, even those schools accustomed to teaching immigrant students.

The present chapter seeks to identify some of the critical issues facing students with limited formal schooling through the analysis of the legal documents associated with the lawsuit introduced in chapter 1. I will show how attempts to describe learners can be easily turned around to *explain* or *justify* failing to educate this subset of English language learners and explore the consequences of a deficit discourse that thoroughly pervades the way adolescents with limited formal schooling are discussed and their needs identified in courts as much as in the media and even the scholarly literature.

Context for the Research

I examine how official and authoritative texts are "read" in ways that empower discriminatory practices. The guiding question was: How are the frames of deficit and discrimination of immigrant/refugee youth constructed in the lawsuit? The data sources for this qualitative inquiry included a number of texts related to the lawsuit:

- Newspaper articles about the lawsuit.
- Memorandum Opinion and Order documents. These documents were produced by federal district judges.
- Motion for Summary Judgment. In this document, the defendants asked for a summary judgment on the lawsuit.
- Memoradum of Law in Opposition to Defendants' Motions for Summary Judgment. This memo was written by the plaintiffs' attorneys arguing against a summary judgment.
- Expert witness report. I was hired to give my opinion on the claim and produced an expert witness report that was cross-examined in a deposition. I prepared this report based on an analysis of documents that the plaintiffs' attorneys gave me.
- Transcript of deposition of expert witness for plaintiffs. This is a transcript of my 7-hr deposition.

The overriding legal strategy of blaming the students' failure on their difference gradually emerged as I became more familiar with the lawsuit. I have come to think of this act as constructing the "ineducability" of the plaintiffs and, by extension, of refugee youth. In hindsight, this should have been clear to me earlier. I had thought that the arguments would revolve around whether the law was violated, not uncovering reasons why the plaintiffs were at fault for not being educable. My interest in examining these documents, therefore, was based on my desire to better understand how this legal strategy occurred rhetorically and the documents I chose were targeted specifically to understand the discursive construction of immigrant adolescents with little print literacy and the policies that apply to them. Laws and policies were used to help me understand the documents in terms of barriers to education. Therefore, I relied on a methodological approach that was qualitative and primarily deductive, guided by my involvement in the deposition and by having prepared the expert witness report, as opposed to the more open-ended and purely inductive approaches many qualitative researchers use. This approach to the analysis allowed me to unmask the ideologies present in the documents. In terms of procedure, the texts were read multiple times and then imported into NVivo (QSR International Pty Ltd., 2008), a software application for qualitative data organization and analysis for open coding of content and descriptors. The search function in NVivo was used to locate missed descriptors by searching for the nouns "students" and "plaintiffs" and coding the words that modified them (e.g., refugee, limited, low).

The analysis explicitly sought to uncover how the ideologies of deficit and discrimination are encoded in the texts produced in this lawsuit. I chose this analysis for its potential to uncover systematic Othering and stereotyping, as done in other studies with minoritized populations (e.g., Gabrielatos & Baker, 2008; Lemmouh, 2008). The main assumptions that tied the inquiry to the people and issues at stake were that the texts examined in the analysis for this chapter are assumed to be small artifacts of larger sociopolitical and historical systems and any text has semantic macrostructures (van Dijk, 1980). In addition, texts have genre-specific (Swales, 1990) propositions that frame the most important part of any text and that are apparent through the coherence of the text. Therefore, for this analysis, the focus was on the larger units and rhetorical structures of the texts.[2]

The Lawsuit in the Media

The lawsuit took place in the state of Minnesota, which has large refugee communities (e.g., Somali, Liberian, Hmong, Oromo) and a very large Latino community. However, the majority of the state, including the urban areas, is White. These facts result in English language learning programs being made up largely of students of color and frequent assumptions that many of the students of color in the plaintiffs' school are in the English language program.

One of the first newspaper articles related to the case had this title "Blacked Out: Immigrants Sue Minneapolis School for the Right to a Decent Education" (Robson, 2005). Most notable is that it fronts race, implying that the reason that the immigrants did not get a decent education is due to their race. At the same time, the subtitle engenders sympathy in its title because any reader would believe that a decent education is a right. This article offered early characterizations of one of the plaintiffs as the following:

1 By his own account, all Ibrahim Mumid wanted was a
2 chance to understand. "I came to U.S. in 1999," says the
3 Ethiopian immigrant. "In five years," he adds, lower lip
4 trembling, "no speak English, no write my name." . . .

This article continued with descriptions of Ibrahim Mumid that evoke sympathy by relating how it must feel to be in school and not learn.

1 Mumid, who wears a hearing aid, describes being kicked
2 out of class and sent to a cafeteria when he asked for help.
3 Through a translator, he tells of the horror he felt when
4 [school] officials scooped him out of class one day
5 and drove him to an adult education center. Frantic and
6 confused, he called his brother to come pick him up.
7 Mumid had been "aged out": At 24, he was too old to stay
8 in school, despite not having completed sufficient work to
9 earn his diploma.

This segment of the article links the common policy in the state of Minnesota (as per state law) of capping the age of high school students to what it means to be a student unfamiliar with this policy and abruptly removed from school. Words like "horror," "confused," and "frantic" evoke the inhumane way this policy was enacted, particularly given that the student has special needs. Nevertheless, the state policy is that students receive public funds until the age of 22. So it seems that Mumid had been in his school 2 years beyond the limits set forth by the policy.

The feelings of injustice expressed in this news story about the case signal discrimination based on race, disability, and age. Although the multiple layers of policies that made these events possible may apply broadly in similarly unfair ways, the feeling of being singled out and discriminated against seems paramount to how sympathy for the plaintiffs is constructed. If we take the stance, as do critical race theorists (e.g., Lopez, 2003b), that racism is normal in U.S. society, this interpretation of events at the school is plausible.

Other newspaper articles presented the lawsuit in less personalized ways and included the perspective of the school. An example is the story that appeared in *The Associated Press State & Local Wire* (2005, September 9) around the same time as the previous news story. The news article represents the claim and the plaintiffs as follows:

1 The lawsuit, filed Tuesday in U.S. District
2 Court, claims the district and [the] school have failed to
3 help students graduate and failed to provide
4 assistance for students with physical or learning
5 disabilities. Most of the students at the . . . school
6 are from Somalia or Ethiopia.
   . . .
7 [A]n attorney for the students said some students
8 can't read or write after spending four or five years
9 at [the] school.

This section explains, through the lens of one of the attorney's, the perspective of the plaintiffs toward the school and evokes outrage that "some students can't read or write after spending four or five years at [the] school" (lines 7–9). In the same article, the perspective of the school's director is summarized by the journalist. The text of the article focuses mainly on the students:

1 The executive director of the [institution], which
2 runs [the] school, hadn't seen a copy of the
3 lawsuit Tuesday but said the basic allegations are
4 false. He said half or more of the students enter
5 the school with little or no formal education.

6 "It's a complicated set of students," he said. "Our
7 goal is to put them in an English immersion
8 program and then move them along as fast as they
9 are capable of moving."

In this segment, the executive director is reported as describing the students with descriptors such as "little or no formal education" (line 5) and "complicated" (line 6). These words indicate that the school views the plaintiffs as deficient and problematic. In the quote above, the academic approach is "English immersion" (line 7), but the director hedges that the students' progress depends on their own capabilities (line 8). The onus for progress is placed primarily on the students.

The following day, the local newspaper reported more details of the lawsuit, which the journalist extracted from a report from the Minnesota Department of Education (MDE) after an initial complaint against the school was filed. The MDE found that the school had no system for screening students with disabilities, did not evaluate or monitor students' needs, and did not explain graduate requirements to students, and it found that students were passing the mandated graduation tests at a rate less than half that of the English language learners statewide (Brandt, 2005).

In sum, the newspaper articles reveal early on the binary conflict embodied in the lawsuit. The defendants (the school and related institutions) claim that the students are difficult to educate and the plaintiffs (the students) claim that the school did not deliver on its mission to educate them.

The Expert Witness's Position: The Lau Remedies and Failing to Educate

To organize the expert witness report, I used the Lau Remedies. The Lau Remedies (Office of Civil Rights, 1975) were a byproduct of the *Lau v. Nichols* (1974) lawsuit that reached the U.S. Supreme Court. The court ruled in favor of Lau, a Chinese student who claimed that he had been denied his constitutional rights through social promotion and even graduation despite not learning English. The suit prevailed not on constitutional grounds but on the 1965 Civil Rights Act, which forbids discrimination based on national origin. The resulting Lau Remedies were established by the Office of Civil Rights to help school districts understand their responsibilities to linguistic minority children, even though they never became formal regulations. They include the following:

- identifying and evaluating national origin minority students' English language skills;
- determining appropriate instructional treatments;
- deciding when English learning children were ready for mainstream classrooms; and
- determining the professional standards to be met by teachers of language-minority children.

In my expert witness report, I added the following terms because the research has shown that they matter a great deal in terms of student achievement:

- employing school staff qualified to work in a public school (e.g, Darling-Hammond, 2000); and

- offering in-service professional development opportunities geared toward their student population (e.g., Guskey & Sparks, 2004).

I found much evidence in the documents that the school did not have systems in place to guarantee that any of the above criteria for adequate schooling for English language learners occurred for the plaintiffs and presumably for other students in the school as well. My expert witness report included the following list of ways that the school did not overcome language barriers to educate the plaintiffs:

- *Assess language ability.* I examined assessments the school used for placement purposes. Most focused on metalinguistic skills, or declarative grammatical knowledge. What one might expect for this population is a native language literacy measure as well as an assessment of basic literacy skills in English. In addition to being ill-suited to the students, the assessments were not aligned to course outcomes and thus using them in valid and reliable ways for placing students was impossible. When the staff was surveyed by the state, they indicated that the school was only beginning to assess students in ways that would inform instruction. In addition, there was no available evidence that students and their parents knew how to exit a program or to see a clear path to graduation before turning 22 or in the event they needed to transition to another program where they could continue working toward this goal.
- *Identify student needs.* Failing to assess and monitor students resulted in lack of knowledge about what students' educational needs were. One locally created policy was that the school should wait for 3 years to assess a student for a disability. This policy does not follow MN rule 3525.0750, which states that "school districts shall develop systems designed to identify pupils with disabilities beginning at birth . . . and shall be developed according to the requirement of nondiscrimination." This policy accounted for the low numbers of students identified as having received special education services. Teachers from this school who were surveyed by the state agreed that the school was able to meet the needs of students receiving special education services at a much lower rate (32%) than the district (60%), which was one of many indicators of failing to identify student needs. More problematic was that if needs were identified, they did not have a mechanism to be met, as stated in the next point.
- *Teaching style.* Students were afforded little opportunity to build language and literacy skills through standards-based content learning. This was an artifact of the strict separation of language and content classes as well as

the traditional approach to teaching English, which resembled foreign language teaching methods for highly literate students rather than instruction for students who were emergent readers. There was no indication that the native language was used strategically or that culturally relevant topics were used in any way. Rebecca Callahan (2005), in a study of the effects of tracking on English language learners, found that high-quality instruction was more important than English language proficiency for English language learners' academic achievement. Features of the high tracks such as challenging curriculum, high expectations, respect for learners, and access to academic content and discourse all resulted in higher achievement among learners with many different characteristics, including limited formal schooling.

- *Appropriate program.* As stated previously, the school fashioned itself as an "English immersion" school. This conceptualization of meeting the needs of students with limited formal schooling through a particular program indicates a lack of familiarity with the fields of both immigrant education (e.g., Faltis & Wolfe, 1999) and immersion education (e.g., Fortune & Tedick, 2008). "Immersion," used imprecisely or colloquially, expresses a glossing over of the many ways that language is intentionally taught, rather than simply "absorbed." However, many of the plaintiffs spent much time in beginning ESL classes in which there was apparently no exposure to academic content, much less immersion in it. Plaintiffs often languished in the lowest level classes until they aged out. In general, the structure of the program was not conducive to students gaining the skills to acquire content at the level that would allow them to accumulate the credits they needed to graduate. "English immersion" is not the accurate term for the program that the school used. They had chosen an instructional model, which, although providing instruction in and through English, is not well suited to their student population. Immersion programs are defined by being linguistically and culturally additive (www.carla.umn.edu), which makes it impossible for a program that advocates using only English with nonnative English speakers to be immersion. The understanding of English immersion in this context seems to be that English is the language of instruction. If this is so, and it plays out in practice, the native languages of the students are not maintained or developed. When a program develops from a simplistic understanding of SLA, lay-person terminology (i.e., colloquial use of the term "immersion") is often incorporated into the school discourse. Unfortunately, simplistic programmatic solutions such as English immersion is often accompanied by incomplete conceptualizations of what constitutes English language instruction and few programmatic or pedagogical structures to scaffold learning for a wide range of academic backgrounds, language proficiency, and academic levels.

- *Train bilingual teachers.* Although the school had many bilingual cultural advisors and staff, they were, ironically, not supposed to use their first languages (L1s) because the school used an immersion approach. There were no licensed bilingual teachers. This issue folds back into problems with program design and appropriate instruction.
- *Employ and develop qualified school staff.* A significant problem the school faced was training their staff to teach adolescents with low print literacy. There were few opportunities to participate in extended and meaningful opportunities to improve their practice with this subset of learners. There were also problems over the years with administrators and teachers not being appropriately licensed to teach in their respective fields.

Constructing a Defense, Constructing Ineducability

This section describes a segment of the deposition in which I participated and analyzes how the characteristics of the students that most distinguished their need for unique instruction were construed to explain why they should not expect to graduate. The attorneys defending the school and school district also used literature from the field that is typically used to advocate for English language learners in order to support the argument that the students had challenges that were insurmountable.

Thomas and Collier and "The Gap"

In the deposition, the first key event in this regard included asking if I agreed with the following text taken directly from the Minnesota English Language Proficiency Guidelines:

1 Collier (1989) reviewed results of large-scale proficiency testing of ELL
2 students in public schools across the country, and found that academic
3 success was related to several crucial factors including (1) whether a learner
4 is already literate in his or her native language, and (2) the learner's age upon
5 arrival in the U.S. Collier concludes that some children—those who already
6 are literate in their native language, and who are less than 12 years old when

7 they enter English-only programs— might take five to seven years to become
8 literate in English and to catch up with children who are native speakers of
9 English. Policy definitions of ELL seem more or less tailored to this segment
10 of the population. However, Collier's findings show that learners who are
11 NOT already literate in their native language or who are 12 years of age and
12 older will take much longer, anywhere from seven to ten years, to reach
13 desired cut-off scores. These learners have a great deal more to learn, both of
14 the language and of content, and it would not be unusual for them to take ten
15 years before their test scores approximated those of native speakers. ELLs
16 who are newcomers in the higher grades AND not literate in their native
17 language usually require even more than ten years to close the gap between
18 themselves and native English-speaking peers.

This text attempts to summarize the research done more than two decades ago by Virginia Collier and Wayne Thomas (Collier, 1989; Collier & Thomas, 1989).[3] In lines 7–8, the text states that it "might take five to seven years to become literate in English." This is not what Collier (1989) or Collier and Thomas (1989) claimed. In fact, they claim that it takes 5–7 years to close the gap with native English speakers in terms of academic achievement. It does not take this long to acquire literacy in English. Lines 17–18 read that it takes "more than ten years to close the gap between themselves and native English-speaking peers." This is also problematic in that this research is entirely oriented toward non-English language learner averages on standardized tests, as opposed to levels of language and content knowledge that would permit content learning and secondary school graduation. Thomas and Collier do, however, assume native-speaker norms in their work. When I was questioned in the deposition about this, my reply did not address the misquote above, but it did attempt to contest the problem with "the gap":

> I guess it depends on what, you know, the author means by—the gap." It could be that, you know, somebody who comes with limited formal schooling and low alphabetic print literacy, it could be that they never, in fact, become exactly a native speaker of English, of course that's possible.

But the gap in terms of academic terms, it's very possible that they will be able to graduate from high school, to go to college . . . to be successful like a native speaker peer, but I guess I'm just not—I'm not sure . . . what [the author] means by "the gap."

Collier's (1989) conclusions, upon which the previous quote (and thousands of other similar quotes) was based, are worth reprinting in order to examine them better, particularly given how frequently they are cited in publications related to English language learners and their education:

1. When students are schooled in two languages, with solid cognitive academic instruction provided in both the first and second languages, both language minority and language majority students generally take from 4 to 7 years to reach national norms on standardized tests in reading, social studies, and science (measures of thinking skills), whereas their performance may reach national norms in as little as 2 years in L1 and L2 tests in mathematics and language arts (the latter testing spelling, punctuation, and simple grammar points). Social class background does not appear to make a significant difference in academic achievement in a dual-language program. (pp. 526–527)

This first conclusion focuses on findings from dual language programs for elementary age learners and is based on quite a bit of evidence if taken collectively. Studies cited by Collier (1989) come from Australia (Gale, McClay, Christie, & Harris, 1981), South Africa (Malherbe, 1978), Sweden (Skutnabb-Kangas, 1979), and the United States (e.g., McConnell & Kendall, 1987; Plante, 1977; Tempes, et al., 1984; Troike, 1978). The estimate that it takes *both* language majority *and* language minority students 4–7 years to reach national norms is relevant and often ignored when discussing these findings.

The second conclusion discussed in the article is as follows:

2. Immigrants arriving at ages 8 to 12, with at least 2 years of L1 schooling in their home country, take 5 to 7 years to reach the level of average performance by native speakers on L2 standardized tests in reading, social studies, and science when they are schooled exclusively in the second language after arrival in the host country. Their performance may reach national norms in as little as 2 years in mathematics and language arts. (Colliers, 1989, p. 527)

The conclusion, however, is based on extremely scant empirical evidence, as recognized by Virginia Collier (1989) herself. She conceded that "very few ESL program evaluations have been reported" (p. 524). She cited her work (Collier, 1987; Collier & Thomas, 1988) but noted that there were no comparison groups in the 6-year study and that students in this study received very little ESL instruction. She also mentioned another study with 19 children by Saville-Troike (1984) that showed development of English vocabulary and continuing cognitive develop in the L1 important for second language (L2) achievement and one by Gersten and Woodward (1985) that summarizes evaluations of students who receive little ESL support. Collier noted that the findings of these studies are not generalizable. Therefore, the second conclusion is based *only* on two studies: Collier (1987) and Collier and Thomas (1988). In other words, conclusions based on two studies conducted 20 years ago are the studies that the field still quotes on the topic of how long it takes English language learners to behave similarly to native speakers on standardized tests. These results are bolstered by Cummins's (1981a) similar findings.

The third conclusion is again based on Collier (1987) and Collier and Thomas (1988), both of which analyzed the length of time required for 2,014 immigrants who are schooled exclusively in English to reach native-speaker norms on standardized achievement tests in the content areas:

3. Young arrivals with no schooling in their first language in either their home country or the host country may take even longer to reach the level of average performance by native speakers on L2 standardized tests: possibly as long as 7 to 10 years in reading, social studies, and science, or indeed, never. Very little longitudinal research has been conducted in this area, however. (Collier, 1989, p. 527)

Collier (1987) hedged that standardized tests are not an adequate measure of academic language and do not measure a range of language proficiency skills (e.g., oral or writing skills, pragmatic skills). Furthermore, these tests are not an adequate measure of content knowledge because they are administered in English, which makes the reliability of the results questionable. A better way to compare achievement among English language learners is how well they achieve in content classes designed to overcome language barriers and assess learning in authentic, and perhaps bilingual, multimodal, ways.

Collier's (1989) fourth conclusion is particularly dismal for late arrivals:

4. Adolescent arrivals who have had no L2 exposure and who are not able to continue academic work in their first language while they are acquiring

their second language do not have enough time left in high school to make up the lost years of academic instruction. Without special assistance, these students may never reach the 50th NCE or may drop out before completing high school. This is true both for adolescents with a good academic background and for those whose schooling has been limited or interrupted. (p. 527)

Nevertheless, this conclusion, like the two before it, is based on little research. Furthermore, it is a perplexing claim because "students who tested below grade level in L1 skills during placement testing upon entry as well as older students with little or no formal schooling in L1" (p. 620) were eliminated from Collier (1987), the original study.

To summarize, it is alarming how little evidence there is for backing up the claims that are so often cited about how long it takes for English language learners to "catch up" with native-speaking peers. There have been critiques of this research (e.g., Crawford, 1999; Salzar, 1998), but they do not seem to dampen the enthusiasm for citing the amount of time that this research claims it takes learners to achieve at grade level and attributing the claims almost exclusively to research by Thomas and Collier (Collier, 1992; Collier & Thomas, 1989). Thomas and Collier's (1989) research is, admittedly, convenient for the field because it advocates for much needed specialized language services for language-minority students, which include bilingual programs and teachers, and intensive work building academic language. In the absence of better, more recent research, I assume that these studies will continue to be used to support programs for English language learners. This becomes important in the next analysis of a segment of the expert witness deposition.

Mace-Matluck et al. and Constructing Deficit

This section annotates, dialogically, an excerpt of the expert witness deposition that focuses on the book *Through the Golden Door: Educational Approaches for Immigrant Adolescents with Limited Schooling* by Mace-Matluck, Alexander-Kasparik, & Queen (1998). This book is a good practitioner resource on adolescents with limited formal schooling and one I have assigned as required reading in classes I teach on the topic. The following analysis, which centers on the rhetoric used by the attorneys to explain failure, moves fairly methodically through the first chapter in Mace-Matluck et al.'s book, which describes the way interrupted or limited formal schooling matters among immigrants and refugees in U.S. public schools.

Transcript	*Annotations*

Attorney Question (hereafter "Q"): Now, showing you what has been marked as Exhibit No. 6. Is this a copy of the reference material that you were citing from Mace-Matluck?[4]

The attorneys are showing me an authoritative source to explain students' failure to learn due to low L1 literacy and academic skills.

Bigelow answers (hereafter "MB"): "Yes."

Q: Now, do you—On page 33 Mace-Matluck states that one of the most important distinguishing factors or distinguishing characteristics is between ELL students with some native literacy and academic skills and those without native literacy and academic skills, do you agree that that's an important distinction between English language learners?

MB: Yes.

Q: Why is that?

MB: Well, they say "native language literacy and some mastery of academic content," both, and the reason for that is because it doesn't matter what language you've learned content in or what language you've developed print concepts in, you only become literate once in your life, unless you're moving to a logographic script or, you know, a totally new alphabet. But print, alphabetic print literacy easily transfers from one language to another, so when you begin reading in a second language, it's not like you're starting from scratch.

I go on for another 165 words and regret that I haven't caught on to where the questions are leading. I'm simply trying to explain conventional wisdom from the field. Then the attorney repeats this conventional wisdom.

Q. So if you know how to read and write in your native language, it probably is easier for you to learn to read and write in a second language than it would be for a student who's not literate in their native language?

MB: Yes.

Q. Looking at that second full paragraph towards the end, Mace-Matluck states that "Students that lack rudimentary literacy skills in their native language," "may need many years of intensive work in order to graduate or make the transition to an appropriate program." Do you agree with that statement?

Then the attorney uses the book again to lay out the consequences of low L1 literacy.

MB: Well, I do in part. It depends on what she means by—or what they mean by "many," and there's a lot of individual factors that matter. So I would say I agree broadly and generally, but I may disagree if there are other circumstances, you know, so it could take many, it could take few, it could take many, many.

I try to add nuance to this statement, but I stay within the frame arguing individual differences are to blame for academic failure.

Q. Would many, many be, say, more than ten?

MB: That would—That would depend on probably other issues going on, so every person—every person is different, right, and so if the student has—it's not just English language—maybe they don't only have English language issues, they might have learning disability issues or psychological trauma that takes years to overcome, so it could take—it could take a very long time. On the other hand, it could take three, four years.

At this point, the attorney chooses Thomas and Collier's (1997) claim that it takes 7–10 years for students with limited prior schooling to catch up. I attempt to add other factors that could delay progress and try to hedge about how long it may take.

Q. Okay. Would three, four years be on the low end of the amount of time you would expect someone who was not literate in their native language to become able to read and write English?

MB: Not in my experience, no. It's pretty normal.

Q: Three to four is pretty typical?

MB: Yeah, I would say. If they—Like, if they come as a 9th grader, it's typical that they can graduate as a 12th grader.
Q: And is that for students who are literate in their native language, or students who are not literate in their native language?
MB: In my experience, both.
Q: Would you agree that all students do not learn at the same pace?
MB: Yes.
Q: Is there significant differences in the amount of time that it may take one individual to master a skill as opposed to another individual?
MB: Yeah. That's what I was trying to say.
Q. Okay. And do the—What other factors influence a student's academic success?
MB: Their teachers and the program they're in.
Q. What about socioeconomic status, do students with low socioeconomic status tend to be less successful in school than students from high socioeconomic status homes?

I finally have come to understand the line of argumentation that the attorneys are building and I am now trying to challenge conventional wisdom.

This question was an opportunity for me to refocus on the possibility that the students are not to blame. The attorney drops this possibility and returns to generating additional reasons why the students' individual differences may explain their failure.

This transcript mirrors similar framings in the media, discussed earlier, in that students with limited formal schooling are described according to their needs. Throughout all of the documents for this case, the students/plaintiffs are repeatedly characterized by what they lack: formal schooling, L1 literacy, passing grades on standardized tests. They are also characterized by what makes them unique from other students: refugees, lived in refugee camps, born in Somali or Ethiopia, late teens. However, what is happening is that their needs, which are not objectionable as such in the Mace-Matluck et al. (1998) publication, are being used *to explain* why the plaintiffs failed to be successful in school and graduate. The book's aim is to help educators understand their needs in order to educate them, not to explain why they cannot be educated. The attorneys' legal strategy, based on the book and other scholarly literature, is to construct the ineducability of the plaintiffs and, by extension, of refugee youth.

As a witness, I did not understand the tack the attorneys were taking until they began to discuss how many years it takes to graduate, at which point I became oppositional and drew from my research with individuals with limited formal schooling who did graduate in short amounts of time. The conversation stemming from Mace-Matluck et al. (1998) ends when I have the opportunity to note that teachers and programs influence a student's academic success. This is the crux of the lawsuit: Was it the school's fault that the students did not achieve or were the plaintiffs' circumstances and individual attributes to blame?

The rationale that the students were at fault was carried over into the defendants' written "motion for summary judgment":

> This lawsuit is the unfortunate result of plaintiffs' unrealistic expectations about how quickly immigrant students with no educational background can both learn English and satisfy U.S. high school graduation requirements. While plaintiffs may believe ALHS could have done a better job of educating them, none of their allegations rises to the level of a Title VI claim for intentional discrimination on the basis of national origin. (Motion, 11/15/2007, p. 47)

This statement attributes the students' failure to their lack of formal schooling rather than the educational system that was created with "typical" English language learners in mind. It is through an argument based on the students' deficits that discrimination in a school, a public institution, is somehow permissible. However, this argument is made possible only through literature from the fields of immigrant education and SLA. Studies that are commonly cited and books that are commonly used were subverted in ways that pitted individual differences squarely against the schools, which are precisely the institutions obligated to address individual differences.

The Construction of Deficit Through Scholarship and Writing Through an Advocacy Lens

In addition to attributing the plaintiffs' life circumstances for their failure, there were multiple ways that knowledge about language learning from both folk theories and SLA research were used to support a rationale for why the plaintiffs should not have expected to graduate from high school.

For example, the opposing attorneys drew on the common belief that it is better to learn a language as a child, rather than as an adolescent. However, the field of SLA has explored this question since the 1970s with mixed conclusions about the role of age and ultimate L2 attainment (Birdsong, 1999). Ten years later, Ortega (2009) concluded that "age may exert universal influences on the learning of a second language, but context moderates these universal effects" (p. 17). In other words, although the field has given nuance to how age matters in SLA, folk theories still hold that younger is better. For the plaintiffs, amount and quality of exposure to comprehensible input would be essential for English acquisition and academic success. Together with Muñoz (2008), I argue that amount and quality of exposure to comprehensible input hinges on high-quality instruction. Therefore, although age may be important, the learning context of the plaintiffs was likely not linguistically rich enough for them to obtain academic success.

Another construct that was used in the lawsuit was the distinction between academic and social language. The attorneys drew heavily on not only the Thomas and Collier (1997) research but also the widely accepted notion that academic language takes longer to acquire than social language (Cummins, 1979, 1981a, 1991). Most researchers and practitioners would agree that academic English includes particular linguistic features, vocabulary, and rhetorical structures that are needed for the communicative functions most frequently found at school. The construct of social and academic language as two broad categories of language skills has been and remains useful in helping those outside the field of language learning and teaching understand that although a learner may seem fluent, he or she still may struggle to use the language needed to do well in school, across all disciplines (Collier, 1989). However, how academic language was framed in the lawsuit was problematic, in that it suggested that the difficulty of acquiring academic language is the result of limited formal schooling, which, in turn, leads to the inevitability of not having the language to finish high school. However, the truth is that neither the fields of SLA nor education know *exactly* what amount of academic English is required to complete high school. This is an empirical question that cannot be measured by standardized tests, which all assess test-taking strategies and have cultural bias (Menken, 2008; Stone, 2008). In addition, dichotomizing language as social and academic perpetuates the false notion that social language is not used for academic learning (Edelsky, 1991; Edelsky et al., 1983; Rivera, 1984). Social language use and academic language use rest along a continuum with a range of registers, speech communities, and types of literacies further delineating these two somewhat contrived categories. In sum, it is a misunderstanding that these two dimensions of language are autonomous and independent of each other and of the settings in which they are used. Furthermore, the time it takes to acquire academic language, although certainly tied to the quality and quantity of prior schooling, relies heavily on the ways educators carefully integrate academic language instruction into learning across subject areas.

Unfortunately, SLA scholarship was used by the school's attorneys to explain student failure. SLA scholars typically write for an audience that is curious about exploring how language is learned and ways to incite learning across the life span. I assume that SLA researchers rarely consider the ways our research could be used to the detriment of learners, particularly in an adversarial context such as the one presented in this chapter. What can SLA researchers do, in their writing, to counter common and simplified assumptions among the public about who can and cannot learn an additional language? The analyses of the lawsuit records in this chapter offer a cautionary note to L2 researchers: Our research may be misused and misapplied among readers of a wider audience (i.e., policy makers, lawyers). Consider, for example, the fact that my colleague Elaine Tarone and I have said in print that "researchers rarely study adult and adolescent immigrant learners with very low literacy . . . none of the studies published in *TESOL Quarterly* during the past 10 years documents the SLA processes of post-critical period L2 learners who have low L1 literacy" (Bigelow & Tarone, 2004, pp. 689–690). Although it is common in academic writing to indicate a gap in the existing knowledge of the field, as we did, the opposing counsel reasoned that if this quote were true, then researchers were unqualified to make any recommendations in court about how to educate adolescent English language learners with low print literacy. The subtleties of what the differences are between conventions in SLA research writing and the conventions used in more general publications in the field of education about this population were largely lost in this adversarial discussion. Nevertheless, the critique against the field of SLA stung.

The education of immigrant and refugee youth hinges not on their deficits but rather on the informed actions that the adults charged with their education take—the programs chosen and instruction that offers access to the curriculum while building English language skills. The stories of Magol, Fadumo, and Sufia in chapter 3 stand in contrast to that of the plaintiffs in this lawsuit, whereas Fatima's story of high school was more mixed, although even she seemed to have more opportunities to learn content than the plaintiffs seemed to have. What I believe Fatima needed was more time in an adult program to meet high school graduation requirements. The plaintiffs were not given the tools or the avenues to get a high school diploma.

Conclusion: The (Re)Production of Discrimination

To date, this lawsuit has not prevailed. It is currently under appeal. Briefly, the judge argued the following:

> Whether District 1 took "appropriate action to overcome language barriers" facing students . . . is, on the record before the Court, a disputed question of fact. Plaintiffs offer expert testimony that [the school] used an "English immersion" curriculum that was pedagogically unsound in theory and badly implemented in practice. Inst. Ex. 21. District 1 responds by criticizing various aspects of plaintiffs' expert report. Dist. 1 SJ Mem. at 36–42. The Court recognizes the force of some of District 1's criticisms, but the Court nonetheless finds that *plaintiffs' evidence suffices to create a jury question as to the appropriateness of District 1's efforts to overcome plaintiffs' language barriers.*

> District 1 is, however, entitled to summary judgment for a different reason: *Plaintiffs' injuries, if any, are not redressable by this Court. Plaintiffs seek both injunctive and monetary relief. But, as is explained below, monetary relief is not available for violations of the EEOA, and the injunctive relief sought by plaintiffs would do nothing to redress their injuries.* [my emphasis]

In other words, the court questioned whether the school did enough to overcome the plaintiffs' language barriers. Nevertheless, because the court could not award monetary compensation for damages and because closing or changing the school would not impact the plaintiffs, the case was dismissed. This is regrettable because awarding money damages could have been used to help finally educate the students. Many of the plaintiffs, after leaving the school, have been unable to obtain the equivalent of a high school education. It is also regrettable that the school was not mandated by the court to improve their program for the students with limited formal schooling who remained.[5]

The types of discrimination evident in the data are in some part due to the (re)production of ethnic and racial prejudice against minoritized youth in the broader national context in which they fall outside schooling norms. Because the plaintiffs were all African and phenotypically Black, there is the overlay of racism implicit in the case. The way the plaintiffs were portrayed in the media seemed to give them leverage as merely wanting a "decent education" but they were "Blacked out." Although race and racism was an element in the texts analyzed, discrimination was verbalized through the ways the participants were Othered as older language learners with particular backgrounds that made them problematic for the school system. They were discriminated against because of their national origin and the fact that they were learning English. Discrimination unfolded through the school's inability to overcome language barriers to give the plaintiffs' access to the district's curriculum, like they are obligated to do for all students. The expert witness report had ample evidence to explain their failure in school through policies and programs that they confronted. The rhetorical structure of the deposition, on the other hand, persistently attempted to leverage authoritative scholarly references on individual differences to explain the students' failure.

I would like to see educators, and the systems we (re)produce, show more recognition that limited formal schooling among some adolescent immigrants is a fact with material consequences for our everyday work. I would also like to see ways educational policies, programs for newcomers, and instructional strategies change from their being currently "limiting" for refugee adolescents in the ways shown in this chapter and this book, to becoming "unlimiting" for these youth, their families, and their communities (Bigelow, 2009b).

In terms of unlimiting programs, state accountability systems must change for all English language learners and particularly for this population (Anderson, 2004; Henderson, 2007; Magnuson, 2003; Stone, 2008). Unlimiting testing policies would include lowering the stakes (not the standards) of the state-mandated tests and using a wider range of measurement tools to measure the standards. Another example of a limiting statewide policy is to limit funding for English language learners to 5 years. An example of a way that a district chose to unlimit this policy is to use general district funds "to provide service to students for as long as they need it" (St. Paul Public Schools, ELL Handbook, 08–09). "Aging out" of high school at the age of 22, despite the availability of many alternative high schools that have suitable environments for adults, is another limiting policy that could be remedied by better transitions to adult diploma programs and clearer paths to graduation for nontraditional students.

In terms of unlimiting programs, we must strive to overcome the failings of programs such as the one described in this chapter, which are limiting to students because they offer little access to academic content learning while students are learning English oral and literacy skills. The contrary would be achieved through unlimiting programs that capitalize on integrated, interesting, and culturally relevant curricular elements. Curricula should be articulated, standards-based, and aligned with placement and exit criteria. Schools can create short-term programs within existing programs, as St. Paul did with their Transitional Language Centers for Hmong Newcomers (Bigelow, Basford, & Smidt, 2008; Ngo, Bigelow, & Wahlstrom, 2007). Culturally specific schools can often offer unique programming as well (Basford, 2008). In all of these schooling possibilities, families and communities should be included to lend expertise and advice to educators.

Teaching must also change to be unlimiting. Educators need the skill and the will to support the academic and language needs of Somali youth without prior schooling. It is essential to maintain high standards, collaborate with colleagues, and broaden teaching repertoires to include more oral language in all instructional phases. Freeman and Freeman (2001) offered one of the best guides to teachers who are working with students with limited formal schooling and Birch (2007) offered one of the most in-depth books for educators who wish to learn more about the underpinnings of how to teach beginning literacy to English language learners.

Abu El-Haj (2006) remind us that, "schools are important sites for change, hope, and possibility, but they do not float free of the broad inequalities embedded in our larger society" (p. 6). The lawsuit discussed in this chapter was a valiant effort to obtain the opportunity to be educated, put forth by some of the most marginalized and minoritized students and their families in our society. They had placed their hope in their school's commitment to educate them, but what occurred was they wasted time in programs and classes that did not address their learning needs during the crucial years before they became ineligible to attend secondary school. There are certainly other students whose needs go unaddressed in public schools. Tragically, the plaintiffs were like Guinier and Torres's (2002) miner's canary:

> Miners often carried a canary into the mine alongside them. The canary's more fragile respiratory system would cause it to collapse from noxious gases long before humans were affected, thus alerting the miners to danger. The canary's distress signaled that it was time to get out of the mine because the air was becoming too poisonous to breathe.

> Those who are racially marginalized are like the miner's canary: Their distress is the first sign of a danger that threatens us all. We watch the canary, seeking to improve the air quality in the mines, and to reconnect individual experiences to democratic faith, to social critique, and to meaningful action that improves the lives of everyone in the mine. (p. 11)

Educators and society at large must pay attention to those who are distressed and not succeeding at school for the good of these individuals and ultimately for the good of society. Their distress threatens us all because it perpetuates social inequities that can last for generations.

Notes

1 Metaphors such as this have been found to be common in the media when referring to immigrants, asylum seekers, migrants and refugees. Gabrielatos and Baker (2008) did a corpus analysis of discursive constructions of how such groups are referred to in the U.K. press and found these and other mainly negative terms (e.g., fleeing, sneaking, flooding) in all major newspapers as well as nonsensical terms such as illegal refugee or bogus migrant. The authors showed how the prosodic choices newspapers make communicate sociopolitical stances against groups of people or public policies and have the power to shape public sentiment.

2 The court transcriptions are not detailed and do not include backchannels, pauses, overlapping, or nonverbal gestures, making it is impossible to do a close linguistic analysis.

3 Thomas and Collier are not the only researchers who have synthesized findings related to the question of how long it takes to develop language and academic skills. Scholarship by Hakuta, Butler, and Witt (2000) and Cummins (1981a) have explored this issue, but these publications have not been cited as enthusiastically as the work by Collier and Thomas, which is often reported but not referenced. It has become professional lore with the specifics of the source material rarely recalled.

4 Another source that was used for similar deficit-oriented argument building was Short and Fitzsimmons's (2007) report entitled *Double the Work: Challenges and Solutions to Acquiring Language And Academic Literacy for Adolescent English Language Learners.*

5 However, in July 2008, a federal judge gave the state of Texas until the end of January to improve the education programs for secondary school English language learners. This was the result of a lawsuit brought against the Texas Education Agency (TEA) by advocacy groups of mainly Spanish speakers in Texas. The judge ruled that the 1981 Bilingual and Special Education Programs Act, a measure passed by the Legislature that staved off court action addressing discrimination in Texas schools, has not improved the schooling of secondary students with limited English proficiency. "The clear failure of secondary Limited English Proficient (LEP) students unquestionably demonstrates that, despite its efforts, TEA has not met its obligation to remedy the language deficiencies of Texas students," Justice wrote."After a quarter century of sputtering implementation, defendants have failed to achieve results that demonstrate they are overcoming language barriers for secondary LEP students. Failed implementation cannot prolong the existence of a failed program in perpetuity" (Carlton, 2008).

Language Learning   ISSN 0023-8333

CHAPTER 6

Researching and Educating Somali Immigrant and Refugee Youth

> And if you meet someone
> in your adopted country,
> and think you see in the other's face
> an open sky, some promise of a new beginning
> it probably means you're standing too far.
>
> Or if you think you read in the other, as in a book
> whose first and last pages are missing,
> the story of your own birthplace,
> a country twice erased,
> once by fire, once by forgetfulness,
> it probably means you're standing too close.
>
> From Li-Young Lee's poem,
> *Self-Help for Fellow Refugees*

Youth have always created new ways of acting and talking, and Somali and Somali American youth are no exception. In the process of adjusting to life in Minnesota, they might try on, reject, and embrace any number of identities through adolescence. My hope is that these processes are better understood so that the institutions and individuals in direct contact with these youth can better support a healthy self-esteem and sense of agency. I hope for spaces at school, at home, and in communities where new and never-before-seen identities can be created and enacted and where immigrant youth can grow into positive role models for other youth and immigrant youth in particular who are engaging in the hard work of identity construction. I also hope for the powerful institutions of our society—like schools, the police, and the courts—to work hard for social justice and equity such that these institutions facilitate or at least do not stand in the way of the hard-won identities that teens are crafting for themselves.

In all contexts, this means not making assumptions about race, religion, or gender. In education in particular, this means seeing academic potential in all Somali youth and seeing their families and communities as sources of strength.

Adolescents are often misunderstood by adults, teachers, and others, but when powerful institutions discriminate against youth based on entrenched xenophobia, racism, and Islamophobia, a democratic, plural society in the making has much to lose. Understandably, minoritized youth may come to distrust society's institutions and justifiably disengage from them. Sadly, the research reported in this book documents that distrust and disengagement often develop with more time in the United States and increased interactions with U.S. institutions. This disengagement is at least partially explained by ways minoritized youth can be discursively constrained, confined, or delimited by how they are identified by institutions in terms of racial, religious, gendered, and ethnic Othering. The forging of new identities can be limited by what youth understand as possible based on how institutions have behaved and based on the long-term effects of institutions on whole groups of people. We must worry about institutions, but also about individuals.

I hope that this book works to complicate the assumptions adults and adolescent peers have of the inner worlds of Somali youth. I also hope it offers ways to reflect on the potential for imposed identities to do harm. Specifically, harm is done when Somali (American) youth are Othered through essentialized, inaccurate, and imposed identities such as false notions of Islam and misconceptions of ethnicity. Racialization occurs through interactions with people who are within and outside the Somali co-ethnic communities. There is, however, a great amount of nuance when negotiated identities are explored among Somali youth. I have tried to reveal this nuance through analyses of their language use (chapter 3) and through their negotiation of racial and religious bias (chapter 4). It is my intention that by providing additional views to those often presented and perpetuated in the media, adults in charge of classrooms, community organizations, and institutions will see immigrant youth as multidimensional and ever-changing works in progress. All immigrant and refugee youth must be educated and chapter 5 explored what can happen when schooling institutions fail students and their families.

Language and Literacy Among Somali Youth

Weedon (1987) notes that "language is the place where actual and possible forms of social organization and their likely social and political consequences are defined and contested. Yet [language] is also the place where our sense of ourselves, or subjectivity, is constructed" (p. 21). The case of the Saturday tutoring group for girls (chapter 3) explores these issues of identity, culture, and literacy as the girls choose how to find links between the literacies they know, such as poems and folktales, and their English language learning. These cases potentially approximate the experiences of other students for whom identity intertwines with how they engage with the literacies they use in and out of school. The high school experience of Somali, refugee, Muslim youth with limited formal schooling and low levels of print literacy offers an intense intersection of social, cultural, and educational issues. The girls showed how Somali language literacies could be used to inspire literacy in English through, for example, poetry and folktales. Their work at school was not separate from who they were as individuals and individuals in families and in communities. The girls essentially created for themselves ways their education was relevant to their lives. The girls used language to find their place in at least some of their high school curricula (Weedon, 1987).

Schools are places where cultural norms and values are created and re-produced (Bourdieu, 1977). Bourdieu (1977) referred to these cultural norms and values as cultural capital—a system of accumulated knowledge specific to the dominant race and class. Immigrant and refugee youth are not immune from the power and status of cultural capital. In fact, they seek it. Norton Peirce (1995) extended the metaphor of cultural capital to language learning, in particular by drawing from Ogbu's (1978) work. She argued that the effort spent acquiring cultural capital must be commensurate with the investment. For most Somali youth in my work, their most valued piece of cultural capital is education. Among many Somalis living in the Diaspora, the need for education, as cultural capital, is fueled by the cultural expectation to finan-cially help family members in the United States or still in Somalia, Ethiopia, or Kenya.

Education, and specifically literacy, is not neutral or context-free. Instead, it must be framed according to the terms of the social and cultural values of that culture. What counts as educated or literate varies as well within family narratives and changes over time due to events such as migration or the economy (Menard-Warwick, 2005). Furthermore, there are certain literacy values and practices that are sanctioned and others that are not (Devine, 1994). How these literacies develop, are maintained, or fall out of use is the focus of this research as well as how literacies serve to inform, question, or maintain the participants' identities as they go through high school in their first years of living in the United States.

The Future for Somali Language Use

I expect that literacy, language, and identity will be mediated more and more through digital communication. Culture is produced and reproduced in the school, work, home, and community settings that Somali youth inhabit and all of these settings are touched by digital communication. However, what is the likelihood that immigrant and refugee youth will find ways to use Somali print literacy to the extent that it will survive or even develop?

The United States is infamous as a context hostile to the maintenance or development of languages other than English. Therefore, one would predict that it is unlikely that widespread use of Somali will persist indefinitely, despite continued chain migration and strong connections to Somali speakers on the Horn of Africa and elsewhere. Indeed, Spanish is still being replaced by English in the United States despite large communities of Spanish speakers and ongoing transnational migration to and from Spanish-speaking countries.

The Somali youth who populated these pages suggest that although they are acquiring multiliteracies in English, there may be little hope for sustaining or developing literacy in Somali. Durgunoğlu and Verhoeven (1998, p. 297) outlined some of the necessary conditions for multiliteracy to continue and I offer here my analysis of how these conditions unfold in Minnesota for Somali youth.

Durgunoğlu and Verhoeven (1998) argued that, historically and politically, the home language must be valued and supported in the society by the majority-language speakers. Currently, there is very little support of Somali print literacy by majority-language (English) speakers. The Minnesota Literacy Council has collaborated with Somali authors to produce bilingual Somali folktales in the form of children's books. This is, however, mainly a symbolic support for Somali literacy. Somali has very little perceived utility beyond the folktale genre and in the form of children's books. Somali classes are not widely offered to heritage speakers, much less majority-language speakers. Durgunoğlu and Verhoeven also argued that for native language literacy to prevail, there must be a perceived economic reason to do so, perhaps because of return migration. Currently, the Somali immigrant and refugee populations have a low rate of print literacy, and because of the ongoing civil war in Somalia, literacy rates continue to decrease. Somali print literacy seems to offer few economic rewards because of the diminishing contexts in which it is required. Although the oral uses of Somali abound, there are few social reasons for Somali text to persist in a community with such low levels of print literacy. English texts are much more likely to be used for interactive storybook reading in homes because Somali texts are so uncommon. Durgunoğlu and Verhoeven said that for literacy in a minority language to persist, there must be a writing system, along with books and literacy materials in that language. Somali has had a writing system since 1972 and books and materials exist, but they are not widely available or prevalent in homes. There is a Somali newspaper that is printed locally in Minnesota, and there are Somali texts available to read digitally, but Somali texts are far from ubiquitous in this context. An important topic of further inquiry that seems to emerge concerns the role of the Diaspora in Somali language development. Diaspora communities may have more resources to produce Somali texts (digital and otherwise) and therefore more power to influence how the language evolves within which genres and across which linguistic functions.

In order for Somali youth to develop or maintain Somali print literacy, there would have to be a drastic shift in the level of importance that it holds for the majority-language speakers as well as for the Somali communities of Minnesota and, I would argue, Somalis worldwide. Somali literacy on the Horn of Africa is even at risk of being replaced by English because of the urgent need for Somalis to engage with the world and the lack of ways to engage with Somali print worldwide. The critical question lies with intergenerational transmission and how, for example, parents use Somali with their children, how adolescents use Somali with their younger siblings, and how all Somali immigrants choose to use Somali with their children born in the United States.

The Future for Academic Literacy in English

By comparison to Somali literacies, English literacies do not appear to be at immediate risk. Durgunoğlu and Verhoeven (1998) concluded that students will learn English and develop academic literacy if another set of conditions exist. For example, does instruction take into consideration the cultural and linguistic backgrounds of the English language learners, as evidenced in the teachers' preparation, the overarching curriculum, and the everyday materials? Does the home environment value literacy development in general, and in English? Is there a match between the values and practices of homes and schools? Do students have access to resources in English through schooling, media, and interaction with people who speak with them in English? Is English viewed as essential for social advancement, economic prosperity, and empowerment? Of all the criteria, this last is perhaps the one that is most solidly in favor of the acquisition of academic English literacies. It is supported almost exclusively by Somali families in lieu of native language literacy. Access to fluent English speakers and users of academic literacies are also challenging in heavily tracked schools or in all-immigrant schools. This point requires further exploration, however, because it is much more beneficial for immigrant youth to feel welcomed and to receive appropriate instruction, albeit with other immigrant youth, than to be ignored in mainstream settings. The girls whose literacy development was discussed in chapter 3 reported speaking to very few people during the school day, and their teachers were the only fluent English speakers they typically encountered during their day—in and out of school.

Implications for Educating Adolescent Immigrants and Refugees

Building on this point, chapter 5 demonstrates many ways a school can establish programs that do not support the development of academic literacies. In short, there are many ways that print literacy in English is supported, but just as many conditions upon which this emergent English print literacy is jeopardized among Somali newcomers. The findings from chapter 5 have many implications for policy reforms as well as for language and literacy development that can only come to fruition through the related and intertwined branches of sound educational practices and advocacy. First, there is a clear need for educators and policy makers to support additive multilingualism across U.S. public schools, large and small, urban, suburban, and rural. For this to become reality requires supportive language and education policies, bolstered by a teaching force that invests in the possibility of something different than the loss of the home language. Second, educational reform must address educational disparities that then need to be supported by legislated policy changes. A professional ecology must be cultivated that also includes teacher education institutions, school leadership, and community investment. Third, it is important that schools that serve refugee adolescents with little prior schooling do so in thoughtful ways. They must have a well-prepared staff that can support students in multiple ways, not only academically. They must have strong language programs that develop academic skills and content knowledge through well-mapped, integrated courses with clear entry and exit criteria.

The lawsuit described in chapter 5 served to bring into relief the ways schools can thwart rather than support the education of youth with limited formal schooling. The drastic action to file a lawsuit was a material consequence of immigrant youth's frustration with attempting to communicate with educators and resolve the problems they were having in making progress in their schooling. The lawsuit marked a moment in time when the youth and their families were becoming aware of how their schooling was failing them. The exploration of exactly how immigrant youth with limited formal schooling were underserved served to uncover ways educational programs, policies, and instructional practices could "unlimit" students and dramatically improve their chances of benefiting from formal schooling and finishing high school.

Identity and the Centrality of Race

In chapter 1, I quote Loukia Sarroub (2005) saying that Muslim youth are "triangulators of identity, and, as a result, culture is enacted in the in-between places they occupy in their home and school worlds" (p. 7). It is difficult or impossible to separate identifiers such as language, religion, race, and gender in the data from Somali immigrant youth. The youth I interviewed were active triangulators of identity in and out of school. Furthermore, they were finding their way across their social worlds in terms of their identity, but not without some ambivalence and pain. Sarroub's work with immigrant Yemeni girls has greatly facilitated my understanding of the experiences of Somali youth and the fact that their identity construction does not only occur in response to or in conflict with White mainstream society. It also occurs within their families, across generations, and within their communities. Dynamics between new-comers and those raised in Minnesota seemed to play out in ways similar to those documents in Sarroub's other work as well as that of other scholars (e.g., Olsen, 1998). Furthermore, through my research I have learned that outward expressions of a racialized or religious identity expressed only a small segment of an individual's identity; as the community adds to its already rich diversity and ever-increasing number of years in Minnesota, a wider range of hybridized identity choices becomes available. Optimistically, this is positive and an ar-tifact of increased knowledge of Islam by non-Muslims in Minnesota as well as a greater familiarity with individuals from East Africa among Minnesota-born and immigrant groups in Minnesota. In other words, choices immigrant youth make about their identities are informed by changes in their fellow Min-nesotans. A more pessimistic, but more likely perspective, is that where once there was no knowledge of East Africans, there now exist biases.

Somali youth almost invariably experience a process of racialization in the United States. Hune (2000) pointed out, "[a]ll power and race relations have come to be seen within this framework of subordinate/majority dynamics" (p. 668). The Black/White oppositionality is *the* model for all race relations. However, under this model, interethnic and interracial tensions are disregarded. Contrary to the opposition set up by the Black/White binary, the everyday racial-ized experiences of Somali students cannot be understood within Black/White vertical dynamics. Urban Somalis are lumped as "Black" or "African Ameri-can" despite the fact that they may call themselves "Muslim" and "Somali."

The processes of racialization mask ethnic differences between and among Somalis, other African immigrants, and African Americans. As some Somali participants (or their elders) rejected being racialized, some simultaneously adopted a hip-hop aesthetic. Except for the youth who had had been in the United States for many years, most failed to understand the long-standing social and institutional racism that African Americans have faced in the United States or were confused by the discourse around "acting White."

Racialization, although seemingly based on "race," needs to be conceptualized through the examination of identity intersections. Somali immigrant youth are not only transforming what it means to be "Somali." They are also transforming further what it means to be "student," "female," "male," and "Muslim" in the context of Minnesota, a Midwestern state in the United States. As this study revealed, Somali girls' identities as Muslims intersected with their identities as females. The hijab serves as an identifier that distinguishes them as Somali, possibly "foreign" and thereby side-stepping an imposed (albeit simplified) African American identity. Thus, the ways in which race intersects with and is shaped by ethnicity, gender, religion, and other markers of difference are far from universal to a hypothetical unified immigration or refugee experience. Instead, they are proven to be highly contextualized and specific to communities—in this case, the Somali communities of Minnesota (Hune, 2000; Lowe, 1996). Common identity markers such as those named in this research are constantly shaped and interpreted by selves and others. Performed identity, then, is highly open to interpretation and misunderstanding.

It is my hope that this research with urban Somali immigrant students provides a starting point for researchers, educators, and others to think about race, religion, ethnicity, and the complexities of difference. I hope to have revealed the myriad ways urban Somali youth are misrecognized. However, there is need for more research that attends to ethnic tensions and the ways that race plays out between and among immigrant students and other students of color. It is important to interrogate what happens in the continuum between "Black" and "White" and complicate the Black/White racial discourse. In particular, by looking in the "in-between" spaces of social interactions and everyday practices, we might begin to understand the complexity of race and race relations and the roles they play in the lives and education of immigrant students.

This research argues for the relevance of examining the political, historical, and cultural contexts Somali youth are navigating and the interrelated roles that ethnicity, race, gender, and religion play in and out of school. Naming and understanding decisions of affiliation, the choices implied by those decisions, as well as the documented processes that immigrants tend to experience in U.S. culture may show teens that their experiences adjusting are not unique or that their feelings of living between worlds are not unusual. It is urgent for teachers to understand the process of identity formation among youth and to broaden their notion of multicultural education to include religious diversity.

Conclusion: For Engaged Scholarship

As I reflect on how the experiences of Somali immigrant youth may be different from or similar to that of other Black immigrant youth, it is impossible to ignore widespread fear and ignorance about Islam. Being Muslim in Minnesota, and in contexts in which Islamophobia is commonplace, is part of identity formation among many Somali youth that cannot be ignored. However, there is likely no imposed identity more powerful than race. Applied Linguists must explore this facet of identity more and more often while exploring language and literacy development, language policy, educational practices, and language use. As has been demonstrated in this book, discrimination among Somali Muslim youth may be made up of multiple ways they are Othered and subsequently minoritized. These ways include at least race, religion, gender, and xenophobia. Poverty and inadequate instruction often add to this already harmful system of oppression. Identity theories used to understand the third spaces of immigrant and refugee youth must consider more thoroughly how discrimination plays out in public spheres where the dominant society prevails such as at school, with the police, and in the courts. However, race may be able to exert great power in the identities that youth choose to embrace, blend, and contest. In looking to test the limits of racialization, we must recognize that it is difficult to be agentive in the face of such powerful systems in a racist society. If this is the case, then it is even more important for the field to become more interdisciplinary and activist.

Chapter 5 also uncovered the subtle ways in which disciplinary knowledge lets itself be co-opted and subverted by oppressive forces and becomes an unwitting tool that can be used against the interests of those who are studied. If researchers in Applied Linguistics and SLA hope to join these efforts, they must start to include the more critical research about immigrant education with roots in Sociology and Anthropology (e.g., Ngo, 2010; Ong, 2003; Suarez-Orozco, 2001; Waters, 1999). In essence, we need to read more broadly and outside of disciplinary silos to better understand the educational and social lives of adolescent refugees and immigrants. Furthermore, we need to make better and more connections between our work and the communities we touch. Our symbolic power can be useful and our skills can sometimes be combined with those of community members to great effect and with the result of mutual capacity building. These shifts toward more engaged scholarship would radicalize the fields of Applied Linguistics and SLA in new and extremely relevant ways because we would develop more frames for understanding language learning and language learners in society.

The research reported in this book, I believe, suggests that there is a great "need for reconceptualization of learning founded on recognition of new social, economic, political and cultural givens and the consequent redistributions and contestations around power" (Kress, 2008, p. 265). These givens reside in the particular time period of Somali migration to Minnesota. The community is large and strong, but not without struggles. There are great investments in the ideologies that frame language use, the institutions of society, including schools, the courts, and law enforcement. These investments make it more difficult for minoritized youth to assert their agendas, their educational needs, and their critiques of the givens of the social order. The Somali Diaspora community in Minnesota, as elsewhere, is in a powerful process of adapting and changing and I hope that this book serves to document, through youth lenses, some of the critical issues they face. As researchers, educators, and advocates, there are myriad means to engage that support equity and social justice as Somali youth continue this process.

Language Learning   ISSN 0023-8333

References

Abdi, A. A. (1998). Education in Somalia: History, destruction, and calls for reconstruction. *Comparative Education, 34*(3), 327–340.

Abdi, C. M. (2007). Convergence of civil war and the religious right. *Signs: Journal of Women in Culture and Society, 33*(1), 183–207.

Abo-Zena, M. M., Sahli, B., & Tobias-Nahi, C. S. (2009). Testing the courage of their convictions: Muslim youth respond to stereotyping, hostility, and discrimination. In O. Sensoy & C. D. Stonebanks (Eds.), *Muslim voices in school: Narratives of identity and pluralism* (pp. 3–26). Rotterdam: SensePublishers.

Abu El-Haj, T. (2006). *Elusive justice: Wrestling with difference and educational equity in everyday practice.* New York: Routledge.

Abu Odeh, L. (1997). Post-colonial feminism and the veil: Thinking the difference. In M. Geren & S. Davis (Eds.), *Toward a new psychology of gender: A reader* (pp. 245–256). New York: Routledge.

Adamson, H. D. (1993). *Academic competence: Theory and classroom practice: Preparing ESL students for content courses.* New York: Longman.

Adrian, J. A., Alegria, J., & Morais, J. (1995). Metaphonological abilities of Spanish illiterate adults. *International Journal of Psychology, 3*, 329–353.

Ahmed, A. J. (n.d.). *The Somali oral tradition and the role of storytelling in Somalia.* St. Paul: Minnesota Humanities Center.

Ajrouch, K. J., & Kusow, A. M. (2007). Racial and religious contexts: Situational identities among Lebanese and Somali Muslim immigrants. *Ethnic and Racial Studies, 30*(1), 72–94.

Alim, H. S., Ibrahim, A., & Pennycook, A. (Eds.). (2009). *Global linguistic flows: Hip hop cultures, youth identities, and the politics of language.* New York: Taylor & Francis.

Allen, J. (2007). "So. . ." In M. V. Blackburn & C. T. Clark (Eds.), *Literacy research for political action and social change* (pp. 77–94). New York: Peter Lang.

Allie, M. (2006, March 18). Somalis under siege in South Africa, *BBC News.* Retrieved June 25, 2010, from http://news.bbc.co.uk/2/hi/africa/6066240.stm

Anderson, B. (1983). *Imagined communities.* London: Verso.

Anderson, M. E. (2004). *Intended and unintended consequences of statewide testing for ESL curriculum and instruction.* Unpublished doctoral dissertation, University of Minnesota, Minneapolis.

Anderson, R. (2009). *Minnesota racism: Racism has a newfound fervor when applied to the state's largest migrant population: Somalis.* Retrieved June 25, 2010, from http://www.mndaily.com/2009/03/01/minnesota-racism

Andrzejewski, B. W. (1988). Infills: Nouns and verbs without lexical meanings in Somali oral poetry. *African Languages and Cultures, 1*(1), 1–14.

Angelou, M. (1978). *And still I rise.* New York: Random House.

Anzaldua, G. (1987). *Borderlands: The new Mestiza = La frontera.* San Francisco: Aunt Lute.

Appadurai, A. (1996). *Modernity at large: Cultural dimensions of globalization.* Minneapolis: University of Minnesota Press.

Arthur, J. (2003). "Baro Afkaaga Hooyo!" A case study of Somali literacy teaching in Liverpool. *International Journal of Bilingual Education and Bilingualism, 6*(3&4), 253–266.

Arthur, J. A. (2000). *Invisible sojourners: African immigrant Diaspora in the United States.* Westport, CT: Praeger.

Auerbach, E. (1995). Deconstructing the discourse of strengths in family literacy. *Journal of Reading Behavior, 27*(4), 643–661.

Baddeley, A. (1986). *Working memory.* Oxford: Clarendon.

Banks, J. A. (1998). The lives and values of researchers: Implications for educating citizens in a multicultural society. *Educational Researcher, 27*(7), 4–17.

Barnes, V. L., & Boddy, J. (1994). *Aman: The story of a Somali girl.* New York: Vintage Books.

Basford, L. E. (2008). *From mainstream to East African charter: East African Muslim students' experiences in U.S. schools.* Unpublished doctoral dissertation, University of Minnesota, Minneapolis.

Basford, L. E., Hick, S., & Bigelow, M. (2007). *Educating Muslims in an East African US charter high school.* Retrieved November 15, 2007, from National Center for the Study of Privatization in Education, Columbia University, New York.

Bashir-Ali, K. (2006). Language learning and the definition of one's social, cultural, and racial identity. *TESOL Quarterly, 40*(3), 628–639.

Bell, A. (2007). Style in dialogue: Bakhtin and sociolinguistic theory. In R. Bayley & C. Lucas (Eds.), *Sociolinguistic variation: Theories, methods and applications* (pp. 90–109). Cambridge: Cambridge University Press.

Bell, D. (1992). *Faces at the bottom of the well: The permanence of racism.* New York: Basic Books.

Berns McGown, R. (1999). *Muslims in the Diaspora: The Somali communities of London and Toronto.* Toronto: University of Toronto Press.

Bhabha, H. (1990). The third space. In J. Rutherford (Ed.), *Identity, community, culture difference* (pp. 207–221). London: Lawrence and Wishart.

Bhabha, H. (1994). *The location of culture.* New York: Routledge.

Biber, D., & Hared, M. (1991). Literacy in Somali: Linguistic consequences. *Annual Review of Applied Linguistics, 12*, 260–282.

Bigelow, M. (2007). Social and cultural capital at school: The case of a Somali teenage girl with limited formal schooling. In N. R. Faux (Ed.), *Low-educated adult second language and literacy acquisition proceedings of symposium* (pp. 7–22). Richmond: Literacy Institute at Virginia Commonwealth University.

Bigelow, M. (2008). Somali adolescents' negotiation of religious and racial bias in and out of school. *Theory into Practice, 47*(1), 27–34.

Bigelow, M. (2009a). Texts and contexts for cultural and linguistic hybridity in the Diaspora. *MI TESOL Conference Proceedings*, 74–89.

Bigelow, M. (2009b, April). *(Un)limiting English language learners: Issues in policy, programs, and teaching.* Plenary at the Minnesota ESL and Bilingual Education Conference (hosted by the Minnesota Department of Education), St. Paul.

Bigelow, M., & Basford, L. (2008, November). *Language, society, and education: What do Somali Muslim youth have to say?* Paper presented at the Meeting Minnesota's Muslims Conference, Islamic Center of Minnesota, Fridley.

Bigelow, M., Basford, L., & Smidt, E. (2008). The academic and social transition to school and the role of native language support. *Journal of Southeast Asian American Education and Asian Advancement.* Retrieved June 25, 2010, from http://jsaaea.coehd.utsa.edu/index.php/JSAAEA

Bigelow, M., delMas, R., Hansen, K., & Tarone, E. (2006). Literacy and the processing of oral recasts in SLA. *TESOL Quarterly, 40*(4), 665–689.

Bigelow, M., & Ranney, S. (2005). Pre-service ESL teachers' knowledge about language and its transfer to lesson planning. In N. Bartles (Ed.), *Applied linguistics and language teacher education* (pp. 179–200). New York: Springer Science+Business Media, Inc.

Bigelow, M., Ranney, S., & Hebble, A. (2005). Choosing depth over breadth in a content-based ESL class. In J. Crandall & D. Kaufman (Eds.), *Content-based language instruction in the K-12 setting* (pp. 179–193). Washington, DC: TESOL.

Bigelow, M., & Tarone, E. (2004). The role of literacy level in SLA: Doesn't who we study determine what we know? *TESOL Quarterly, 39*(1), 689–700.

Bigelow, M., & Watson, J. (in press). Educational level and L2 learning. In S. Gass & A. Mackey (Eds.), *Handbook of second language acquisition.* London: Routledge/Taylor Francis.

Birch, B. (2007). *English L2 reading: Getting to the bottom* (2nd ed.). Mahwah, NJ: Erlbaum.

Birdsong, D. P. (Ed.). (1999). *Second language acquisition and the critical period hypothesis.* Mahwah, NJ: Erlbaum.

Blackledge, A. (2005). *Discourse and power in a multilingual world.* Philadelphia: Benjamins.

Blank, R. M., Dabady, M., & Forbes Citro, C. (2004). *Measuring racial discrimination.* Washington, DC: National Academies Press.

Block, D. (2003). *The social turn in SLA.* Washington, DC: Georgetown University Press.

Block, D. (2006). *Multilingual identities in a global city: London stories.* New York: Palgrave Macmillan.

Bourdieu, P. (1977). The economics of linguistic exchanges. *Social Science Information, 16*, 645–668.

Brandt, S. (2005). Students sue alternative high school. *Star Tribune*, p. 4B.

Bryce-Laporte, R. S. (1972). Black immigrants: The experience of invisibility and inequality. *Journal of Black Studies, 3*(1), 29–56.

Buroway, M., Gamson, W., Ryan, C., Pfohl, S., Vaughan, D., Derber, C., et al. (2004). Public sociologies. *Social Problems, 51*(1), 103–130.

Callahan, R. M. (2005). Tracking and high school English learners: Limiting opportunity to learn. *American Educational Research Journal, 42*(2), 305–328.

Canagarajah, S. (2004). Multilingual writers and the struggle for voice in academic discourse. In A. Pavlenko & A. Blackledge (Eds.), *Negotiation of identities in multilingual contexts* (pp. 266–289). Clevedon: Multilingual Matters.

Carlton, J. (2008, July 26). Texas ordered to improve bilingual education: TEA has until the end of January to change program for secondary schools. *Associated Press*. Retrieved June 25, 2010, from http://www.dallasnews.com/sharedcontent/dws/dn/education/stories/DN-bilingual_26met.ART.State.Edition1.4d5e6cb.html

Castro-Caldas, A., Petersson, K. M., Reis, A., Stone-Elander, S., & Ingvar, M. (1998). The illiterate brain: Learning to read and write during childhood influences the functional organization of the adult brain. *Brain and Language, 121*(6), 1053–1063.

Chanoff, S. (2008, May 13). Africa's "forgotten" refugees, *Boston Globe*. Retrieved June 25, 2010, from http://www.boston.com/news/world/blog/2008/05/africas_forgott.html

Chhuon, V. (2009). *How school structures influence ethnic and panethnic identity in Cambodian high school youth*. Unpublished doctoral dissertation, University of California, Santa Barbara.

Cisneros, S. (1995). *Loose women: Poems*. St. Louis, MO: San Val, Inc.

Coffey, A., & Atkinson, P. (1996). *Making sense of qualitative data: Complementary strategies*. Thousand Oaks, CA: Sage.

Collet, B. A. (2007). Islam, national identity and public secondary education: Perspectives from the Somali diaspora in Toronto, Canada. *Race, Ethnicity and Education, 10*(2), 131–153.

Collier, V. P. (1987). Age and rate of acquisition of second language for academic purposes. *TESOL Quarterly, 21*(4), 617–641.

Collier, V. P. (1989). How long? A synthesis of research on academic achievement in a second language. *TESOL Quarterly, 23*(3), 509–531.

Collier, V. P. (1992). A synthesis of studies examining long-term language minority student data on academic achievement. *Bilingual Research Journal, 16*(1&2), 187–212.

Collier, V. P., & Thomas, W. P. (1988, April) *Acquisition of cognitive-academic second language proficiency: A six-year study*. Paper presented at the annual meeting of the American Educational Research Association, New Orleans.

Collier, V. P., & Thomas, W. P. (1989). How quickly can immigrants become proficient in school English? *Journal of Educational Issues of Language Minority Students, 5*, 26–38.

Colombi, M. C. (2002). Academic language development in Latino students' writing in Spanish. In M. J. Schleppegrell & M. C. Colombi (Eds.), *Developing advanced literacy in first and second languages* (pp. 67–86). Mahwah, NJ: Erlbaum.

Condon, P. (2009). *Minneapolis struggles with rise of Somali gangs.* Retrieved June 25, 2010, from http://www.cnsnews.com/news/article/51251.

Crandall, J., & Kaufman, D. (Eds.). (2005). *Content-based language instruction in the K-12 setting.* Washington, DC: TESOL.

Crawford, J. (1999, May 14). *Life in a politicized climate: What role for educational researchers.* Paper presented at the Linguistic Minority Research Institute: Conference on the Schooling of English Language Learners in the Post 227 Era, Sacramento, CA. Retrieved June 25, 2010, from http://www.languagepolicy.net/articles/LMRI.htm

Crenshaw, K., Gotanda, N., Peller, G., & Thomas, K. (Eds.). (1995). *Critical race theory: The key writing that formed the movement.* New York: The New Press.

Crookes, G. (1997). SLA and language pedagogy. *Studies in Second Language Acquisition, 19*(1), 93–116.

Cummins, J. (1979). Cognitive/academic language proficiency, linguistic interdependence, the optimal age question and other matters. *Working Papers on Bilingualism, 19*, 197–205.

Cummins, J. (1981a). Age on arrival and immigrant second language learning in Canada: A reassessment. *Applied Linguistics, 2*, 132–149.

Cummins, J. (1981b). The role of primary language development in promoting educational success for language minority students. In California State Department of Education (Ed.), *Schooling and language minority students: A theoretical framework* (pp. 3–49). Los Angeles: National Dissemination and Assessment Center.

Cummins, J. (1991). Conversational and academic language proficiency in bilingual contexts. *Reading in Two Languages: AILA Review, 8*, 75–89.

Cummins, J. (1994). The acquisition of English as a second language. In K. Sprangenberg-Urbschat & R. Pritchard (Eds.), *Kids come in all languages: Reading instruction for ESL students* (pp. 36–62). Newark, DE: International Reading Association.

Darling-Hammond, L. (2000). Teacher quality and student achievement: A review of state policy evidence. *Education Policy Analysis Archives, 8*(1), 1–44.

DeCapua, A., Smathers, W., & Tang, F. (2009). *Meeting the needs of students with limited or interrupted schooling: A guide for educators.* Ann Arbor: University of Michigan Press.

De Fina, A. (2003). *Identity in narrative: A study of immigrant discourse.* Philadelphia: Benjamins.

De Voe, P. A. (2002). Symbolic action: Religion's role in the changing environment of young Somali women. *Journal of Refugee Studies, 15*(2), 234–246.

Devine, J. (1994). Literacy and social power. In B. M. Ferdman, R. M. Weber, & A. G. Ramírez (Eds.), *Literacy across languages and cultures* (pp. 221–237). Albany: State University of New York Press.

Diaz, K. (2009, March 12). FBI tracks Somali terror link. *Star Tribune,* pp. A5, A8.

Dorian, N. C. (1982). Defining the speech community in terms of its working margins. In S. Romaine (Ed.), *Sociolinguistic variation in speech communities* (pp. 25–33). London: Edward Arnold.

Dörnyei, Z. (2005). *The psychology of the language learner.* Mahwah, NJ: Erlbaum.

Dufresne, J., & Hall, S. (1997). LEAP English Academy: An alternative high school for newcomers to the United States. *MINNE-WI TESOL Journal, 14,* 1–17.

Durgunoğlu, A. Y., & Verhoeven, L. (1998). Multilingualism and literacy development across different cultures. In A. Y. Durgunoğlu & L. Verhoeven (Eds.), *Literacy development in a multilingual context: Cross-cultural perspectives* (pp. 289–298). Mahwah, NJ: Erlbaum.

Dyer, C. (2008). Early years literacy in Indian urban schools: Structural, social and pedagogical issues. *Language and Education, 22*(5), 237–253.

Dyson, A. H. (1993). *Social worlds of children learning to write in an urban primary school.* New York: Teachers College Press.

Dyson, A. H. (2003). *The brothers and sisters learn to write: Popular literacies in childhood and school cultures.* New York: Teachers College Press.

Echeruo, M. J. C. (1999). An African diaspora: The ontological project. In I. Okpewho, C. B. Davies, & A. A. Mazrui (Eds.), *The African Diaspora: African origins and new world identities* (pp. 3–18). Bloomington: Indiana University Press.

Edelsky, C. (1991). Not acquiring Spanish as a second language: The politics of second language acquisition. In C. Edelsky (Ed.), *With literacy and justice for all: Rethinking the social in language and education* (pp. 18–40). London: The Falmer Press.

Edelsky, C., Hudelson, S., Altwerger, B., Flores, B., Barkin, F., & Jilbert, K. (1983). Semilingualism and language deficit. *Applied Linguistics, 4*(1), 1–22.

Egbo, B. (2004). Intersections of literacy and construction of social identities. In A. Pavlenko & A. Blackledge (Eds.), *Negotiation of identities in multilingual contexts* (pp. 243–265). Clevedon, UK: Multilingual Matters.

Ellsworth, E. (1989). "Why doesn't this feel empowering?" Working through the repressive myths of critical pedagogy. *Harvard Educational Review, 59*(3), 297–342.

Ephron, D., & Hosenball, M. (2009, January 24). Recruited for Jihad? *Newsweek.* Retrieved June 26, 2010, from http://www.newsweek.com/id/181408

Espiritu, Y. L. (1992). *Asian American panethnicity*. Philadelphia: Temple University Press.

Faltis, C., & Wolfe, P. (Eds.). (1999). *So much to say: Adolescents, bilingualism, and ESL in the secondary school*. New York: Teachers College Press.

Farid, M., & McMahan, D. (2004). *Accommodating and educating Somali students in Minnesota schools: A handbook for teachers and administrators*. St Paul, MN: Hamline University Press.

Feagin, J. (2000). *Racist America: Roots, current realities and future reparations*. New York: Routledge.

Ferdman, B. M., & Weber, R. M. (1994). Literacy across languages and cultures. In B. M. Ferdman, R. M. Weber, & A. G. Ramírez (Eds.), *Literacy across languages and cultures* (pp. 3–29). Albany: State University of New York Press.

Fine, M., Weis, L., Powell, L., & Wong, L. (Eds.). (1997). *Off white: Readings on race, power, and society*. New York: Routledge.

Fine, M., Weis, L., Weseen, S., & Wong, L. (2000). For whom? Qualitative research, representations, and social responsibilities. In N. K. Denzin & Y. S. Lincoln (Eds.), *Handbook of qualitative research* (pp. 107–131). Thousand Oaks, CA: Sage.

Fishman, J. A., Riedler-Berger, C., Koling, P., & Steele, J. M. (1985). Ethnocultural dimensions in the acquisition and retention of biliteracy: A comparative ethnography of four New York City schools. In J. Fishman, M. H. Gertner, E. G. Lowy & W. G. Milan (Eds.), *The rise and fall of the ethnic revival: Perspectives on language and ethnicity* (pp. 377–441). New York: Mouton.

Foley, D., & Valenzuela, A. (2006). Critical ethnography: The politics of collaboration. In N. K. Denzin & Y. S. Lincoln (Eds.), *Sage handbook of qualitative research* (pp. 217–234). New York: Sage.

Forman, M. (2001). "Straight outta Mogadishu": Prescribed identities and performative practices among Somali youth in North American high schools. *Topia, 5*, 33–60.

Fortune, T. W., & Tedick, D. J. (Eds.). (2008). *Pathways to multilingualism: Evolving perspectives on immersion education*. Bristol, UK: Multilingual Matters.

Frater-Mathieson, K. (2004). Refugee trauma, loss and grief: Implications for intervention. In R. Hamilton & D. Moore (Eds.), *Educational interventions for refugee children: Theoretical perspectives and implementing best practice* (pp. 11–34). London: RoutledgeFalmer, Taylor & Francis Group.

Freeman, Y. S., & Freeman, D. E. (2001). Keys to success for bilingual students with limited formal schooling. *Bilingual Research Journal, 25*(1&2), 203–213.

Gabrielatos, C., & Baker, P. (2008). Fleeing, sneaking, flooding: A corpus analysis of discursive constructions of refugees and asylum seekers in the UK press, 1996–2005. *Journal of English Linguistics, 36*(5), 5–38.

Gale, K., McClay, D., Christie, M., & Harris, S. (1981). Academic achievement in the Milingimbi bilingual education program. *TESOL Quarterly, 15*, 297–314.

Gardner-Chloros, P. (1997). Vernacular literacy in migrant and minority settings. In
R. B. LePage, A. Tabouret-Keller, G. Varro, & P. H. Gardner-Chloros (Eds.),
Vernacular literacy: A re-evaluation (pp. 189–222). Oxford: Clarendon Press.

Gaspar de Alba, A. (1995). The alter-native grain: Theorizing Chinaco/a popular
culture. In A. Darder (Ed.), *Culture and difference: Critical perspectives on the
bicultural experience in the United States* (pp. 103–122). Westport, CT: Bergin &
Garvey.

Gee, J. P. (1986). Orality and literacy: From *The savage mind* to *Ways with words*.
TESOL Quarterly, 20, 747–751.

Gee, J. P. (1990). *Social linguistics and literacies*. New York: The Falmer Press.

Gee, J. P. (1996). *Social linguistics and literacies: Ideology in discourses* (2nd ed.).
London: Falmer Press.

Gerstend, R., & Woodward, J. (1985). A case for structured immersion. *Educational
Leadership, 43*, 75–79.

Gibbons, P. (2008). "It was taught good and I learned a lot": Intellectual practices and
ESL learners in the middle years. *Australian Journal of Language and Literacy,
31*(2), 155–173.

Gibson, J. (2007). *What's going on in Minnesota? It seems to be on its way to be
America's first Somali-Muslim state*. Retrieved June 26, 2010, from http://www.
foxnews.com/story/0,2933,259761,00.html

Gibson, M. A. (1988). *Accommodation without assimilation: Punjabi Sikh immigrants
in American high schools and community*. Ithaca, NY: Cornell University Press.

Gilroy, P. (1993). *The Black Atlantic: Modernity and double consciousness*.
Cambridge, MA: Harvard University Press.

Gitlin, A., Buendía, E., Crosland, K., & Doumbia, F. (2003). The production of margin
and center: Welcoming-unwelcoming of immigrant students. *American Educational
Research Journal, 40*(1), 91–122.

Goldstein, T. (2003). *Teaching and learning in a multilingual school: Choices, risks,
and dilemmas*. Mahwah, NJ: Erlbaum.

González, N. (2005). Beyond culture: The hybridity of funds of knowledge. In N.
González, L. Moll, & C. Amanti (Eds.), *Fund of knowledge* (pp. 29–46). Mahwah,
NJ: Erlbaum.

Green, K. R., & Reder, S. (1986). Factors in individual acquisition of English: A
longitudinal study of Hmong adults. In G. L. Hendricks, B. T. Downing, & A. S.
Deinard (Eds.), *The Hmong in transition* (pp. 299–329). Minneapolis: The Center
for Migration Studies of New York, Inc. & The Southeast Asian Refugee Studies of
the University of Minnesota.

Griffiths, D. J. (2002). *Somali and Kurdish refugees in London: New identities in the
Diaspora*. Burlington, VT: Ashgate.

Gubrium, J. F., & Holstein, J. A. (1998). Narrative practice and the coherence of
personal stories. *The Sociological Quarterly, 39*(1), 163–187.

Guerra, J. C. (2004). Emerging representation, situated literacies, and the practice of transcultural repositioning. In M. Hall Kelly, V. Balester, & V. Villanueva (Eds.), *Latino/a discourses on language, identity & literacy education* (pp. 7–23). Portsmouth, NH: Boynton/Cook.

Guinier, L., & Torres, G. (2002). *The miner's canary: Enlisting race, resisting power, transforming democracy.* Boston: Harvard University Press.

Gumperz, J. (1982). Conversational code-switching. In J. Gumperz (Ed.), *Discourse strategies* (pp. 59–99). New York: Cambridge University Press.

Guskey, T., & Sparks, D. (2004). Linking professional development to improvements in student learning. In E. M. Guyton & J. R. Dangel (Eds.), *Research linking teacher preparation and student performance: Teacher education yearbook XII* (pp. 233–247). Dubuque, IA: Kendall/Hunt.

Hakuta, K., Butler, Y. G., & Witt, D. (2000). *How long does it take English learners to attain proficiency?* The University of California Linguistic Minority Research Institute, Policy Report 2000–1.

Hall, S. (1989). New ethnicities. In D. Morley & K.-H. Chen (Eds.), *Stuart Hall: Critical dialogues in cultural studies* (pp. 441–449). London: Routledge.

Hall, S. (1990). Cultural identity and diaspora. In J. Rutherford (Ed.), *Identity: Community, culture, difference* (pp. 222–239). London: Lawrence and Wishart.

Hall, S. (1996). Introduction: Who needs "identity"? In S. Hall & P. du Gay (Eds.), *Questions of cultural identity* (pp. 1–17). London: Sage.

Hallman, C. (2006, August 31). Double jeopardy for African American Muslims. *Minnesota Spokesman-Recorder.*

Han, Z.-H. (2007). Pedagogical implications: Genuine or pretentious. *TESOL Quarterly, 41*(2), 387–393.

Hansen, K. (2005). *Impact of literacy level and task type on oral L2 recall accuracy.* M.A. thesis, University of Minnesota, Minneapolis.

Hargreaves, A. (1994). *Changing teachers, changing times: Teachers' work and culture in the postmodern age.* London: Cassell.

Hargreaves, A. (2003). *Teaching in the knowledge society: Education in the age of insecurity.* New York: Teachers College Press.

Haw, K. F. (1998). *Educating Muslim girls: Shifting discourses.* Buckingham, UK: Open University Press.

Haynes, C. (1998). Muslim students' needs in public schools. *Update on Law-Related Education, 22*(1), 17–21.

Henderson, J. (2007). *Five Minnesota districts' perceptions of the No Child Left Behind Act of 2001: English language learner tests and their implications for program instruction and climate.* Unpublished doctoral dissertation, Hamline University, St. Paul, MN.

Hersch, P. (1998). *A tribe apart: A journey into the heart of American adolescence.* New York: Ballantine Books.

Higginbotham, E. B. (1992). African-American women's history and the metalanguage of race. *Signs, 17*(2), 251–274.

Hollingsworth, H. (2007, December 18). Programs work with uneducated immigrants. *The Associated Press.* Retrieved June 26, 2010, from http://www.amren.com/mtnews/archives/2007/12/programs_focus.php

Hopkins, G. (2006). Somali community organizations in London and Toronto: Collaboration and effectiveness. *Journal of Refugee Studies, 19*(3), 361–380.

Horgen, T. (2007, October 7). Feast after the fast: Dining spots come alive at night during Ramadan as Muslims break daylight fasts. *Star Tribune.* Retrieved June 26, 2010, from http://www.startribune.com/entertainment/dining/11502786.html

Hornberger, N. (Ed.). (2003). *Continua of biliteracy: An ecological framework for educational policy, research and practice in multilingual settings.* Clevedon, UK: Multilingual Matters, Ltd.

Hudson, W. S., & Corrigan, J. (1999). *Religion in America: An historical account of the development of American religious life* (6th ed.). Upper Saddle River, NJ: Prentice Hall.

Hull, G., & Nelson, M. E. (2005). Locating the semiotic power of multimodality. *Written Communication, 22*(2), 1–38.

Hune, S. (2000). Rethinking race: Paradigms and policy formation. In M. Zhou & J. V. Gatewood (Eds.), *Contemporary Asian America: A multidisciplinary reader* (pp. 667–676). New York: New York University Press.

Ibrahim, A. (1999). Becoming black: Rap and hip-hop, race, gender, identity, and the politics of ESL learning. *TESOL Quarterly, 33*(3), 349–369.

Integrated Regional Information Networks. (2003). *A gap in their hearts: The experience of separated Somali children.* Nairobi, Kenya: UN Office of the Coordination of Humanitarian Affairs.

Jama, Z. M. (1994). Silent voices: The role of Somali women's poetry in social and political life. *Oral Tradition, 9*(1), 185–202.

Jewitt, C. (2008). Multimodality and literacy in school classrooms. *Review of Research in Education, 32*(1), 241–267.

Joshi, K. Y. (2006). The racialization of Hinduism, Islam, and Sikhism in the United States. *Equity & Excellence in Education, 39,* 211–226.

Kahin, M. H. (1997). *Educating Somali children in Britain.* Staffordshire, UK: Trentham Books.

Kalantry, S., Getgen, J., & Koh, S. A. (2009). Measuring state compliance with the right to education using indicators: A case study of Colombia's obligations under the ICESCR. *Cornell Law School Working Papers Series, Paper 52.*

Kanno, Y., & Norton, B. (2003). Imagined communities and educational possibilities: Introduction. *Journal of Language, Identity, and Education, 2*(4), 241–249.

Kidd, R. (1996). Teaching academic language functions at the secondary level. *Canadian Modern Language Review, 52*(2), 285–307.

Khan, S. (2002). *Aversion and desire: Negotiating Muslim female identity in the diaspora.* Toronto, Ontario: Women's Press.

Kress, G. (2008). Meaning and learning in a world of instability and multiplicity. *Studies in Philosophy and Education, 27*(4), 253–266.

Kusow, A. M. (2006). Migration and racial formations among Somali immigrants in North America. *Journal of Ethnic and Migration Studies, 32*(3), 533–551.

La Vaque, D. (2008, September 17). True to their faith, true to their teams. *Star Tribune.* Retrieved June 26, 2010, from http://www.startribune.com/local/28485049.html?page=1&c=y

Labov, W. (1982). Speech actions and reactions in personal narrative. In D. Tannen (Ed.), *Analyzing discourse: Text and talk* (pp. 219–247). Washington, DC: Georgetown University Press.

Ladson-Billings, G. (2007). Pushing past the achievement gap: An essay on the language of deficit. *Journal of Negro Education, 76*(3), 316–323.

Lam, W. S. E. (2006). Culture and learning in the context of globalization: Research directions. *Review of Research in Education, 30*, 213–237.

Lam, W. S. E. (2009). Multiliteracies on instant messaging in negotiating local, translocal, and transnational affiliations: A case of an adolescent immigrant. *Reading Research Quarterly, 44*(4), 377–397.

Lambert, W. E. (1975). Culture and language as factors in learning and education. In A. Wolfgang (Ed.), *Education of immigrant students.* Toronto: Ontario Institute for Studies in Education.

Lau v. Nichols 414 U.S. 563 (1974).

Lee, L.-Y. (2009). Self-help for fellow refugees. In *Behind my eyes.* New York: W.W. Norton and Company.

Lee, S. (2005). *Up against whiteness: Race, school and immigrant youth.* New York: Teachers College Press.

Lemmouh, Z. (2008). A critical linguistic analysis of the representation of Muslims in the *New York Times. Hermes, 40*, 217–240.

Levin, H. M. (2009). The economic payoff to investing in educational justice. *Educational Researcher, 38*(1), 5–20.

Lewis, C., & del Valle, A. (2009). Literacy and identity: Implications for research and practice. In L. Christenbury, R. Bomer, & P. Smagorinsky (Eds.), *Handbook of adolescent literacy* (pp. 307–322). New York: Guilford.

Lin, A. M. Y. (2008). Modernity, postmodernity and the future of "identity": Implications for educators. In A. M. Y. Lin (Ed.), *Problematizing identity: Everyday struggles in language, culture and education* (pp. 199–219). New York: Erlbaum.

Lin, A. M. Y., Wang, W., Akamatsu, N., & Riazi, A. M. (2002). Appropriating English, expanding identities, and re-visioning the field: From TESOL to teaching English for glocalized communication (TEGCOM). *Journal of Language, Identity & Education, 1*(4), 295–316.

Lincoln, Y., & Guba, E. G. (1985). *Naturalistic inquiry*. Beverly Hills, CA: Sage.

Long, M. H., Inagaki, S., & Ortega, L. (1998). The role of implicit negative feedback in SLA: Models and recasts in Japanese and Spanish. *Modern Language Journal, 82*(3), 357–371.

Lopez, N. (2003a). *Hopeful girls, troubled boys: Race and gender disparity in urban education*. New York: Routledge.

Lopez, G. R. (2003b). The (racially neutral) politics of education: A critical race theory perspective. *Educational Administration Quarterly, 39*(1), 68–94.

Loureiro, C. d. S., Braga, L. W., Souza, L. d. N., Filho, G. N., Queiroz, E., & Dellatolas, G. (2004). Degree of illiteracy and phonological and metaphonological skills in unschooled adults. *Brain and Language, 89*, 499–502.

Lowe, L. (1996). *Immigrant acts: On Asian American cultural politics*. Durham, NC: Duke University Press.

Luria, A. (1976). *Cognitive development: Its social and cultural foundations* (M. Cole, ed.; M. Lopez-Morillas & L. Solataroff, Trans.). Cambridge, MA: Harvard University Press.

Lyster, R. (1998a). Negotiation of form, recasts, and explicit correction in relation to error types and learner repair in immersion classrooms. *Language Learning, 48*(2), 183–218.

Lyster, R. (1998b). Recasts, repetition and ambiguity in L2 classroom discourse. *Studies in Second Language Acquisition, 20*(1), 51–80.

Lyster, R., & Ranta, L. (1997). Corrective feedback and learner uptake: Negotiation of form in communicative classrooms. *Studies in Second Language Acquisition, 19*(1), 37–66.

Mabandu, P. (2009, March 18). Somali refugees fear further xenophobic attacks. *Mail & Guardian Online*. Retrieved June 26, 2010, from http://www.mg.co.za/article/2009-03-04-somali-refugees-fear-further-xenophobic-attacks

Mace-Matluck, B. J., Alexander-Kasparik, R., & Queen, R. M. (1998). *Through the golden door: Educational approaches for immigrant adolescents with limited schooling*. McHenry, IL: Center for Applied Linguistics and Delta Systems Co., Inc.

Magnuson, P. (2003). *The interplay between Minnesota's accountability system and adolescent English language learners with limited formal schooling*. Unpublished doctoral dissertation, University of Minnesota, Minneapolis, MN.

Malherbe, E. G. (1978). Bilingual education in the Republic of South Africa. In B. Spolsky & R. Cooper (Eds.), *Case studies in bilingual education* (pp. 167–202). Rowley, MA: Newbury House.

Mathur, S. L. (2005, June 29). For Somalis, Eden Prairie is a little closer to home. *Star Tribune*. Retrieved June 26, 2010, from http://www.encyclopedia.com/doc/1G1-133657268.html

Matsuda, P. K., & Matsuda, A. (2009). The erasure of resident ESL writers. In M. Roberge, M. Siegal, & L. Harklau (Eds.), *Generation 1.5 in college composition: Teaching academic writing to U.S.-educated learners of ESL* (pp. 50–64). New York: Routledge.

Maynard, M. (2002, May). I against I: Why can't Somalis and Blacks get along? *The Rake: Secrets of the City*. Retrieved June 26, 2010, from http://slowdog.com/journEx_IAgainstI_p.html

McCluhan, M. (1994). *Understanding media: The extensions of man*. Cambridge, MA: MIT Press.

McConnell, B. B., & Kendall, J. R. (1987, April). *Application of the cohort model to evaluate bilingual programs: The "BELEPS" program*. Paper presented at the American Educational Research Association, Washington, DC.

McIntosh, P. (1988). White privilege and male privilege: A personal account of coming to see correspondences through work in women's studies. *Working Paper 189*.

McIntosh, P. (1990). White privilege: Unpacking the invisible knapsack. *Independent School, 49*(2).

McKay, S., & Wong, S.-L. C. (1996). Multiple discourses, multiple identities: Investment and agency in second-language learning among Chinese adolescent immigrant students. *Harvard Educational Review, 66*, 577–608.

McNeil, D. G. (2009, March 16). An outbreak of autism, or a statistical fluke? *The New York Times*. Retrieved June 26, 2010, from http://www.nytimes.com/2009/03/17/health/17auti.html?_r=1&partner=rssnyt&emc=rss

Medina, J. (2009, January 25). In school for the first time, teenage immigrants struggle. *New York Times*. Retrieved June 26, 2010, from http://www.nytimes.com/2009/01/25/education/25ellis.html?_r=1&sq=limited%20formal%20schooling&st=cse&scp=1&pagewanted=print

Menard-Warwick, J. (2005). Intergenerational trajectories and sociopolitical context: Latina immigrants in adult ESL. *TESOL Quarterly, 39*(2), 165–185.

Menken, K. (2008). *English learners left behind: Standardized testing as language policy*. Philadelphia: Multilingual Matters.

Menken, K., & Garcia, O. (2010). *Negotiating language policies: Educators as policymakers*. New York: Routledge.

Milner, H. R. (2007). Race, culture, and researcher positionality: Working through dangers seen, unseen, and unforseen. *Educational Researcher, 36*(7), 388–400.

Minnesota Statewide Racial Profiling Report. (2003). Institute on Race and Poverty, Council on Crime and Justice, Minneapolis, MN.

Mohan, B., & Beckett, G. H. (2001). A functional approach to research on content-based language learning: Recasts in causal explanations. *Canadian Modern Language Review, 58*(1), 133–155.

Moore, L. C. (2006). Learning by heart in Qur'anic and public schools in northern Cameroon. *Social Analysis, 50*(3), 109–126.

Morais, J., Bertelson, P., Cary, L., & Alegria, J. (1986). Literacy training and speech segmentation. *Cognition, 24*, 45–64.

Morais, J., Cary, L., Alegria, J., & Bertelson, P. (1979). Does awareness of speech as a sequence of phones arise spontaneously. *Cognition, 7*, 323–331.

Morais, J., Content, A., Bertelson, P., & Cary, L. (1988). Is there a critical period for the acquisition of segmental analysis? *Cognitive Neuropsychology, 5*, 347–352.

Morais, J., & Kolinsky, R. (2002). Literacy effects on language and cognition. In L. Bäckman & C. v. Hofsten (Eds.), *Psychology at the turn of the millennium* (pp. 507–530). Hove, East Sussex: Psychology Press.

Muñoz, C. (2008). Symmetries and asymmetries of age effects in naturalistic and instructed L2 learning. *Applied Linguistics, 29*, 578–596.

Nabei, T. (2003). *Recasts in classroom interaction: A teacher's intention, learners' attention, and second language learning*. Ph.D. dissertation, University of Toronto, Toronto.

Native Language Literacy Screening Device. (n.d.). Glenmont: The University of the State of New York, The State Education Department.

Ngo, B. (2004). *The complexities of difference: "Diversity," race and immigrant identity at an urban high school*. Ph.D. dissertation, University of Wisconsin-Madison.

Ngo, B. (2008). Beyond "culture clash" understandings of immigrant experiences. *Theory into Practice, 47*(1), 4–11.

Ngo, B. (2009). Ambivalent urban, immigrant identities: The incompleteness of Lao American student identities. *International Journal of Qualitative Studies in Education, 22*(2), 201–220.

Ngo, B. (2010). *Unresolved identities: Discourse, ambivalence and urban, immigrant students*. Albany: State University of New York Press.

Ngo, B., Bigelow, M., & Wahlstrom, K. (2007). The transition of Wat Tham Krabok Hmong children to Saint Paul Public Schools: Perspectives of teachers, principals, and Hmong parents. *Hmong Studies Journal, 8*, 1–36.

Norton, B. (2000). *Identity and language learning: Gender, ethnicity and educational change*. Essex, UK: Pearson Education.

Norton Peirce, B. (1995). Social identity, investment, and language learning. *TESOL Quarterly, 29*(1), 9–31.

Norton Peirce, B. (1997). Language, identity, and the ownership of English. *TESOL Quarterly, 31*(3), 409–429.

O'Brien, D. G. (1998). Multiple literacies in a high-school program for "at-risk" adolescents. In D. E. Alvermann, K. A. Hinchman, D. W. Moore, S. F. Phelps, & D. R. Waff (Eds.), *The literacies in adolescents' lives* (pp. 27–50). Mahwah, NJ: Erlbaum.

Ogbu, J. U. (1978). *Minority education and caste: The American system in cross-cultural perspective*. New York: Academic Press.

Ogbu, J. U. (1988). Class stratification, racial stratification, and schooling. In L. Weis (Ed.), *Class, race, and gender in American education* (pp. 163–182). Albany: State University of New York Press.

Olsen, L. (1998). *Made in America: Immigrant students in our public schools*. New York: The New Press.

Olson, D. R. (2002). What writing does to the mind. In E. Amsel & J. Byrnes (Eds.), *Language, literacy, and cognitive development: The development and consequences of symbolic communication* (pp. 153–166). Mahwah, NJ: Erlbaum.

Omi, M., & Winant, H. (1994). *Racial formations in the United States: From the 1960s to the 1990s* (2nd ed.). New York: Routledge.

Ong, A. (2003). *Buddha is hiding: Refugees, citizenship, the new America*. Berkeley: University of California Press.

Ong, W. J. (1982). *Orality and literacy: The technologizing of the word*. London: Routledge.

Ortega, L. (2005). For what and for whom is our research? The ethical as transformative lens in instructed SLA. *Modern Language Journal, 89*(3), 427–443.

Ortega, L. (2009). *Understanding second language acquisition*. London: Hodder Education.

Parker-Jenkins, M. (1995). Children of Islam: A teacher's guide to meeting the needs of Muslim pupils. Trentham, UK: Stoke-on-Trent.

Pavlenko, A., & Blackledge, A. (Eds.). (2004). *Negotiation of identities in multilingual contexts*. Clevedon, UK: Multilingual Matters.

Persson, J. (2009). Album review: K'naan—Troubadour. Retrieved June 26, 2010, from http://consequenceofsound.net/2009/02/26/album-review-knaan-troubadour/

Philp, J. (2003). Constraints on "noticing the gap": Nonnative speakers' noticing of recasts in NS-NNS interaction. *Studies in Second Language Acquisition, 25*(1), 99–126.

Pienemann, M., & Johnston, M. (1987). Factors influencing the development of language proficiency. In D. Nunan (Ed.), *Applying second language acquisition research* (pp. 45–141). Adelaide, Australia: National Curriculum Resource Centre, Adult Migrant Education Program.

Pienemann, M., Johnston, M., & Brindley, G. (1988). Constructing an acquisition-based procedure for second language assessment. *Studies in Second Language Acquisition, 10*(2), 217–243.

Pires-Hester, L. J. (1999). The emergence of bilateral dispora ethnicity among Cape Verdean-Americans. In I. Okpewho, C. B. Davies, & A. A. Mazrui (Eds.), *The African Diaspora: African origins and new world identities* (pp. 485–503). Bloomington: Indiana University Press.

Plante, A. J. (1977). *A study of effectiveness of the Connecticut "pairing" model of bilingual/bicultural education* (Vol. 68). Hamden: Connecticut Staff Development Cooperative.

Platt, E., & Troudi, S. (1997). Mary and her teachers: A Grebo-speaking child's place in the mainstream classroom. *Modern Language Journal, 81*, 28–49.

Polio, C., & Gass, S. (1997). Replication and reporting: A commentary. *Studies in Second Language Acquisition, 19*(4), 499–508.

Pollock, M. (2004). *Colormute: Race talk dilemmas in an American school*. Princeton, NJ: Princeton University Press.

Portes, A., & Rumbaut, R. G. (1996). *Immigrant America: A portrait*. Berkeley: University of California Press.

Pressley, M. (1998). *Reading instruction that works: The case for balanced teaching*. New York: Guilford.

QSR International Pty Ltd. (2008). NVivo qualitative analysis software (Version 8). Melbourne, Australia: Author.

Rackley, L. (2006). Kenya: Humanitarian conditions worsen in Dadaab refugee camps. Retrieved August 22, 2008, from http://www.startribune.com/local/11577656.html

Rampton, B. (1995). *Crossing: Language and ethnicity among adolescents*. London: Longman.

Ravid, D., & Tolchinsky, L. (2002). Developing linguistic literacy: A comprehensive model. *Journal of Child Language, 29*, 417–447.

Read, C., Zhang, Y., Nie, H., & Ding, B. (1986). The ability to manipulate speech sounds depends on knowing alphabetic spelling. *Cognition, 24*, 31–44.

Reder, S. (1994). Practice-engagement theory: A sociocultural approach to literacy across languages and cultures. In B. M. Ferdman, R.-M. Weber, & A. G. Ramírez (Eds.), *Literacy across languages and cultures* (pp. 33–74). Albany: State University of New York Press.

Reis, A., & Castro-Caldas, A. (1997). Illiteracy: A cause for biased cognitive development. *Journal of International Neuropsychological Society, 3*, 444–450.

Reis, A., Faísca, L., Mendonça, S., Ingvar, M., & Petersson, K. M. (2007). Semantic interference on a phonological task in illiterate subjects. *Scandinavian Journal of Psychology, 48*, 69–74.

Reis, A., Guerreiro, M., & Petersson, K. M. (2003). A sociodemographic and neuropsychological characterization of an illiterate population. *Applied Neuropsychology, 10*(4), 191–204.

Reisigl, M., & Wodak, R. (2000). "Austria first": A discourse-historical analysis of the Austrian "Anti-Foreigner Petition" in 1993. In M. Reisigl & R. Wodak (Eds.), *The semiotics of racism* (pp. 269–304). Vienna: Passagenverlag.

Reisigl, M., & Wodak, R. (2001). *Discourse and discrimination: Rhetorics of racism and antisemitism*. London: Routledge.

Rich, S., & Troudi, S. (2006). Hard times: Arab TESOL students' experiences of racialization and othering in the United Kingdom. *TESOL Quarterly, 40*(3), 615–627.

Richardson, E. (2006). *Hip hop literacies*. New York: Routledge.

Rivera, C. (Ed.). (1984). *Language proficiency and academic achievement*. Clevedon, UK: Multilingual Matters.

Roble, A., & Rutledge, D. (2008). *The Somali Diaspora: A journey away*. Minneapolis: University of Minnesota Press.

Robson, B. (2005, September 28). Blacked out: Immigrants sue Minneapolis school for the right to a decent education. *City Pages*. Retrieved September 21, 2008, from http://www.citypages.com/2005-09-28/news/blacked-out/

Romaine, S. (1995). *Bilingualism*. Oxford: Blackwell.

Rymes, B. R., & Pash, D. (2001). Questioning identity: The case of one second language learning. *Anthropology & Education Quarterly, 32*, 276–300.

Salzar, J. J. (1998). A longitudinal model for interpreting thirty years of bilingual education research. *Bilingual Research Journal, 22*(1), 1–12.

Santos, T. (1989). Replication in applied linguistics research. *TESOL Quarterly, 23*(4), 699–702.

Sarroub, L. K. (2001). The soujourner experience of Yemeni American high school students: An ethnographic portrait. *Harvard Educational Review, 71*(3), 390–415.

Sarroub, L. K. (2005). *All American Yemeni girls: Being Muslim in a public school*. Philadelphia: University of Pennsylvania Press.

Sarroub, L. K. (2008). Living "glocally" with literacy success in the Midwest. *Theory into Practice, 47*, 59–66.

Saville-Troike, M. (1984). What really matters in second language learning for academic achievement. *TESOL Quarterly, 18*(2), 199–219.

Sawyer, D. J., & Fox, B. J. (1991). *Phonological awareness in reading: The evolution of current perspectives*. New York: Springer-Verlag.

Schieffelin, B., & Ochs, E. (1986). Language socialization. *Annual Review of Anthropology, 15*, 163–191.

Schmidt, R. (2002). Racialization and language policy: The case of the U.S.A. *Multilingua, 21*, 141–161.

Scribner, S. (1984). Literacy in three metaphors. *American Journal of Education, 93*(1), 6–21.

Scuglik, D. L., Alarcón, R. D., Lapeyre, A. C., Williams, M. D., & Logan, K. M. (2007). When the poetry no longer rhymes: Mental health issues among Somali immigrants in the USA. *Transcultural Psychiatry, 44*(4), 581–595.

Shah, A. (2000, June 24). Somali girls coming of age are caught in cultural tug of war. *Star Tribune*. Retrieved June 26, 2010, from http://www.startribune.com/stories/462/4183113.html

Shah, S. (2006). Leading multiethnic schools: A new understanding of Muslim youth identity. *Educational Management Administration & Leadership, 34*(2), 215–237.

Shepard, R. M. (2008). *Cultural adaptation of Somali refugee youth*. New York: LFB Scholarly Publishing.

Short, D., & Fitzsimmons, S. (2007). *Double the work: Challenges and solutions to acquiring language and academic literacy for adolescent English language learners*. New York: Carnegie Corporation of New York.

Skutnabb-Kangas, T. (1979). *Language in the process of cultural assimilation and structural incorporation of linguistic minorities*. Rosslyn, VA: National Clearninghouse for Bilingual Education.

Sorenson, J. (1991). Politics of social identity: "Ethiopians" in Canada. *Journal of Ethnic Studies, 19*(1), 67–87.

Steele, C. M. (1997). A threat in the air: How stereotypes shape the intellectual identities and performance of women and African-Americans. *American Psychologist, 52*, 613–629.

Stone, K. R. (2008). *Making sense of testing: English language learners and statewide assessment*. Unpublished doctoral dissertation, University of Minnesota, Minneapolis.

Street, B. (Ed.). (1993). *Cross-cultural approaches to literacy*. Cambridge: Cambridge University Press.

Street, B. (1995). *Social literacies: Critical approaches to literacy development, ethnography, and education*. Reading, MA: Addison Wesley.

Suarez-Orozco, M. (2001). Globalization, immigrant and education: The research agenda. *Harvard Educational Review, 71*(1), 345–365.

Swain, M., & Fathman, A. (1976). Some limitations to the classroom applications of current second language acquisition research. *TESOL Quarterly, 10*(1), 19–32.

Swales, J. M. (1990). *Genre analysis: English in academic and research settings*. Cambridge: Cambridge University Press.

Tarone, E., & Bigelow, M. (2007). Alphabetic print literacy and processing of oral corrective feedback in the L2. In A. Mackey (Ed.), *Interaction and second language acquisition* (pp. 101–121). Oxford: Oxford University Press.

Tarone, E., Bigelow, M., & Hansen, K. (2009). *Literacy and second language oracy*. Oxford: Oxford University Press.

Tarone, E., Swierzbin, B., & Bigelow, M. (2006). The impact of literacy level of features of interlanguage in oral narratives. *Rivista di Psicolinguistica Applicata, 6*(3), 65–77.

Taylor, C. (1994). *Multiculturalism*. Princeton, NJ: Princeton University Press.

Tempes, F., Burnham, L., Piña, M., Campos, J., Matthews, S., Lear, E., et al. (1984). *Implementing theoretically sound programs: Do they really work?* Paper presented at the Annual Conference of the California Association for Bilingual Education, San Francisco.

TESOL Quarterly Submission Guidelines. (2009). *TESOL Quarterly*. Retrieved June 26, 2010, from http://www.tesol.org/s_tesol/sec_document.asp?CID= 476&DID=1031

Thandeka. (1999). *Learning to be white: Money, race, and God in America*. New York: Continuum Press.

Thomas, W. P., & Collier, V. (1997). School effectiveness for language minority students. *NCBE Resource Collection Series, 9*. Retrieved June 26, 2010, from http://www.thomasandcollier.com/Downloads/1997_Thomas-Collier97.pdf

Traoré, R., & Lukens, R. J. (2006). *"This isn't the America I thought I'd find": African students in the urban U.S. high school*. Lanham, MD: University Press of America.

Troike, R. (1978). Research evidence for the effectiveness of bilingual education. *NABE Journal, 3*(1), 13–24.

Tuan, M. (1998). *Forever foreigners or honorary Whites? The Asian ethnic experience today*. New Brunswick, NJ: Rutgers University Press.

Tummala-Narra, P. (2004). Asian trauma survivors: Immigration, identity, loss, and recovery. *Journal of Applied Psychoanalytic Studies, 3*(3), 243–258.

Twine, F., & Warren, J. (Eds.). (2000). *Racing research, researching race: Methodological dilemmas in critical race studies*. New York: New York University Press.

UNICEF. (n.d.). *Despite all odds*. Retrieved June 26, 2010, from www.unicef.org/somalia/SOM_NewDawndoc.pdf.

Valdés, G. (2001). *Learning and not learning English: Latino students in American schools*. New York: Teachers College Press.

Valenzuela, A. (1999). *Subtractive schooling: U.S.-Mexican youth and the politics of caring*. Albany: State University of New York Press.

van Dijk, T. A. (1980). *Macrostructures: An interdisciplinary study of global structures in discourse, interaction, and cognition*. Hillsdale, NJ: Erlbaum.

Vickerman, M. (1999). *Crosscurrents: West Indian immigrants and race*. New York: Oxford University Press.

Walker-Leigh, V. (2006, March 18). Refugees: Tiny Malta is finally heard. *Inter Press Service News Agency*. Retrieved June 26, 2010, from http://ipsnews.net/africa/nota.asp?idnews=34036.

Ward, L. M. (2004). Wading through the stereotypes: Positive and negative associations between media use and black adolescents' conceptions of self. *Developmental Psychology, 40*(2), 284–294.

Waring, H. Z. (2007). The multi-functionality of accounts in advice giving. *Journal of Sociolinguistics, 11*(3), 367–391.

Warsame, A. A. (2001). How a strong government backed an African language: The lessons of Somalia. *International Review of Education, 47*(3–4), 341–360.

Waters, M. C. (1994). Ethnic and racial identities of second-generation Black immigrants in New York City. *International Migration Review, 28*(4), 795–820.

Waters, M. C. (1999). *Black identities: West Indian immigrant dreams and American realities*. New York: Russell Sage Foundation.

Watson, J. (2010). *Interpreting across the abyss: A hermeneutic study of initial literacy development by high school English language learners with limited formal schooling*. Unpublished doctoral dissertation, University of Minnesota, Minneapolis.

Weedon, C. (1987). *Feminist practice and poststructuralist theory*. Cambridge, MA: Blackwell Publishers.

Weinstein, G. (1986). *From mountaintops to city streets: An ethnographic investigation of literacy and social process among the Hmong of Philadelphia*. Ph.D. dissertation, University of Pennsylvania, Philadelphia.

West, T. R. (2002). *Signs of struggle: The rhetorical politics of cultural difference*. Albany: State University of New York Press.

Woldemikael, T. M. (1989a). *Becoming Black American: Haitians and American institutions in Evanston, Illinois*. New York: AMS Press.

Woldemikael, T. M. (1989b). A case study of race consciousness among Haitian immigrants. *Journal of Black Studies, 202*(2), 224–239.

Wong Fillmore, L. (1991). When learning a second language means losing the first. *Early Childhood Research Quarterly, 6*, 323–346.

Yin, R. K. (2003a). *Applications of case study research*. Thousand Oaks, CA: Sage.

Yin, R. K. (2003b). *Case study research: Design and methods* (3rd ed., Vol. 5). Thousand Oaks, CA: Sage.

Yon, D. A. (2000). *Elusive culture: Schooling, race, and identity in global times*. Albany: State University of New York Press.

Zhou, M., & Bankston, C. L., III. (1994). Social capital and the adaptation of Vietnamese youth in New Orleans. *International Migration Review, 28*, 821–845.

Zine, J. (2001). Muslim youth in Canadian schools: Education and the politics of religious identity. *Anthropology & Education Quarterly, 32*(4), 399–423.

Zwiers, J. (2006). Integrating academic language, thinking, and content: Learning scaffolds for non-native speakers in the middle grades. *Journal of English for Academic Purposes, 5*(4), 317–332.

Language Learning   ISSN 0023-8333

Index

Index

Made in the USA
Lexington, KY
16 November 2012